Praise for
The Conversation C...

When customers ring a call centre, they often have .... automated waiting lines first before they can ask their question ....o often that customers are not helped sufficiently. Many compan, ...ers consider their call centre to be a debit entry. They think that every call solves a problem. However both satisfied and unsatisfied customers share their experiences and sometimes their frustrations with family and friends. Their image of your 'brand' is determined by all customer interactions, not only by the smooth advertising messages. Steven Van Belleghem gives tangible and strong examples which explain the power of turning the vicious circle around. How does the supermarket help teach the management a lesson, and which basic elements compose the success of a successful Conversation Company. **Philippe Rogge, CEO, Microsoft Belgium**

Imagine the power at your control. If you have ten thousand happy customers who each have a hundred Facebook or Twitter friends, that's potentially a million positive conversations about your company! Steven Van Belleghem shows you how to tap that amazing free resource to grow your business now. **David Meerman Scott, Author**

At Zappos, we found that the more we invested into customer service and the customer experience, the more we grew from word-of-mouth. *The Conversation Company* is for anyone interested in transforming a company's service level.
Tony Hsieh, *NY Times* best-selling author of *Delivering Happiness* and CEO of Zappos.com, Inc

Studio 100 strongly believes in a 'we'-culture. An open and authentic company culture is the foundation of a successful company. The vision and insights from *The Conversation Company* will inspire any company manager to see culture as the foundation of positive and influential marketing. A must read for every manager.
     Like nobody else, Steven Van Belleghem again puts the consumer literally at the CENTRE of modern company management, the main difference being that 'consumer ownership' is not only contained in the marketers' job description, but in that of all employees. In the end conversation with consumers becomes the responsibility of all employees, not just of marketers. Steven helps you start appealing to this underused conversation potential. **Hans Bourlon, CEO, Studio100**

The customer should not know only the marketing department. The entire company should be close to the customer, in order to listen to his needs. By closing the gap between customer and company, you created an openness to involve customers in the company's policy. That is how customers and collaborators become the best salesmen together. Steven succeeded again in inspiring via his book.
Piet Decuypere, CEO, Danone, The Netherlands

All signs point at consumers wanting to connect and have conversations on a personal, one-on-one basis with brands and the companies that make them. Consumers want to be personally engaged and entertained on a human level through the stories the brands have to tell. Steven Van Belleghem's latest work provides new insights into the role company culture plays in creating a consistent story and the untapped potential employees represent for connecting with consumers. *The Conversation Company* is a recommended read for those wishing to bring more consumer orientation into their company.
Jef Van De Cruys, Global leader digital connections, ABInBev

The world is changing and with it the role of communications. This book is a must read guide to the shift from communications to conversations, encompassing both the cultural and the practical, leaving the reader in no doubt about the importance of action. A tour de force of common sense in our upside down world.
Peter Boterman, Corporate Communications Director, Heinz Continental Europe

In the age where consumers are the ones shaping the brand and where organizations are still clinging to the illusion of control, Steven offers invaluable lessons of unlocking unused conversation potential of your company that will allow you to excite and delight your customers. This book is about shifting from the mentality of drive-by marketing to genuine caring... *about your customers, employees and partners*. Using 4 Cs in his book – Customer Experience, Conversation, Content and Collaboration – Steven will give you actionable insights on how to take your brand to new heights. **Ekaterina Walter, Social Media strategist and well respected thought leader, Intel**

Great case studies and lessons. There are a growing number of businesses around the world that talk about the importance of social networks, social media and social engagement. A much smaller number of businesses 'really get it'. And it's the few that will make the difference. In his book, *The Conversation Company*, Steven Van Belleghem has identified companies who are leading the way and sharing their journey with others. The cases that Steven has captured and the lessons that are shared will be valuable to businesses, both large and small, who lead with relationship and are intent on making the customer the focus of their purpose. I'm delighted that PEMCO Insurance, the company where I am Chief Marketing Officer, is included among that group. **Rod Brooks, VP and CMO PEMCO, 2011 Board President WOMMA (Word-of-Mouth Marketing association)**

The
Conversation
Company

Publisher's note

Every possible effort has been made to ensure that the information contained in this book is accurate at the time of going to press, and the publishers and author cannot accept responsibility for any errors or omissions, however caused. No responsibility for loss or damage occasioned to any person acting, or refraining from action, as a result of the material in this publication can be accepted by the editor, the publisher or the author.

First published in Great Britain and the United States in 2012 by Kogan Page Limited

120 Pentonville Road	1518 Walnut Street, Suite 1100	4737/23 Ansari Road
London N1 9JN	Philadelphia PA 19102	Daryaganj
United Kingdom	USA	New Delhi 110002
www.koganpage.com		India

© Steven Van Belleghem, 2012

ISBN   978 0 7494 6473 8
E-ISBN   978 0 7494 6474 5

British Library Cataloguing-in-Publication Data

A CIP record for this book is available from the British Library.

Library of Congress Cataloging-in-Publication Data

Van Belleghem, Steven.
    The conversation company : boost your business through culture, people and social media / Steven Van Belleghem.
        p. cm.
    Internet marketing–Social aspects, Customer relations, Social media, Management–Social aspects
    ISBN 978-0-7494-6473-8 – ISBN 978-0-7494-6474-5   1. Marketing–Social aspects.
2. Internet marketing–Social aspects.   3. Customer relations.   4. Social media.
5. Management–Social aspects.   I. Title.
    HF5415.V28 2012
    658.8'02–dc23
                                                                    2012000161

Typeset by Graphicraft Ltd, Hong Kong
Print production managed by Jellyfish
Printed and bound by CPI Group (UK) Ltd, Croydon, CR0 4YY

Contents

Foreword

Join the conversation. Seems like a cliché these days, except for the fact I coined the phrase (or at least no one has told me otherwise). I've written three books (and I'll be busy writing my next one as soon as I finish writing this foreword) – *Life after the 30-second spot*, *Join the Conversation* and *Flip the Funnel*.

At one point (this would be when CNN's Anderson Cooper kept using the phrase as a super on his show), I wondered why I didn't trademark the phrase, but then realized it would have gone against everything I stand for. And everything author of this book, Steven Van Belleghem, stands for as well.

So when Steven asked me to pen this foreword, I wondered to myself, 'Does the world need another book on social media?' 'Does the industry need another call to action to join the conversation?' 'Do marketeers need another jibe in the gut to avoid going the way of the dinosaur?' The answer is no, but fortunately that's not what this book sets out to do.

Whereas Steven's first book, *The Conversation Manager*, looks to answer the **why** (see the earlier paragraph), this book focuses on the all important **what** and **how**. I came up with an acronym I've used – and continue to use – across my books: COST. It stands for cultural, organizational, strategic and tactical and it's a simplified (arguably over-simplified) change management continuum for business and brands in general.

The fact remains, companies today are still mired in the tactics of social media.

We need to be on Twitter.

Why?

We don't know...

Brands today are still looking at social media, but only really seeing the 'media' part, ie buying attention (paid media), creating attention (earned media), building attention (owned media), when in actual fact they should be focusing on **paying** attention (what I call non-media). They're trying to teach an old, tired dog new tricks and worse still, they're measuring their efforts and success using staid and out-of-touch metrics.

Thankfully there are ways to navigate to a better place; a better space; a better way to work. It's called the Conversation Company. And it's as much attitude as it is aptitude. In the Conversation Company, everything and everyone communicates. That includes customers. And it includes employees.

The journey ahead is one of cultural transformation, but cultural change is the single most difficult thing to achieve in a corporation that is hardwired to resist, bypass and obfuscate.

Trust me, this is easier said than done. In all my travels and keynote speeches to companies around the world, there are two sticking points which refuse to budge: How do we cope with negativity or criticism? How do we deal with loss or lack of control?

Companies are just not built or structured to be flat, transparent, open... social. It's a REACH to be responsive, empathetic, accessible, connected and human. But that doesn't mean it isn't worth the effort and it isn't – arguably – the most important journey you will ever undertake in your professional lives. To be sure, at times it feels like climbing Mount Everest and most of you reading this will most likely walk away with a defeatist attitude; some of you will turn away with an air of scepticism, denial or haughty arrogance.

And then there's the segment of people who will attempt to implement steps towards a new way of working; a new approach to conducting business that acknowledges a bigger picture and a longer time frame. What is required is a strategic framework and process. Like a solid foundation supported by four central pillars – the four Cs: customer experience, conversation, content and collaboration – and a three-step process beginning with building up knowledge, conducting pilot projects and finally, integration.

The first time is often the hardest, but by reading this book you're essentially taking that first step. And what you'll find along the way is an endless pipeline of opportunities and challenges that can be taken advantage of and overcome. For example, like starting with the 28 per cent of 'very satisfied' customers Steven has identified (and talks about in the Introduction). How are you acknowledging them, engaging them in dialogue, recognizing and rewarding their loyalty, tenure and investment and ultimately, activating their advocacy. This is what I call 'flipping the funnel' and it's part of the process of what Steven calls unused conversation potential.

As legendary Yankees catcher and captain, Yogi Berra once said, 'when you come to a fork in the road, take it.' Well, this is your fork. Which road will you take? I'm guessing this isn't your first book that deals with the cataclysmic change brought on through new media and social media. But I hope it's your last. I hope you stop reading and start doing.

Steven uses the phrase 'smart marketeers' when referring to you, but I'm not going to be as complimentary. Our business is full of smart people making dumb decisions, which by my judgement makes you dumb. It's not an excuse anymore to blame the machine, the bureaucratic and political dysfunction of the people and processes around you. You are part of that machine. You are complicit – tacitly or explicitly.

You're only as smart as your actions. And yes, your results – the impact you make on your business, your brand and your earnings. The challenge is time. With so many results being self evident over time, it's a balancing act to bridge the gap between short-term results and long-term transformational change. I'd argue both are as important. Today's pilot programme is tomorrow's cultural and strategic imperative.

You may never become a conversation manager or work for a Conversation Company in your professional lifetimes, but that in no way, shape or form means you shouldn't devote increasing and significant amounts of time to prove otherwise.

Joseph Jaffe is author of three books, including *Flip the Funnel: How to use existing customers to gain new ones*. He blogs, podcasts and video blogs at **www.jaffejuice.com** and **www.jaffejuice.tv**. Find him on Twitter: **@jaffejuice** or e-mail him: **jaffe@getthejuice.com**

Acknowledgements

THANK YOU!

An awful lot of work goes into making a book. I had the pleasure of actually penning *The Conversation Company*, but I could not have done it without the help of very many other people.

First and foremost, I must mention the entire team at InSites Consulting. They assisted me with the writing of stories and the preparation of customer cases, as well as casting a critical eye over my new ideas and offering words of encouragement when they were needed. Special thanks to my co-partners Tim, Kristof, Niels, Joeri, Christophe, Sam, Filip and Magali. I appreciate more than I can say that you were willing to give me the time and space to write this book.

In addition, I would also like to thank all the companies and organizations which have hired my services in recent years for speeches or workshops. It was during these moments that the idea for *The Conversation Company* was first planted in my mind. Of course, the plentiful feedback from Facebook fans and Twitter followers was vital for the development and testing of this idea, and also provided much useful input. The experience of the managers I was able to interview was another crucial element. My thanks go to Mobile Vikings, Studio100, AB InBev, ABB Benelux, Nokia, Zappos, Intel, Kodak, Cisco, ING Nederland, Dexia, Carglass, Unilever, Van Leeuwen, RTBF, Van Marcke, Colruyt, Porter Novelli, Diageo, Microsoft, PEMCO, Telenet and Danone. I really am most grateful!

The content for the book was developed in co-creation with Professor Dr Kristof De Wulf, Professor Dr Niels Schillewaert, Joeri Van den Bergh, Annelies Verhaeghe, Polle De Maagt, Dado Van Peteghem, Dennis Claus, Tom De Ruyck and Sam Berteloot. Furthermore, I was always able to rely on the critical opinions of Professor Gino Van Ossel (Vlerick School of Management), Professor Dr Rudy Moenaert (TiasNimbas Business School), Marc Michils (Saatchi & Saatchi Brussels), Jef Vandecruys (AB-InBev) and my father, Pol Van Belleghem. Thank you all!

The choice of title came after a brilliant brainwave from Guillaume Van der Stighelen. Thanks for the golden tip, Guillaume!

Before I started InSites Consulting, I worked as a researcher at the Vlerick Leuven Ghent Management School. I have continued to give lessons there and in 2010 was appointed as its Deputy Professor of Marketing. I would here like to express my deep appreciation to those at the school for the opportunities they have given me and the confidence they have shown in me.

My publishers Kogan Page (Jon Finch), Van Duuren Media (Ina Boer and Roderik Teunissen) and Lannoo Campus (Hilde Van Mechelen and Peter Saerens) have believed in this project from the start. For this, too, I am grateful.

Last but definitely not least, there is also my wife Evi. She supports me every day in my mission to make companies think in a more customer-oriented way. Thanks Evi for always being there and for your constant encouragement.

How my sons Siebe and Mathis inspired me, you can read at the very end of the book. They don't know it yet, but even they made a contribution to *The Conversation Company*. Thank you, young men.

Introduction

Everyone is a marketeer

Marketeers are the masters of the fine promise. These promises are launched onto the market with lots of noise and plenty of visibility. And marketeers hope that, on the basis of these promises, consumers will then buy the product. This is how marketing works. Or this, at least, is how marketing used to work. Smart marketers now understand that it is no longer enough just to make fine promises. Nowadays, you need to give consumers a pleasing experience, exceed their expectations, listen to their ideas, and collaborate with them in development of those ideas. This is the basis of successful modern marketing. Even more importantly, it is the basis of a successful modern company. But the marketing department cannot do all this by itself. Every employee has a contribution to make. Every employee is a potential spokesperson, salesperson or manager. Even the customers can help with the marketing, sales and research of a company. Customers have the means and the motives to help you – and are often more than willing to do so.

In my previous book, *The Conversation Manager*, I introduced companies to the modern consumer. A consumer who has become highly flexible. A consumer who can make or break your brand. A consumer who is a part-time marketing manager in his or her own right. A consumer who enjoys having an emotional relationship with a brand. In order to get the most out of this modern consumer, I also introduced companies to a new management role: the conversation manager. The conversation manager is able to transform traditional advertising into a series of conversations about the brand. The conversation manager observes, facilitates and participates in conversations with consumers (both online and offline). It is a new philosophy based on dialogue with the consumers instead of the more classical one-way flow of information. By applying what I wrote in that book, you can bring your marketing closer to the modern consumer.

Helping your marketing department to think and act differently is just the first step. Many companies today also use conversation management to polish up their external image. Unfortunately, marketeers sometimes think that a successful Twitter or Facebook page can change their organization. I call this the 'checklist' philosophy: just ticking off the boxes for the next 'cool' campaign. Making a cool app currently scores big-time with checklist marketeers!

However, we all need to take a step further. In order to cater to the needs of the modern consumer, we need to change our entire business philosophy. Who you are as an organization is more important than what you say. A company that invests millions of euros in the market to say that they offer excellent service will only have an impact if it is indeed excellent in providing service of quality. Good service and good products are the things that consumers actually experience. The proof of your marketing claims is to be found (or not) in this experience, and not in the message that you transmit through your advertising. The modern consumer will only believe in you if your whole company radiates this attitude.

In our modern society every employee of a company is jointly responsible for the experience of the consumer. On the one hand, every employee works actively towards creating this experience. On the other hand, every employee is a 'medium' who can converse positively or negatively about the company. In other words, marketing has become much broader than in the past and stretched far beyond the confines of the marketing department. But this is a good thing: marketing is much too important to be left to the marketeers alone. Everyone is responsible for marketing.

Your company almost certainly has unused conversation potential

On average, 28 per cent of customers are very satisfied with the services provided. However, nobody ever talks about this happy 28 per cent.[1] This is an example of unused conversation potential. Proud staff who fail to share their experiences are another example.

Every company has unused conversation potential of this kind. Many companies are still excellent at devising creative marketing tools, but by using the power of your staff and your customers in a positive way, you can create an additional conversation lever.

Imagine that your staff and your customers could share their satisfied feelings with the rest of the world. This is like a pot of gold that is available to every company in every sector. The tapping of this unused conversation potential is the reason why you should transform your company into a Conversation Company. The philosophy of these modern companies is easy to define: the Conversation Company succeeds in ensuring that every interaction between the company and the customer ends with a positive, high-impact conversation. This is how you find your pot of gold. This sounds obvious – and easy. But in this book you will discover that many companies still take decisions that fail to optimize their conversation potential.

Bringing the customer into the boardroom

The origins of these wrong decisions are to be found in the huge gulf between the customer and the company. In most companies, the staff are still very far removed from the daily realities with which the customer is confronted. This encourages companies to make decisions that work in their own favour, rather than to the benefit of the customer. In other words, their interactions do not always end with a positive conversation. This is not a question of 'ill will', it is just that companies fail to see what is good for the customer – and therefore also good for the company. A few months ago, the CEO of a leading company vented his frustrations to me. He said: 'Look Steven, we have a really exciting and forward-looking company here. It really annoys me that everyone seems to see us as the big bad wolf!' However, it soon became clear that there were valid reasons to explain why consumers sometimes (but certainly not always) see this company in a poor light. In reality, it is very difficult for the CEO of a large modern organization to get an insight into what the customer is thinking and feeling. This explains why the credo of the Conversation Company seeks to involve the customer in a structural way in all aspects of the company, from R&D to marketing and from HR to senior management. The idea is to bring the customer into the boardroom, so that the CEO can hear about (and learn from) the customer's story at first hand. By bringing everyone in your company closer to the customer, you can optimize your conversation potential. The more people in your company are plugged into the outside world, the better you will be able fully to exploit your conversation potential.

Your mission: the Conversation Company

Take a good look at the world. In recent times it has undergone huge structural changes. Just a few short years ago there was no such thing as Twitter, Facebook had only a couple of million users, YouTube was just a pipedream and mobile internet was still in its infancy. In the last five years or so, this has all changed – and so has the behaviour of the people who use these new tools. These radical changes mean that it is necessary to reinvent our companies. In this book I will describe how you can transform your company into a Conversation Company, with the aim of allowing you to utilize fully your conversation potential. It bears repeating: your mission is to ensure that every interaction with your company ends with a positive, high-impact conversation.

People are the most important source of conversations for a company. Customers and staff talk to each other about their experiences and so influence public opinion about your organization. All the parties to these conversations now have new technologies, such as social media, at their disposal, so that their impact is greater than ever before. A successful Conversation Company is able to create value in a positive manner from the conversational power of these people.

The basis for this process is an open, authentic and positive company culture. A culture in which the customer stands central is essential if you want to win the conversation game. This culture is carried and spread by people. Your staff are the tangible proof of your culture. They create the customer experiences that will determine your positioning. The great challenge for companies is to become more 'human' again, more people-oriented – and this is only possible through your staff. By formulating values that both your customers and your staff can identify with, your company can create its own conversation guide. The values ensure that the staff know how to behave and that the customers know what to expect. This leads to consistent conversations. Everything that the Conversation Company does or says must reflect its company culture and its company values. And culture says what the company stands for – not what it sells.

In this respect, social media are the lever that will allow you to increase the number of conversations about your company. Social media are a mirror on society. They magnify both the good things and the bad things. Social media are therefore the ideal accelerator for your company's story. Moreover, they allow you to collaborate constructively with your consumers. The correct and clever use or management of these new tools is a key characteristic of a Conversation Company.

The Conversation Company makes full use of its conversation potential. To achieve this, the company relies on four central pillars – the four Cs – customer experience, conversation, content and collaboration. The most important conversation starter with consumers is their (online and offline) experience of your company's products and services. The managing of the customer experience – before, during and after the sale – is therefore the first pillar of the Conversation Company. The use of these products and services often leads to questions from consumers. If the customer asks a question, the Conversation Company must give a proper answer. This is self-evident when using classic channels of communication – e-mail, telephone, sales points, etc – but the Conversation Company adds to this list the management of online conversations. This is the second important pillar. Moreover, it is crucial to remember that you can use the new social media not only reactively to deal with comments and complaints, but also proactively to spread high-impact content. Content about your company is a key conversation starter. You offer relevant information without being overtly commercial. This builds up the credibility of your company. Content leads to conversion and sale – and is therefore your third important pillar. Finally, the Conversation Company builds a bridge between its staff and its customers on a foundation of structural collaboration. Through your external and internal communication, there is a constant interaction between your company and the market. In this way, customers become involved in almost every important company decision. Consequently, collaboration is the fourth and final pillar.

FIGURE 0.1

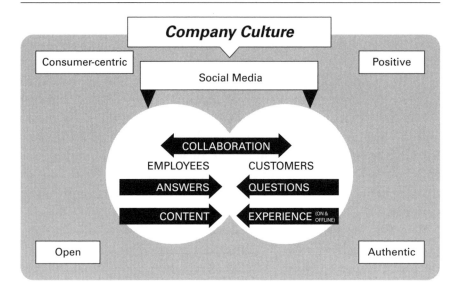

How best to read this book

The first part of this book provides insights into different aspects of your unused conversation potential. We will also confront you with several company paradoxes. You mean well, but you sometimes do the opposite of what you should be doing if you want to reduce your unused potential.

The second part brings us to the real heart of the Conversation Company. Here the key role of company culture is explained. You will read why staff and customers are the most important source of conversations and how you can best make use of their conversational power. Finally in this section, we will also look at the role of social media.

The third part will outline the most important management dimensions which you will need to guide your Conversation Company in the right direction. This relates to the four pillars mentioned earlier (the four Cs): customer experience, conversation, content and collaboration.

The fourth part describes the change process that every company will need to undergo. To become a Conversation Company, you will need to implement a major restructuring of the way your company thinks and works. This restructuring is based on three distinct phases and 10 strategic change projects.

The first three parts of the book are therefore inspirational. They offer you a new vision of a modern company. The fourth part serves a different purpose. This is intended as an instruction guide for implementing change. You can use it as a detailed step-by-step plan to transform your company into a Conversation Company.

The basis of the Conversation Company

This book is based on market research carried out by the InSites Consulting team, supplemented with further insights gleaned from a thorough study of the professional literature; customer projects; the many reactions to our workshops, presentations and articles; and (of course) my own vision and beliefs. Because this book has been the work of a whole team, the 'we' form of address is used in preference to the 'I' form.

During the past two years, the InSites Consulting team has carried out the following special studies specifically for the preparation of this book:

- Twenty-five in-depth interviews with companies from many different sectors and countries, relating to the integration of social media and customer-oriented thinking into their organization.

- A quantitative survey of 400 senior marketeers from the United States and the UK, concerning the integration of conversations into their organizations. Thank you to our partner SSI. InSites Consulting and SSI conduct this project in close partnership.

- An analysis of one million conversations on the Twitter and Facebook fan pages of more than two hundred global brands. This study revealed insights about the things people like to say about brands on social network sites.

- A quantitative survey of more than 7,000 consumers worldwide, in order better to understand their behaviour with regard to conversations in general, social media and conversations at work.

Thank you for reading this book. I wish you every success in your new mission!

Steven Van Belleghem

All feedback, suggestions and new examples are welcome on **Steven@InSites.eu** *or via Twitter:* **@Steven_InSites**

Part One
A world full of contradictions

Chapter One
Your company has unused conversation potential

Companies in 'checklist' mode

During the past three years, companies have been overwhelmed with stories relating to the impact of social media and the modern consumer. The same companies have been simultaneously bombarded with new trends and new evolutions. As a result, most companies are now aware of the radical changes that have taken place in our world. At the beginning of 2010, 45 per cent of US marketeers said that social media was their top priority.[2] In other words, social media awareness has become a fact. Most companies were already taking necessary corrective action. A recent study conducted in both the United States and the UK showed that only 12 per cent of companies are currently doing nothing at all in the field of social media.[3] In other words, there is both awareness and action.

Very good, you might think. Mission accomplished! Unfortunately, not. In fact, very definitely not.

Seven out of 10 companies who have adjusted their marketing strategy to reflect the expectations of the new consumer regard these changes from a purely tactical perspective.[4] They have what we call a 'checklist mentality'. They have heard that you need a Facebook page – and so they create a Facebook page. Check, done that! Twitter is becoming increasingly popular? Check, done that! Mobile apps are cool? Okay, I suppose we'd better do that as well... This is all very good, and possibly well intended, but its purpose is tactical rather than strategic. For example, companies of this kind will set up a new Twitter account for each of their events. But they don't always do the necessary follow-up. In other words, they are making repeat investments in followers who are then left to their own devices after the event. Perhaps investments are occasionally made to win new fans for a company's Facebook page. However, new content of interest is only posted on this page during campaigns. And the rest of the time? Little or nothing at all. Not really the best way to create satisfied fans, is it? These actions fail, because they are not framed within the context of a specific vision. They are just opportunistic, tactical pin pricks.

The most successful cases of this kind relating to social media are nearly all advertising campaigns which use the media in a creative manner. Indeed, marketeers regularly win awards for such campaigns. Unfortunately, these actions alone are not sufficient to guarantee structural change within the companies in question. If your company really wants to adjust itself to the demands of the new consumer, you will need to go further. Much further. Just tarting up your external image by implementing a few clever social media campaigns will not be sufficient to convince this new empowered generation of modern consumers. Don't forget: they are better informed than ever before.

It is not just about social media

The biggest problem with the checklist mentality is that it places its focus too squarely on social network sites, such as Facebook and Twitter. In reality, the focus must be placed on conversations between people, since it is these conversations that have the power to influence opinions. Billions of conversations about brands are conducted between consumers each day. In the United States alone, there are 3.4 billion such conversations every 24 hours.[5] People talk about new products, new variants, new promotions, the prices of good or services and their experiences (both good and bad) of different brands.[6] These types of conversation strongly affect the opinions and the purchasing behaviour of consumers. The conversations take place both online and offline. In fact, a surprising 94 per cent of the conversations are currently offline.[7] Even so, online conversations have the advantage of being able to reach large audiences quickly, easily and cheaply. In addition, there is more chance that online conversations will be included in a Google search carried out by someone looking for information about your brand – which is an immensely powerful tool in its own right. In terms of customer perception, the credibility attached to a conversation increases by 25 per cent if it appears in the results of an online search.[8]

If you can find the right people (positive people, reliable people, experts, etc) to talk about your company in the right way (relevant content), you will always be more successful than the companies that are never talked about or are talked about by the wrong people in the wrong way.[9] It sounds simple, but that is the reality of the situation.

Conversations form the basis for the decisions and perceptions of consumers. In the past, numerous studies have underlined the relationship between positive conversations and good sales figures.[10] In other words, conversations also form the basis for the growth of your company. Our research has shown that 73 per cent of all marketeers claim to apply this philosophy, but only 20 per cent manage their conversations in a strategic manner.[11] We are convinced that every company has conversation potential. Of course, some companies (eg Disney, Apple) intrinsically have more conversation potential than others (eg heavy B2B), but this does little to alter the fact that by managing your conversations wisely you can optimize your existing potential and tap new sources of possible future conversations. However, the majority of conversations are still not strategically managed, so that there is still a significant amount of unused conversation potential in every company.

In short, your company may already be doing fantastic things in this field. Conversations with customers initially develop in a tactical and/or organic way. By not managing these conversations strategically, you are not always able to get the most out of them. This is your unused conversation potential. If you are better able to exploit this potential, this can only lead to positive results for your company. It will certainly enhance people's perception of your company image. You will also note an increase in sales and will suddenly find it easier to recruit new staff. In this book we will search together for the path that will show you where your unused conversation potential can be found and how it can be used more effectively.

FIGURE 1.1

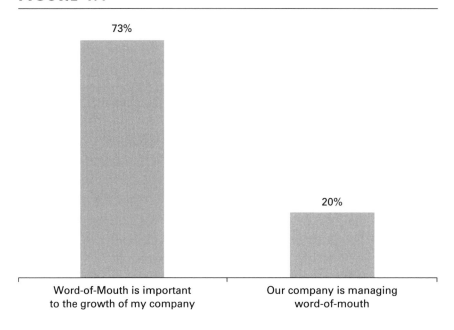

73%

20%

Word-of-Mouth is important
to the growth of my company

Our company is managing
word-of-mouth

Every company is sitting on top of a potential goldmine

The highest proportion of unused conversation potential is to be found among your existing customers and staff. Everyone reading this book will agree that satisfied customers are important. Satisfied customers who talk about your company are even more important. A European survey of various sectors showed that 28 per cent of customers were very satisfied with particular products or services they have received, but did not talk with anyone else about them. In other words, almost one third of customers had a good experience of a product or service, but said nothing to anyone about it. This is a massive unused potential for positive conversations. The same is true of your staff. Every company has its own ambassadors on its payroll – but doesn't always realize it. Too often these people are given too few opportunities to speak about their pride in the company they work for. If you can find a way to activate these two groups, you could find yourself sitting on a goldmine.

If your company reduces the level of unused conversation potential, everything it does will have a wider reach and a greater impact.

In short, managing the conversations of your customers and your staff in a strategic manner will create a lever effect. The Conversation Company succeeds in ensuring that every interaction between a customer and a member of staff ends with a positive, high-impact conversation. The better you use this conversation potential, the faster your organization will grow and the stronger it will become.

Regrettably, the current checklist attitude does not lead to the optimization of conversation potential. It may sometimes work in the short term, but will have no long-term structural impact. Remember: the challenge is to use the conversation potential of your company fully. Once you accept this and start looking at your business in this light, you will start to see unused potential everywhere.

CASE STUDY Old Spice: probably the campaign with the greatest unused potential in the world

Many people will be familiar with the Procter & Gamble (P&G) 'Old Spice' campaign. It all began with the famous TV commercial: 'The man your man could smell like.' In this spot, Isaiah Mustafa, a former US football star, was portrayed as the ideal man. Thanks to clever casting and the equally clever build up of the commercial, it was an instant hit.

FIGURE 1.2

The message was targeted at female viewers and can be summarized as follows: your man may not look as good as the man in this advert, but if he uses Old Spice he can at least smell like him. The commercial was first broadcast during a break in the Superbowl final in 2010. In the following days, it attracted millions of fans and followers and later in the year even won the Grand Prix at Cannes – the highest accolade for any television commercial. In the meantime, P&G was already working on a follow-up. In June, the interactive version of the campaign was launched. Via Twitter, people were able to put questions to Mustafa. During the first 12 hours, 117 additional videos were recorded to answer possible questions. These answers covered topics ranging from simple 'home and garden' advice to a proposal of marriage. The response of the public to the campaign exceeded all expectations and resulted in countless conversations and interactions with Old Spice. Almost overnight, the Old Spice YouTube channel became the best viewed channel ever, with more than 40 million viewers. In just days, the brand had an additional 120,000 followers on Twitter.

According to P&G, sales increased by 107 per cent during the month of the campaign,[12] although objective figures from SymphonyIRI data showed that there was no increase in market share for Old Spice.[13] Sales figures apart, everyone was agreed that it was a brilliant and unique interactive campaign. Nothing like it had ever been seen before. Congratulations, Old Spice, for so much creativity!

On the basis of this description, you might be forgiven for concluding that there was very little unused potential in this instance. Everyone who saw the campaign, talked about it. Almost every blogger in the world wrote about it. So where is the remaining potential? Is there, in fact, any remaining potential?

Of course there is! Huge amounts of it! In reality, P&G dealt very carelessly with the conversation potential. You must bear in mind that this was not a cheap campaign: the combination of a television commercial with a state-of-the-art interactive follow-up is hugely expensive, especially in the United States. To pay for all this, P&G really needed to make use of every last scrap of the conversation potential at its disposal. But this is not what happened.

During a 90-day period between June and September 2010, the Old Spice Twitter account only sent 20 or so tweets. Moreover, these tweets were mainly one-way tweets, which encouraged little interaction with the fans – and this was at a time when there were 120,000 wildly enthusiastic new fans, all anxious for feedback and new content. In short, no effort was made to build up strategic conversations with the fans, which would have built up the potential and helped to cement possible relationships for the future. Little wonder that a September 2010 magazine article about the campaign was entitled 'Old Spice fades into history...'.[14] This says it all.

An analysis of Google Trends shows that the Old Spice brand enjoyed a huge conversation peak during the period February to June 2010, but that this level gradually returned to normal once the campaign period was finished. The problem with this case is that it is still linked to a specific, individual campaign. A brilliant campaign, but a campaign nonetheless. And campaigns come and go. And the all-so important conversations go with them.

The real art of conversation management is to build up a process of continuous interaction with your target group. You can turn campaigns on and off, but you should never do the same with conversations: this only increases your levels of unused potential.

CASE STUDY 'The Voice': very little unused potential

Between 1990 and 2000, television was dominated by big entertainment shows. Between 2000 and 2010, the reality programmes took over. In 2011 'The Voice' arrived with a totally new concept that will no doubt be used more and more in the years to come. For the first time the public was confronted with a television 'event' that runs 24/7 on various different media. This new format started in the Netherlands as a John De Mol production (he also dreamed up 'Big Brother') but has since been adopted in a number of other countries, including the United States.

At first glance, 'The Voice' seems just like any other talent show of the 'X Factor' or 'Idol' genre. Its purpose is essentially the same: to find a new top singer. Even so, there are important differences. For example, the auditions are organized in a completely different way: namely, exclusively on the basis of vocal talent. The members of the jury are not able to see the candidates; in fact, they act more as coaches than as a jury. On the basis of these blind auditions, each coach can select his or her own team of eight candidates, who compete with the other teams week after week. The candidates are gradually eliminated, until 'the voice' will finally be chosen after an exciting final.

Both in the Netherlands and in the United States (the first country where the concept was televised), the programme inspired a seldom-seen number of conversations on social media. During the first live show in the Netherlands, no fewer than 120,000 tweets were sent. During the final, an average of 70 tweets per second – 80,000 per hour – were posted. Subsequent analysis showed that 26 per cent of the entire Dutch Twitter population had talked about the programme at some point.[15] By analysing the tweets, it was possible to predict the winner of the final 24 hours in advance. And the prediction was spot on. In both countries, 'The Voice' attracted a huge viewing audience, with phenomenal peaks at key moments in the series. The CEO of a major media company recently said to me: 'In the old days, the success of a TV programme was judged by the conversations at the office coffee machine; now it is judged by the conversations on social media.'

Was 'The Voice' a chance success? Just another lucky shot? No, it was nothing of the kind. It was the result of very careful planning during the pre-production phase. 'Even at the very first meeting, the importance of the link between the programme and social media was stressed,' says Nicole Yaron, the producer of the US show.[16] 'In our digital world, integration with social media is not something that you can leave to chance, like some kind of afterthought. To be successful, you need a concrete strategy, clear planning and tight implementation.'

The viewers were able to converse with both the candidates and the coaches (jury). The creation of new content was also non-stop. The content that could not be shown on television was transmitted around the world via various online channels. In this way, 'The Voice' is no longer 'just' a television programme. It has become an ongoing story to which new elements are added each day. And to complement this story – the icing on the cake, as it were – the viewers are treated to a new live show each week.

The way of thinking demonstrated by 'The Voice' dramatically reduces the level of unused conversation potential. Consumers are regularly provided with fresh content and conversations are launched by or with many of the key players (candidates, jury). These conversations are also cleverly facilitated, while the live shows offer excellent opportunities for further customer acquisition and retention. Commitment to the brand is also additionally strengthened by the voting process and by the possibility of viewer input for the choice of songs. In other words, the conversational thinking goes much further than the pure product itself. In fact, the conversations continue almost irrespective of the programme. If this is properly planned and implemented, the results can often be truly spectacular.

Look everywhere – unused conversation potential is in every corner of your business

We have a challenge for you. Try and look at your own company purely from the perspective of unused conversation potential. Can you see it now? If you look carefully, you will find potential that is not being used in every corner of your organization. But by thinking and acting differently, you can put that potential to very good use. What is at stake is the creation of new conversations, with more impact, about who you are, what you do and what you sell.

The most important conversation starter with consumers is their experience of your company. The impression made by your products and services is the most important reason for talking about you and your organization.[17] In addition, customers can ask questions about your company via both online and offline channels. If you respond cleverly, these questions can lead to successful conversations. Companies can also encourage consumers to talk about them through the careful composition of their content. High-impact content leads to conversion and new customers.

The basis of these three conversation starters (customer experience, conversations and content) is to be found in the interaction between different people (staff, customers, opinion makers, etc). Taken together, these aspects frequently exhibit a great deal of unused conversation potential.

Better use of the interaction between people

People are the most important source of conversations. Everyone talks to someone about the companies and brands with which they have a relationship. This can be as a customer or end-user, but also as a member of staff, supplier, shareholder, etc. All these people have conversation potential. But this potential is seldom managed. However, a Conversation Company is different. A Conversation Company adopts a consistent policy to manage these interactions between people carefully in order to make maximum use of its conversation potential.

The realities relating to the unused conversation potential of customers include the following:

- As previously mentioned, every company has an average of 28 per cent of satisfied customers who never talk about the company. This is an unexploited goldmine of potential conversations. People like to help, but don't always know how. You need to give them a gentle push in the back.

- Many companies only begin to manage their customer conversations during times of crisis. Companies such as Comcast and Dell are now well advanced in terms of their change process, but their initial decision was forced on them by the financial crisis of 2008. T-Mobile only woke up to the importance of conversations in the Dutch market when they were ridiculed for poor service in the social media by a famous stand-up comedian. But why should a company wait for a crisis to occur before it decides to manage its conversations with customers in a positive manner? By waiting until negative conversations begin to appear, you are not only getting off on the wrong foot but are also missing numerous opportunities for positive conversations.

- Companies usually approach their customers from an opportunistic perspective. They expect near-miracles in the short term (particularly from social media), so that they often end up disappointed. It is important to realize that the optimization of conversation value is a structural process. Magical conversation starters that cost next-to-nothing do exist, but they are the exception rather than the rule.

- Companies are inclined to reward new customers; for example, with a discount on a first purchase. But why only reward new customers? Your existing customers are your biggest treasure trove of conversational potential. These are the people you should be encouraging. Transform your customers into ambassadors and reward them as such.

- Most customers will be keen to work with your company in some form or other. More than half will be prepared to assist you in the development of new products or marketing campaigns.[18] This type of collaboration is ideal for starting conversations, but the opportunities remain all too frequently unexploited.

CASE STUDY Diageo focuses media on fans

(Based on a presentation from the IAB Conference Europe, 2011.)[19]

Diageo, the manufacturer (among other things) of alcoholic drinks under brand names such as Johnnie Walker, J&B, Baileys and Smirnoff wants to sharpen the focus of its fan management. In 2011 the company instructed its media bureaus to concentrate more directly on the fans of its different brands. Until now, each brand has had its own socio-demographic profile. Johnnie Walker, for example, was targeted at men between the ages of 25–40 years. Likewise, all the media attention for the brand was directed at this age group. However, more recent market research has revealed that this profile does not really coincide with the profile of many of the real brand fans. For example, it became clear that many women are also fans of Johnnie Walker. As a result, the brand profiles have been rewritten and there has also been a corresponding shift in media emphasis. The impact of this decision was quickly felt. The number of fans on Facebook increased fivefold during the months following the changes.

- In addition to the unused conversation potential of your customers, the conversation potential of your own staff is seldom exploited to its fullest extent. Two out of every three employees are proud of their job and the company they work for, and the majority of them are also happy to talk about this fact.[20] In this respect, social media are the ideal platform for telling people about your everyday life. Unfortunately, many companies have decided that their staff should not be permitted to tell stories about their jobs on social media sites. This has effectively blocked an important flow of potential conversations. In Europe and the United States less than 20 per cent of employees converse about their job on social networks, despite the fact that 50 per cent of the same employees have indicated a willingness to share information about new products with these networks.[21]

- A few months ago I did a workshop for a large manufacturer in the foodstuffs sector. While I was there, I learnt that their marketing team had been forbidden from sharing their latest advertisement with their friends via Facebook. This is unbelievably short-sighted, since there is more chance that someone will look at the work of a friend on Facebook than that the individual will actually see it on television.

FIGURE 1.3

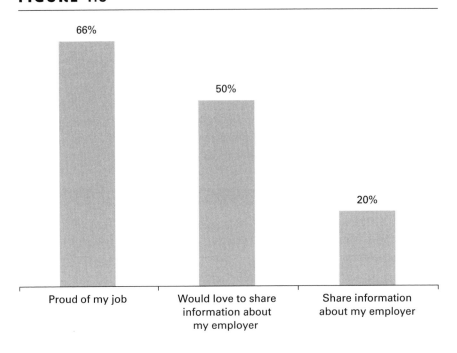

66%

50%

20%

Proud of my job

Would love to share
information about
my employer

Share information
about my employer

CASE STUDY
HP turns its employees into ambassadors for the company[22]

Every year, HP organizes a number of demo days. During these days, the company staff give information about HP products to potential customers in local shops. The interesting thing about this programme is the fact that it is not only the sales staff who are involved. HP asks all its employees, irrespective of their function or experience, if they are willing to take part. This is just one of many activities designed to promote a more customer-oriented approach at all levels of the organization. The idea is that if everyone gets feedback directly from the customers, the gap between the internal world of HP and the external world of the market will be closed. It is also worth noting that the employees do this in their own free time and do not receive any form of financial recompense. During the first demo days held in 2007, just 10 per cent of staff were willing to participate. Since then the number of participants and the level of their enthusiasm has increased systematically. Using your own employees as ambassadors is a clever way to optimize conversation potential.

CASE STUDY Johnnie the Bagger

(Based on Glanz, 2009)[23]

Is it a myth or is it true? Nobody really knows for sure. Johnnie was a young man with Down's syndrome. He worked for a grocer's store in the United States. His job was to help people to put their groceries into carrier bags while they were checking out at the cash desk. On his own initiative, he decided to offer the customers a little something extra. In each bag he added a short, handwritten note, in which he thanked the customers for their visit. He never told anyone, but after a short time the till where Johnnie worked was always the busiest and most popular. People were pleasantly surprised, touched even, by the warmth of the messages; to such an extent that they were prepared to wait longer in the queue, just to get a message from Johnnie. After a time, the management discovered (via a customer) what was going on. Everyone was amazed at the impact that this simple, human act had generated. From this moment onwards, the store began to look at its customers in a different light – and tried to act accordingly. Everyone was encouraged to think of new ways in which the customers might be pleasantly surprised.

No doubt many of your own staff also have valuable ideas about how the conversation potential of your customers can be increased. You would be wise to listen to these ideas as part of the change process which will accompany your transformation into a Conversation Company.

The better use of content

The focus of content is very often placed on formal communication (financial information, crisis warnings, etc) or on campaigns, whereas every company has its own interesting stories to tell. As a result, the average company woefully underuses its content potential:

- The launching of an innovative product is often kept quiet for as long as possible. In other words, you have something great, but nobody is supposed to know about it! That's not very sensible, is it? The last months of production usually generate interesting content which you can use to warm up the market for what is to follow. It is understandable that companies are concerned about the proper timing of the launch, but if you wait until the product is fully ready, you will inevitably reduce the number of conversations about it. This 'open' technique is used by Apple for each of its launches. The iPad was made public a full eight months before it actually became available in the shops. This whets the market's appetite for the product, so that people are almost queuing up to buy it before it is even on the shelves.

- By planning its marketing activities in terms of campaigns, a company creates the illusion that it can start and stop communicating whenever it likes. In reality, a company can **never** stop communicating – nor should it want to. Every interaction (via staff, products, letters, etc) between your company and the outside world is a form of communication. Thinking exclusively in terms of campaigns drastically reduces the breadth of your vision and results in a narrow approach to your customers. In contrast, if you can generate relevant content on a daily basis, your unused conversation potential will diminish significantly.

- Content is often used at a single moment in a single place. But it doesn't always have to be this way. Check to see whether content can be spread by more than one channel. Consider carefully whether a small content spin-off can provide a lever for the profitability of your initial investment. In the case of 'The Voice', for example, a television production is an extremely expensive way to generate content creation. Greater content impact was achieved through various spin-offs, which cost significantly less but yielded a higher return.

Companies often overlook the importance of informal content. Every organization has interesting stories to tell about what actually goes on behind the scenes. A photograph of a meeting, a YouTube film of a work floor prank, a picture of your New Year reception: these are all informal elements, but they help to bring your company culture to life. In short, they give your organization a human face and make it more accessible.

CASE STUDY Martel Home Builders

Martel Home Builders is a Canadian company that, as the name implies, builds houses. Originally, the company focused its marketing and sales activities on architects and other building promoters. Direct selling to end-users was not written into the company's DNA. However, in recent years Martel Home Builders has radically remodelled its strategy. By using its professional knowledge (ie its content) cleverly, it has now developed new channels that get its message directly to potential home buyers. It starts with a blog directed at the housing market in general. This blog contains practical tips about how to buy, build or renovate your home. In just a few years' time, the number of leads via the end-user has increased from 0 per cent to 86 per cent. The success of the blog was in large measure due to its focus on e-mail registration. Readers were encouraged to receive new blog posts in their mail box. In this way, the content was transmitted to an ever-increasing number of people. This smart combination of relevant content, new media and 'good old' e-mail reduced the level of unused conversation potential month after month.

The better use of conversations

Consumers talk about companies. These conversations present many interesting opportunities, which most companies simply let pass:

- Just 20 per cent of companies listen to the conversations of their consumers.[24] The failure to do anything with this mass of potential feedback is a waste and a shame.

- By failing to facilitate the sharing of content, many companies are missing out on a substantial number of quick wins. Offering your consumers interesting information, but in a form that makes it difficult for them to share it via social media, is a missed opportunity.

- Conversations are generally more positive than most people think. Only 14 per cent of Facebook conversations are truly negative.[25] If they have had a good experience, consumers like to recommend companies. By not reacting to a positive recommendation from one of your customers, you are simply throwing away conversation potential. If you react and thank them, their loyalty level will increase still further.

- Consumers are asking companies more and more questions in public forums. If you fail to answer these questions, you are not only limiting your conversation potential but may actually be encouraging negative conversations.

- Many companies restrict themselves to very meaningless conversations. The number of useless Facebook updates is almost beyond counting. Superficial conversations and an absence of avenues for structural collaboration will mean that your approach will lack depth and substance.

The better use of customer experience

For your customers, their personal experience of your products and services is the most important reason for talking about your company.[26] Throughout the entire purchasing process (before, during and after sale), your customers are in intimate contact with many different aspects of your organization. Every interaction of this kind is a potential source of conversation. Yet again, however, many of these opportunities are allowed to slip by:

- Many companies have a single team that is responsible for customer service. As a result of this very specific positioning, the rest of the organization can sometimes feel less responsible for providing 'good service'. In reality, of course, the provision of good service is the responsibility of everyone in the company, although this is seldom well managed. In addition, good service is a crucial conversation starter.

- Many companies focus on the conversation value to be gained from the phase which precedes the actual purchase. This is logical, since this is the phase in which the 'heart' of the customer still needs to be won. However, from your customers' point of view, they are always in a purchase phase: before the purchase they are in the information phase, during the purchase they are in the selection phase and after the purchase they are in the evaluation phase. By overlooking the conversation value inherent in all these different phases, it is possible that your conversation potential may not be fully used.

- Try to identify the channels that have a wide range but a low conversation value, since this is where much of your unused potential is to be found. For many companies, their most important interaction moment is when they send out the monthly invoices. This is the case, for example, with telecom companies, where there is often little direct contact with end-users, except when the bill eventually drops into their letter box. You should try to make these channels conversation-worthy in a creative manner. Sometimes something small will do the trick. For instance, your 'out-of-office' message is an interaction that potentially brings you into contact with dozens of people each day, even though you are not there. These messages are usually short, impersonal and boring. But you can easily turn them into a conversation starter, with a little creative thinking. As we have said, unused conversation potential can be found in every corner of your organization, no matter how small.

- In addition, it is also useful, of course, to try and develop channels that have a wide range and a high conversation value, such as a blog, Twitter or Facebook. In mid-2011 about half of all US and UK companies had a Twitter account and 70 per cent had a Facebook page.[27] However, there is no correlation between the number of Facebook fans and the level of interaction on that page.[28] This means that many companies have a large number of Facebook fans, but that they don't actually converse with them to any significant degree. It is yet another missed opportunity to reduce the level of unused conversation potential.

CASE STUDY The Zappos cards

Zappos.com, the online shoe seller, has become the world reference in its sector in just 12 years. In 2010, a mere decade after its foundation, it was sold to Amazon.com for an astronomical USD 1.2 billion. In 2010, the company was good for turnover of USD 2.2 billion. The mission of Zappos is to have the most satisfied customers in the world. To realize this goal, the company operates a very unique (and extreme) form of customer service. The strategy has a strong focus based on a very powerful company culture. Zappos is without doubt a company where the level of unused conversation potential is kept to an absolute minimum. It achieves this in part by building surprise elements into every phase of the purchasing process. I made a guided visit to carry out interviews at the Zappos HQ in Las Vegas in 2010. During my visit even I was surprised by one of the details I noticed in its call centre. The call centre operators all have a pile of greetings cards lying on their desks in front of them. If it becomes clear during the call that the customer is buying shoes for a particular reason or occasion, the operative will quickly write a personalized card for that particular customer. For example, if the shoes were bought for a birthday, the customer will receive a birthday card from Zappos the very next day. This requires very little effort at relatively low cost, but it is outstanding conversation management. Just consider what happens to such a card. It will no doubt be displayed (along with all the other cards) at some prominent location in the customer's home, where it can be seen by all that person's family and friends. And that, of course, is a perfect opportunity for the customer to start a positive conversation about the Zappos approach. It is a strategic conversation starter with few parallels in my experience. The touchpoint experience of the call centre is extended via a separate conversation-worthy channel, with minimal effort and expense. Simple, but brilliant.

The challenge: build a conversation lever

After reading this chapter, you will now no doubt be looking at your company with different eyes. You will already be seeing dozens of opportunities to optimize your conversation potential. Fantastic! Remember, however, that the highest impact results from interactions between staff and customers. Your staff provide the content and your customers provide the experience. They ask each other questions and converse with each other, both online and offline. If you can succeed in building a conversation lever via your staff and customers, you will be well on the way to solving your problem of unused conversation potential.

You will have noticed, perhaps, that many of the things we have discussed are relatively simple, even self-evident. Nevertheless, there are relatively few companies that succeed in keeping their unused conversation potential to a minimum. This can be explained to a large extent by the classic manner in which we all grew up. In addition, the current checklist mentality creates the illusion that companies have adjusted (or are adjusting) to the new situation. But nothing could be further from the truth. It is only by integrating strategic and structural conversations at every level of your organization that you will be able to evolve in the right direction.

In Chapter 2 you will be confronted with a number of marked contradictions that typify the modern world of business. Most companies have the best of intentions, but are blocked in their attempts to realize these intentions by their own, stereotyped, classical way of thinking. As a result, they often take decisions which reduce rather than increase their conversation potential. We will be looking closely at these contradictions, so that they can be eliminated. Only then will it be possible to start building a Conversation Company that is capable of maximizing your conversation potential.

KEY CONVERSATION POINTS

Possible conversation starters

- Break through the checklist mentality. Your company has not made the adjustment to the new media simply because you have a Facebook page and a Twitter account.

- Every company has unused conversation potential. You may already be doing many good things, but you are still letting too many opportunities for positive conversations slip by unnoticed. A large group of customers – 28 per cent – is very satisfied with your company, but they never talk about this to anyone else. Similarly, the ambassadors in your staff do not receive enough support. This is a shame.

- Unused conversation potential can be found everywhere in your company, even in the smallest corner. Your customers can still converse more about you, but so can your own staff. Also pay more attention to the smart presentation of your content and never miss an opportunity for a conversation, if you can help it.

- The majority of conversations with customers start because of the customers' own experience of your company. Examine how you can build a conversation-worthy experience into every phase of the purchase process.

Questions you must ask yourself

- How large is the group of customers that is satisfied with your company but never talks about it? As we have seen, the average figure is 28 per cent but what is the situation in your case?
- Which content are you not using enough?
- Do you control or facilitate the conversations of your staff?
- Do you only reward new customers, or also your loyal ones?
- Is your customer experience conversation-worthy in every phase of the purchasing process?
- Which channels are not conversation-worthy, but nonetheless have a wide reach?
- What are three quick wins that your company can implement tomorrow to reduce your level of unused conversation potential?

Further information

Use these links for further interesting information on:

- the Old Spice film: **www.youtube.com/oldspice;**
- the Diageo example: **www.slideshare.net/stevenvanbelleghem/ how-diageos-digital-strategy-started.**

Chapter Two
Your company is full of paradoxes

The gap between intentions and deeds

Is there a company that does not want to optimize its conversation potential? Of course there isn't! That's something everyone wants!

Unfortunately, good intentions do not always lead to positive deeds. For example, 80 per cent of European marketing managers claim that they intend to listen to the conversations of their consumers, but only 20 per cent of them effectively do so.[29] This difference between words and action is a typically human failing. In much the same way, everyone is convinced of the need for a healthy diet, but the fast-food restaurants are still packed to overflowing every lunchtime. Psychologists refer to this as 'procrastination'. (See more about this on Wikipedia.) Procrastination is the psychological effect that causes our deeds to deviate from our original intentions. Or as the popular saying puts it: 'The road to hell is paved with good intentions.' A classic example is the postponement of urgent matters to attend to less urgent matters. This is caused by an implicit fear to begin a new and often unknown task. We all have problems with this from time to time, but the problem increases in intensity during times of major structural change. Dan Ariely describes the problem as follows: 'The surrender of long-term objectives for short-term pleasure is the basis of all procrastination'.[30] This may mean that in one company (where the attitude is open and adventurous) there is an increase in tempo, whereas in another company (where the attitude is more conservative) there is actually a decrease in tempo.

Today's companies need to take many decisions in areas where they have little or no experience. Should we allow our staff to use

Facebook during working hours? Should we open a Twitter account? How should we react to the negative comments of an influential blogger? These are all very real problems for many companies; problems for which they were never trained in business schools. Companies feel – quite rightly – that they are less in control of things than they used to be. They have the intention to adjust their company to the new way of doing business, but they either lack the courage or the know-how to actually do it. An imperfect understanding of the modern consumer and the latest technological trends cause uncertainty – and uncertainty is always damaging to change. And so a gap is created between intentions and deeds.

During the last 20 years companies have invested heavily in more efficient processes and a hierarchical company structure. The focus was placed primarily on the creation of a better internal organization. However, recent developments on the consumer side of the business equation mean that this classic manner of managing a company is no longer adequate. There is a widening gulf between consumers and companies. The challenge facing contemporary companies is to bridge this gulf. Modern business organizations need to place the customer at the centre of their thinking, but this requires them to jettison a number of traditional management principles. Some companies cling with determination to the old systems; others are more prepared to let them go.

We compare this situation with trying to hold on to a slippery bar of soap. One person will try to close his or her fist as tightly as possible, so that the soap shoots out of the person's grip and falls to the ground. Another person will simply relax his or her hand, so that the soap remains in the open palm.

CASE STUDY The obvious choice for 'Mad Men'

Fans are good at making new content for their favourite brand. The television programme 'Mad Men' discovered this to its cost. 'Mad Men' tells the story of the US advertising world during the 1960s. A fan decided to add a new character to the story line. He gave his character the name Bud Melman (his real name is Bud Cadell). He created a Twitter account for this character and via his Twitter updates he acted along in the show. He added content which perfectly matched the storyline, and the viewers of 'Mad Men' followed this added dimension with pleasure. Before too long, members of the production team became aware of this new personage. How did they react, do you think? Did they give Bud a walk-on role in an episode, so that they could extrapolate on their fans' conversations, or did they ask Bud to immediately shut down his Twitter account?

They went for the second option, asking Bud (with some degree of insistence) to quietly bury his character. Bud agreed to their request without discussion.[31] This was his reaction:

> Your brand kidnapped? Your copyright infringed? Or was it just passion? You can call it what you like, but I call it the thin line between consuming content and creating content, and this is something that will never go away. The content creators are the biggest fans. If the programme is ever stopped, we will be the first one to start a petition. Talk to us. Be friends with us. Ask our help. But please... don't treat me as a criminal.[32]

In this situation, it was very obvious that the right choice was to give the fan the credit he deserved. Bud meant (and caused) no harm to the brand. Exactly the opposite, in fact. The production team made the type of decision that can easily turn a fan into a hater. And this story is by no means an exception. We have seen other world-famous brands do precisely the same with fans who started up Facebook pages and Twitter accounts. It is almost as if the companies cannot recognize a fan when they see one, or that they are frightened that the fan is not just an ordinary man or woman in the street (or behind a computer). But surely it must be the companies' objective to try and attract these fans, not scare them away through heavy-handed overreaction.

Focus on the positive, not just on the negative

Sadly, the reality is that many companies have actually widened the gap between themselves and their customers, rather than narrowing it. One of the reasons for this is their tendency to focus on the negative. Managers who learnt their craft in the previous century give much less attention to things that go right than to things that go wrong. As a result, the companies they lead develop a kind of 'fear' for their own customers.

Almost every company is convinced that there are more negative conversations about their brands than positive ones. This is one of the biggest misconceptions held by today's managers. During a conversation analysis conducted for one of our customers, we discovered that 80 per cent of the comments were favourable. The customers were so happy with the products that many of them had even taken the trouble to write letters of thanks. Nevertheless, within the company there was a clear perception that most of the customers had a negative attitude. The reason for this is simple: the company only replied to the relatively few negative comments they received. Positive comments were ignored. After our analysis, the company also decided to reply to the positive letters and e-mails. This was a sensible decision: thanking its fans and communicating with them is the smartest thing that any company can do. If you don't already do this, start tomorrow!

Because companies focus on the negative, they want to cover themselves against every possible eventuality and guard against every possible misuse of their brands. This often leads them to make the wrong decisions. In the case of 'Mad Men' a loyal fan was effectively silenced, because the television company was convinced that his expression of his loyalty was actually motivated by negative considerations. For some reason, managers fail to appreciate that some fans – in fact, most fans – have a positive attitude towards their brands. Wearing the management glasses of the 20th century, Bud Cadell was seen as someone who wanted to damage the brand – and therefore he had to be stopped.

Compare this situation with a concert by U2. If U2 should attempt to guard its brand in the same way as the producers of 'Mad Men', this would mean that Bono and the boys would stop singing as soon as the audience started to join in. The group's legal advisers would then warn the public that they had only paid their 200 euros per ticket to listen, not to join in. In fact, their singing represented a serious diminution of the quality of the concert, so that the U2 brand might suffer irreparable damage. Can you ever see something like this happening? No, neither can we: the idea is just too silly for words. Rock groups have the advantage that they can see their fans in front of them, so that they have better contact with them and a better understanding of just how much they need them. Companies seem to have more trouble getting used to this idea.

The right thing to do is often so obvious that we can't believe it is true – and so we do the opposite. Talk about a paradox!

Companies are full of paradoxes

Thanks to my first book, *The Conversation Manager*, I have had the luxury of being able to brainstorm with more than 100 companies about the impact of contemporary consumers on their businesses. The conclusion is – as we saw in the previous section – that most companies are full of the strangest paradoxes. And each and every one of these paradoxes results in the further underuse of conversation potential.

Here are the most important of these paradoxes:

- Almost every company thinks that word-of-mouth advertising is important, but they make no effort to manage it. There is a (mistaken) perception that companies can do little to influence consumer conversations.

- The companies communicate impersonally, while their customers are demanding a more human approach. The customer wants just one thing: to be treated in a manner that makes him or her happy. Companies seem more concerned with processes, structures and budgets.

- One of the global trends in the business world is a growing requirement for good service. Many companies see customer service as a budget post on which savings can and should be made.

- Customers want to help companies, to be their friends. The companies do not think that 'just' a few hundred fans are worth investing in.

- The companies spend a small fortune on advertising in which they essentially make promises. The modern consumer wants proof, not promises; wants action, not just communication.

- Consumers talk to each other, and often have interesting and relevant things to say. Companies make little effort to track down these comments and even less effort to take account of them.

- Consumers now have relatively sophisticated technology at their disposal. Many companies are still working with outdated technology. Indeed, Peter Hinssen has described 'a job' as 'the eight hours a day when you work with ageing technology'.[33]

- Staff are often proud of their companies and would like to talk about them, but are forbidden to do so by their employers. But the biggest paradox of all is this: we keep on saying every day that satisfied customers and satisfied staff are important, but our actions do little or nothing to reflect these words. This is the fundamental cause of unused conversation potential.

During a presentation to 100 European marketeers, I asked two simple questions:

'Who thinks that satisfied customers are important?' 100 hands shot up into the air, accompanied by 100 baffled looks that anyone could ask such a stupidly obvious question.

'Who dares to say that they do absolutely everything possible to make their customers satisfied?' Just three hands remained up...

Enough said.

Positive word of mouth is important – so why don't we manage it?

Our research has shown that 73 per cent of European marketeers think that word of mouth has a strong impact on the growth of their company. However, just 20 per cent make any serious effort to manage conversations.[34] This is a huge and scarcely understandable paradox: almost everyone agrees that something has a major influence on company growth, but few seem prepared to devote any management attention to this key element. Strange, very strange...

Brands such as Ben & Jerry's have prospered by focusing on positive word of mouth about their products. They know that word of mouth can be managed.

CASE STUDY Ben & Jerry's

One of the key components of Ben & Jerry's strategy to gain positive word of mouth, which the company introduced almost from the start, was the distribution of free ice creams. It has been doing this regularly since the second anniversary of its founding, back in 1979. The annual highpoint is 'free cone day', when every consumer in the world is gifted an ice-cream: free, gratis and for nothing. Since 2010, Ben & Jerry's has added an online aspect to this event. During the summer lorries loaded with Ben & Jerry's products drive through the streets of Boston and New York. Fans of the brand can use Twitter and Facebook to say where the lorries should stop. In this way the fans know where they can get their free ice-cream. In the past, it used to be the other way around: Ben & Jerry's said to the fans: 'Here we are, come and get it.' Now the fans are able to say: 'Here we are, come and bring it.' Moreover, the free sampling process is expanded and magnified through the use of other social media. Via Foursquare, the lorry notifies its location to fans in the vicinity. At each stopping point, photographs and videos are made, which are spread via Flickr, Facebook and Twitter. In addition to the random selection of sampling sites, the company also tries to seek out star names and influential people. This means that Twitter users with plenty of fans who work for a large company are much more likely to find the lorry stopping outside their front door. Once the lorry has distributed its free samples, the fans start to converse enthusiastically about the brand on social media. In this way, the company does something positive for its fans, while at the same time maximizing its conversation potential. As outlined in the 2010 Womma Summit presentation, 'Ben & Jerry's and Edelman', during the first 12 weeks of the programme, Ben & Jerry's reached more than 17 million people in this way. In the meantime, the programme has been extended to cover other major cities in the United States.

Companies see service as a cost, not a conversation starter

A survey of 500 European marketeers[35] revealed some startling conclusions:

- Of the 500 marketeers, 10 per cent never answer the service-related questions of their customers. Never...

- Even on their own Facebook and Twitter pages, 24 per cent never answer questions received from their fans or customers. Never...

FIGURE 2.1

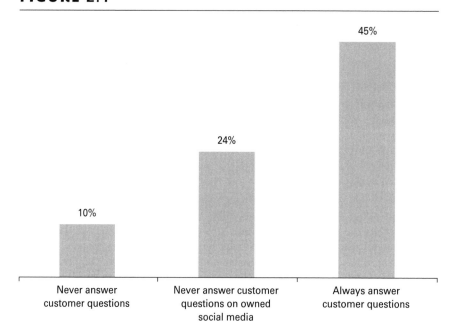

- Only 45 per cent of the companies always answer the service-related questions of their customers. In other words, less than half...

What exactly is the problem with customer service? Well, service cannot easily be hived off to a single department of the company. Service is more a state of mind, in which all the departments need to be involved. In other words, it must be an integral part of the philosophy and culture of the organization. Top restaurants and top hotels have understood this perfectly. From the receptionist to the manager, everyone in a hotel knows that the customer comes first. The things that happen behind the scenes are not the customer's problem.

The second difficulty with customer service is that it is generally regarded as a budgetary cost. And indeed, good service is expensive. The average cost of a single telephone call to a US call centre is 7.5 dollars.[36] During times of financial hardship, customer service is therefore one of the first posts where managers seek to make savings. Some companies even organize 'call avoidance' programmes. This is a concrete, step-by-step plan to significantly limit the number of calls being made to call centres. This might include measures such as:

- non-notification of the call centre number on the company's website;
- changing this number every two weeks;
- answering the phone after a minimum two minutes of ringing.

In the short term, this can certainly reduce calls, cut costs and increase profitability. But months later, the damage in terms of dissatisfied customers and lost revenue will be almost incalculable. In addition, there is also a high opportunity cost. If a complaint is dealt with quickly and efficiently, the level of customer satisfaction rises significantly. This type of experience increases customer loyalty and results in numerous positive conversations. However, these benefits are lost completely if too stringent efforts are made to save on service.

The positive effects of good service are woefully underestimated by many companies. In a world where it is becoming increasingly difficult to differentiate your products from those of your competitors, quality service can be an important distinguishing factor. The figures from the 2011 American Express global customer service barometer show that customers are anxious to see greater investment in service:

- Consumers are willing to pay 13 per cent more for the products of a company that offers them excellent service.
- Sixty per cent want companies to focus greater attention on excellent service.
- Sixty per cent are prepared to change to a different supplier, if that supplier can guarantee better service.
- Seventy-eight per cent have terminated a planned purchase because of a bad feeling about the likely quality of the after-sales service.

Moreover, there is a direct relationship between service and conversations. Between 60 per cent and 70 per cent of all conversations are linked to a direct experience of the company concerned. More than half of these conversations relate to an interaction between the customer and the customer service department of that company.[37] It must therefore be as plain as a pikestaff that good customer service is of vital importance. Mustn't it? Apparently not. Organizations still consistently ignore the conversation potential of service-related matters and continue to regard service as an inconvenient cost rather

FIGURE 2.2

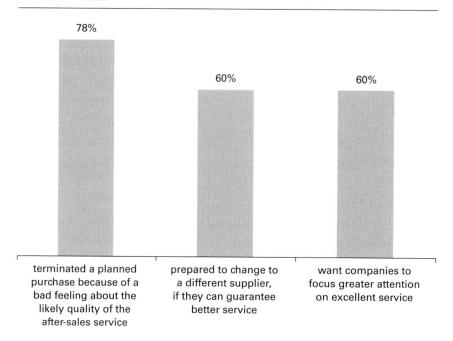

than an excellent conversation opportunity. It is just another one of those paradoxes we have been talking about.

Of course, we understand that not every company pursues – or can pursue – the same strategy. Companies with a low-price positioning cannot offer the same service as a premium player. However, it is not the intention that everyone should provide perfect service, but they should at least provide correct service. And when the moment arrives that every company strives to provide better service, then the business world will be evolving in the right direction.

CASE STUDY   Service – the Nordstrom way

Fortunately, not everyone falls into the paradox trap. Nordstrom, a large US clothing chain, has been able to book good financial results in recent years, notwithstanding the financial crisis.

Since 2007, its turnover has increased by 10 per cent. Between 2009 and 2011, its profits rose by 50 per cent, from USD 400 million to USD 600 million. According to *Business Week*, July 2011 investors' page, these figures are better than the figures for most of the other companies in its sector. The reason for its success is excellent customer service. Nordstrom has been focusing on customer needs for decades. And even during the crisis that followed the 2008 crash the company was unwilling to make cuts in this crucial area. In 1996 its philosophy had been written into a bestselling book: *The Nordstrom Way*, with its famous motto: 'customer service is not a department; it is a way of life'.[38] Nordstrom has always found the idea of a separate department for customer service to be a nonsense. Its leaders believe that everyone is jointly responsible for ensuring that the customer receives top quality service. They have translated this into a simple policy: 'think like a customer, and treat them the way you would want to be treated yourself.' Staff are given enough independence to make the necessary decisions on the spot. Since 2010 Nordstrom has also been playing the online service card. Their website is a magnificent example of user-friendliness. With just three clicks of your mouse, you can select any piece from their range. You can even phone up a style adviser while you are considering your choice! And of course the company is present on Facebook and Twitter, so that it can answer any questions its customers may have.

Companies talk too much: the customer wants proof

Advertising creates an atmosphere of promises, promises and more promises. Good advertising seduces consumers into making a purchase. And for many years brands succeeded in persuading consumers in this manner. If the reality came close to matching the promises, this was usually enough. Or at least it used to be enough. Not any more. Consumers now understand that advertising always portrays the world as being more beautiful – and reliable – than it really is. They have become more critical than ever before. They expect honest communication.

Nowadays, the best way to convince consumers and make maximum use of their conversation potential is to show them openly what you are worth and what you can mean for them. Rather than investing in an advert that promises good service, you should invest the money in actually providing good service. Some years ago, McDonald's replaced the red in its logo with green; it wanted to send a powerful message that it was an environmentally-friendly company. This was a nice piece of visual marketing, but customers will only believe it if they experience greater environmental awareness in their dealings with McDonald's.

Besides, truly top products and companies don't really need advertising. Robert Stephens expressed this nicely when he said: 'Advertising is the price you pay for being unremarkable.' 'Advertising must not only say and promise, but also do and prove,' states Marc Michils, CEO of Saatchi & Saatchi.[39] The advertising budget for Apple is much lower than for Samsung and Nokia, yet Apple outperforms them both in the marketplace. Google's advertising budget is almost non-existent, but every surfer in the world knows who Google is. If your products and services are strong, conversations will do the rest.

CASE STUDY   'United breaks guitars' scores on all paradoxes

(Based on the 2010 Harvard Business School case study 'United breaks guitars'.)

In March 2008 singer Dave Carroll was sitting on board a United Airlines flight. The plane was still on the tarmac, and through the window he could see how the baggage staff were dealing less than gently with his luggage. In his case, this included his expensive guitar, so he warned the United Airlines staff on the plane that he was concerned for its safety. He was not being difficult; all he wanted was that the handlers should exercise a little more care. Surely there was nothing unreasonable in that? The cabin crew showed little interest and said that they could not 'interfere' with the work of their colleagues on the ground. They simply referred Carroll to the ground crew at his place of final destination. When he arrived, Carroll found that his fears had been justified: his costly Taylor guitar had been badly damaged. As he had been told, he reported to the ground personnel and explained his problem. No one was really prepared to listen and he was passed from one person to another. Nobody did anything and nobody accepted responsibility. In the end, Carroll gave up in frustration. He tried to claim compensation through the airline's head office, but at the end of another frustrating nine months he was finally told 'no'. He never received a penny.

Carroll decided to put his frustration to creative use and so he wrote a song about his experiences: 'United breaks guitars'. Unexpectedly, it became a monster internet hit. In less than a week, more than a million people had seen the video. Dave was by no means a famous singer, but people could associate with his feelings and share in his story: they too had felt the same sense of exasperation and powerlessness when dealing with a giant company. During the first days, more than 100 bloggers also picked up the story. United Airlines decided not to react.

Unfortunately for United Airlines, however, the snowball was already rolling – and there was no stopping it. By the middle of the second week the story had reached the ears of the traditional media. CNN ran a piece on the song, the newspapers followed, and all of a sudden Dave was a popular guest on several radio stations. The story seemed to have a life of its own.

Because no reaction from United Airlines was forthcoming, Dave launched a second song, which really put the boot in hard on the company. A few months later, he was finally invited to meet three of United Airlines' senior managers. They personally apologized to him for the inconvenience he had suffered. It was the first time since the incident occurred – more than a year previously – that he had heard the word 'sorry'. A week later he was invited to the American Senate, to discuss the rights of airline passengers.

Throughout this entire saga, United Airlines had chosen not to react in public forums. This was a missed opportunity. Dave's story caused many other dissatisfied customers to come out into the open. The best reaction would have been to listen to these people and try to help them. In this whole sorry tale, there is only a single mitigating factor in the company's favour: in the weeks immediately

FIGURE 2.3

following the damage to his guitar, United Airlines personnel did try to contact Dave directly. But because he did not feel this approach to be genuine, he was not at this stage prepared to meet them. Or perhaps he was becoming increasingly aware of the real power of the modern consumer. Or perhaps he was simply enjoying his '15 minutes of fame': his video is now used by United Airlines (and many others) as didactic material during customer service training.

This is hardly surprising. Dave's story brilliantly illustrates all the paradoxes that we have mentioned so far. There were probably other less than satisfied customers in the past, and they had probably talked online about the company's poor service. The major crisis with Dave could have been avoided, if United Airlines had acted earlier to put these matters right. It is also clear that before the incident customer service at United Airlines was a department, not a philosophy. To make matters even worse, it was more than one department, all of whom were keen to pass on the responsibility to each other. The cabin crew on Dave's plane should have taken action immediately: good service means that everyone must be prepared to take their responsibility seriously. Even though airlines are not always directly in charge of their own baggage handling, there still needs to be clear communication and sense of commitment toward the customer.

One of United's slogans is: 'we invite you to come and fly the friendly skies'. It is a good slogan, but the behaviour of the company's staff showed that it was no more than that: the reality behind the slogan, as Dave experienced, was very different. Modern consumers will only believe what you say in your advertising if they see the proof with their own eyes in your actions.

The paradoxical behaviour of United Airlines was not only confined to its underuse of conversation potential. In fact, they actually provoked a flood of negative conversations. The memory banks of Google mean that crises of this kind can continue to haunt a company. In August 2011, three years down the line, the link to the 'United breaks guitars' video still occupies the 15th spot if you search for information about 'United Airlines' and 'baggage'.

CASE STUDY Threadless avoids the paradox

(Based on Inc.com, 2011, 'The customer is the company', www.inc.com/ magazine/20080601/the-customer-is-the-company.html)

Threadless is a clothing company that pays particularly close attention to the needs of its customer community. In fact, it is an excellent example of how the conversation paradoxes can be avoided. The company was founded in 2000 by Jake Nickell and Jacob De Hart. Their starting capital was just USD 1,000, which they had won in a T-shirt design competition.

The unique thing about the company is that all the clothes are designed by its customers. Every week these customers are given a new opportunity to design a T-shirt for the company's range. Each designer is allowed to submit a maximum of 1,500 ideas. The visitors to the website pick the designs they like the most. The winning designs are manufactured and sold in the Threadless stores. The winning designer is paid a fee based on the level of sales for his or her design. The company has never invested in advertising, has no professional designer of its own and has never had a design failure.

FIGURE 2.4

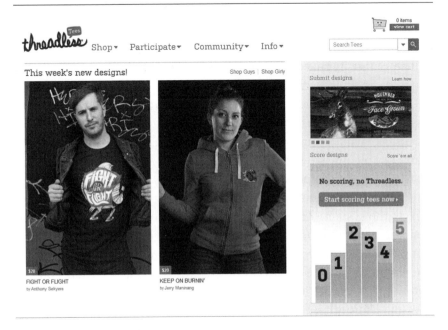

In just 10 years, company's annual turnover has grown to a healthy USD 30 million. The Threadless vision proclaims that 'the customer is the company'. In short, the customers are the staff, and vice versa. Everything that the customers say is immediately integrated into the organization. Growth is based exclusively on word of mouth, which takes advantage of the fact that its 'gimmick' is not just a one-off campaign, but a repeated sequence. Threadless uses this approach continuously, and in so doing breaks the traditional management model.

Traditionally, you have a company. The employees of that company make products and the customers buy those products. With Threadless, the customers make the products for other customers, and the company simply facilitates the production. It is a unique concept.

Our greatest enemy: the 'What if...?' question

Most of the matters discussed in this chapter seem fairly obvious, a question of logic. So why do so many companies fail to avoid these paradoxes? The reason is to be found in our single most potent enemy: the 'What if...?' question. What if our customers abuse our excellent service? What if our staff spend four hours a day on Facebook? What if...? When faced with all these 'What ifs', many companies simply conclude that it is safer to do nothing. This is not only a mistake; it is also an unnecessary mistake.

The reality is that only a minority of people will misuse a good concept. So it is perfectly true that some people will abuse really good customer service; just as it is true that some employees will take advantage of the opportunity to chat for hours on end on Facebook. This is human nature and therefore unavoidable. But how many people are we actually talking about? At Zappos.com, where customers have the possibility to return their shoes 365 days a year, just a few – between 1 per cent and 5 per cent – actually take advantage of the system. Zappos regards this cost as its marketing budget. Besides, its service promise creates so many positive effects for the company, that the 'cost' of the profiteers is minimal in comparison. There will always be profiteers of this kind, no matter what you do. But are you going to base your policy on the (mis)behaviour of this small minority, or are you going to focus your activities on the 95 per cent of ordinary, decent people? This is the question you need to answer – and the answer should be pretty obvious.

It is as if you have a recipe for the most delicious cherry cake in the world, but end up serving your guests a dry and flavourless sponge. Why? Because 5 per cent of people in the world are allergic to cherries. Giving them cherries is a risk you don't want to take – and if they can't eat cherries, no one will eat cherries. This may seem a stupid comparison, but in reality it is the manner in which many crucial business decisions are taken – often with disastrous consequences.

In this respect, McDonald's offers us an example of good practice. If staff forget to include something in your order, all you have to do is tell the company, and it will give you an immediate refund without discussion. In other words, if you want to eat for free, you just phone McDonald's customer service staff and tell them that staff forgot your Big Mac with your last order. They will not dispute or check your claim, even though it may be a lie – they will simply send you a voucher for a free Big Mac. A small number of people make misuse of this system, but McDonald's have no intention of changing its popular customer-friendly approach because of the greed of a few.

The Conversation Company stops the paradox

Your task will not be easy. The path leading to the optimization of your conversation potential is strewn with paradoxes. These are obstacles that you must learn to avoid. Our two introductory chapters make clear that today's consumers want more from companies than just a creative Facebook page or an occasional response to a tweet. Today's consumers want a company that is open and receptive to their opinions, a company that puts the customer first.

In other words, a Conversation Company is not a company full of Twittering employees. Our story is not just a social media story. The Conversation Company really puts the customer in a central position. By eliminating the paradoxes we have mentioned, you will maximize your conversation potential. This will lead to a constant stream of positive conversations about your organization. These conversations will lay the foundations for your future growth.

KEY CONVERSATION POINTS

Possible conversation starters

- Companies have good intentions, but fail to adjust their behaviour quickly enough. Companies say much, but do little.

- Many decisions are based on internal processes, so that the customer does not always occupy a central position in company thinking. Customers sense this and do not like it.

- Conversations are an important driver of growth; manage them actively.

- Customer service is an important conversation starter. The entire company is responsible for service, not just a single department.

- If we listen to conversations carefully, we can predict most crises before they arise.
- Staff are an important source of unused potential. By refusing them access to social media at work, we are forbidding them to talk with other people about their job. Instead of forbidding them to use social media, we should be training them how to use the new media better.
- The story of the Conversation Company is a story of company culture, people and social media.

Questions you must ask yourself

- For which paradoxes do you score well and for which do you score badly?
- Which of your non-implemented good intentions are quick wins that you could easily introduce tomorrow?
- Which of your guidelines and decisions are targeted at the 5 per cent of losers? Is this really necessary?

Further information

Use these links for further interesting information on:

- the 'Stop the paradox' study:
  www.slideshare.net/stevenvanbelleghem/stop-the-paradox;
- the 'United breaks guitars' story (video):
  http://youtube.com/watch?v=5YGc4zOqozo;
- Threadless: **www.threadless.com.**

Part Two
The Conversation Company: culture, people and social media

Chapter Three
The Conversation Company

CASE STUDY
PEMCO made a strategic choice to be 'a little different'

Breaking through the paradox is not always easy, but sometimes a company emerges that has the foresight and vision to advance in a unique and strategic direction. Like PEMCO. PEMCO is a regional US insurer, operating in the northwest states of Washington and Oregon. For years, PEMCO was regularly in the list of the top three insurance carriers 'to be considered' – until, that is, a strong consolidation and competitive wave swept through the insurance sector a few years ago. This renewed competition and significantly increased marketing budgets of PEMCO's national competitors, resulted in a number of intense marketing campaigns. The spending was unprecedented. Unfortunately, PEMCO was unable to match its rivals in this respect and began to lose its coveted position in the 'top three'. This, in turn, had a negative impact on new business sales and market share. The most obvious reaction – an aggressive marketing campaign of its own – was not possible for PEMCO because of budgetary limitations. The competition simply had more money. In this kind of situation, you must choose smartly as a company; you are 'forced' to think differently. You are compelled to examine your strengths and optimize them in ways that others cannot. In other words, drastic situations like the rapid shift in market awareness often call for drastic measures. Rod Brooks, PEMCO's Chief Marketing Officer, believed that leveraging the company's business model – one that for decades has lead with customer relationship and service excellence – and extending the conversations to the point of referral and advocacy was the play that would help the company compete and win in the marketplace. During an extensive interview, Brooks explained his philosophy. His motto (BHAG: Big Hairy Audacious Goal) is: 'we will never have to advertise for a lead again.' The company made the bet that it could be more local than its much larger national competitors; that it could demonstrate that it knew the people of the northwest in ways that its competitors could not; that it was capable of standing in the customers' shoes and delivering a 'world class customer experience' worth talking about at every touchpoint, every time. The emphasis was refocused on the voice of the customer. Listening, listening and more listening became an important aspect of everyone's role. 'You don't learn anything while you're talking', Brooks said.

Brooks's dream is for PEMCO customers to lose sleep at night when they know that a friend or family member isn't insured by PEMCO. And the company has set the bar high. It won't rest until consumers identify PEMCO as one of the top five service experiences they have had – regardless of industry or sector. Brooks and his colleagues knew that succeeding in this task would create a flood of positive conversations. Conversations and relationships offered the only way to fight back against the stronger financial position of PEMCO's rivals.

The first step was to engage the culture of the organization and to re-emphasize the voice of the customer at every opportunity. It was clear right from the start that the staff would have a crucial role to play in optimizing the winning strategy. Every employee who had direct contact with customers was trained in the arts of better service and communication. The values of the company – integrity, responsibility and courage – were transformed into rock-solid reality. Everyone was encouraged to be as helpful as possible to customers and potential customers. The importance of accepting responsibility for every customer interaction – and doing everything possible to help – was emphasized time and again. And, of course, enabling employees to demonstrate the culture of the company via social media sites went hand in hand with the strategy.

After developing and providing the necessary social media training, employees were given permission by the company to engage in conversations with consumers online. It was slow at first, but over time approximately 5 per cent of the staff volunteered to accept this new responsibility. And it worked. The conversations, whether on the phone or online, helped to create more and more satisfied customers. The next stage was to turn some of these satisfied customers into ambassadors; people who would not only recommend PEMCO, but would actually defend its interests. Brooks has developed a model that reflects the customer life cycle and the importance of marketing and remarketing at each step along the way. The model is called 'Awareness to Advocacy'. The three phases of the model are 1) I know you (awareness, perception, preference); 2) I like you (selection and renewal); and 3) I love you (referral and advocacy). Brooks points to advocacy and suggests that if it were its own phase he would call it 4) I defend you.

In addition to this major effort, a number of smaller initiatives were also launched to give the customer a more central place in the company's activities. For example, every management meeting now begins with a customer story from recent days or weeks. Brooks says it's a way to bring the voice of the customer into the room and to demonstrate to everyone present that the company is serious about listening and responding to the customer.

The innovation vision of the company has also changed. The focus is no longer on product innovation, but on service innovation. This was a new concept of customer relations that went much further than mere marketing. It was clear that everyone had a role to play in the successful implementation of this new vision: 'we will never have to advertise for a sales lead again'. In other words, marketing was no longer being left to the marketers. Five years later PEMCO is once again in the list of the top three 'to be considered'. But the impact of the changes on its customer loyalty is even more impressive. At the time of writing, it has a retention rate of 94 per cent, against a sector average of 84–85 per cent. But even now the company is not satisfied. It hopes to push this figure up to 98 per cent. This is the maximum possible, since approximately 2 per cent of its customers move to other states, pass away, or are non-renewed by the company for cause.

PEMCO is well on the way towards becoming a true Conversation Company. It is an excellent example of what can be achieved. Many pundits believed that conversation offered little potential in the insurance sector. PEMCO has proved them wrong. Conversation is important for every company in every sector.

The Conversation Company is based on culture, people and social media

The Conversation Company is much more than a group of Twittering staff and fans. It is a company where the staff and the customers occupy a central position, with the purpose of maximizing conversation potential. Every interaction between the Conversation Company and the outside world must end in a positive conversation, full of impact.

The foundation on which the Conversation Company is built is its company culture. For this reason, the clear formulation of the company's basic values is a crucial first step. Even more importantly, these values must be understood, accepted and actively implemented by everyone in the company, at all levels. Toni Hsieh, the CEO of Zappos.com, puts it as follows: 'The long-term positioning of your company is determined by its culture'.[40] He is 100 per cent correct. Whenever a customer comes into contact with your company, he or she is immediately confronted with your company culture. Every interaction (before, during and after sales) helps to build on your positioning – and culture is the most powerful way to strengthen this positioning. A strong company culture is difficult for competitors to copy, because a culture is embodied in people. For this reason, companies that invest seriously in their culture normally recruit their personnel on the basis of their personality. A strong culture appeals to (and therefore attracts) both new employees and new customers. Why does Google never have problems finding new staff? Because everybody knows that Google has succeeded in combining a culture of innovation with fun. In short, company culture must be the guide of the Conversation Company.

Culture is not about saying what you sell. Culture tells your staff and your customers what your company stands for. Your culture makes clear what things are important to you, and why. It reflects the personality of your company. In fact, it is the personality of your company. Peter Drucker, a marketing legend, formulated this idea as follows: 'Culture eats strategy for lunch.' Culture is the only long-term strategy that your company needs. Surely you are not planning to change the personality of your company every five years? Where would that leave your customers and your staff? A survey of US CEOs suggests that the importance of culture is finally being understood in management circles. According to a 2010 article in *Human Capital Management* magazine, their second most important priority (after the financial aspects of management) is 'the consistent application of a strategy in keeping with the culture of the organisation'.

The culture of an organization is made tangible through its staff. Your staff are the ideal way to make your company seem more 'human'. Customers have much more sympathy for individual employees than for the company as a whole. It is much more difficult to be negative about 100 people you know than about an impersonal company with 100 'staff'. In other words, your employees are largely responsible for the manner in which your customers experience your company. If these employees know and understand how they can contribute towards a better customer experience, this will improve their motivation and lead to more satisfied customers.

The Conversation Company regards each and every member of its staff as a potential spokesperson. The task of the company is to help staff to become good spokespersons. The more good spokespersons you have working for you, the stronger your company positioning is likely to be – on condition that everyone shares the same vision and communicates it with conviction. Your employees must be trained to conduct conversations both proactively and reactively, and in a relevant manner. These conversations may be internal (with other colleagues) or external (with the public). Your company culture must serve as a guide for your conversation teams.

But your employees are not your only spokespersons. Your customers are also an important source of conversations. Every customer is a potential ambassador. If you can reduce the gap between your customers and your staff in a structural manner, your company's bonding with those customers will become tighter. The customers will feel more involved in and committed to your company, so that their willingness to act as ambassadors is likely to increase. In this way, as it were, the Conversation Company can attract new members of 'staff' it doesn't have to pay! In a Conversation Company, the customers and the employees both have the same objective: helping the company forward together.

There is, of course, a third important factor in this conversation equation: social media. Social media spread the conversations about your company on a massive scale. By proactively sharing relevant content and reactively dealing with any customer questions that may arise, the Conversation Company is strongly present in the online conversation community. The objective must be to achieve a well-balanced mix between your own online media (a Facebook page, a Twitter account, a blog) and earned online media (customers who share positive stories, based on their experience of your company). In addition to extending your reach, social media also play a key role in your structural collaboration with your customers. In this

FIGURE 3.1

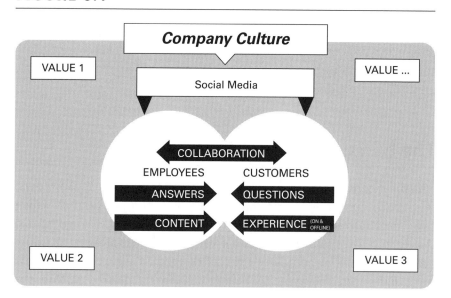

TABLE 3.1 Differences between a traditional company and a Conversation Company

	Traditional company	Conversation company
Positioning	It is determined by product characteristics or brand attributes	It is determined by culture and values
Most important channels of communication	Offline media	Conversations between people
Role of social media	It is an additional channel for spreading the company message	It is used to expand company reach and facilitate conversations and collaboration with customers
Decision-making	The management decides just about everything	Customers and staff are involved in the decision-making process

way (via different online communities), customers can participate in the decision-making processes of your company.

These three elements – culture, people and social media – all contribute towards the creation of a conversation lever. This in turn helps to enhance the public perception of your company in a proactive, credible and positive manner.

The basis: culture and people

The most commonly used definition of company culture is as follows: 'Company culture is a series of shared values and convictions which help individuals to understand the functioning of the company. A clear company culture makes it easy for the employees to know precisely what the company expects of them. Culture gives people an insight into the type of behaviour that is desired within the company'.[41] Research has confirmed that a company culture often forms the basis for the successful implementation of a strategy.[42] A strong company culture also has a positive impact on the performance and productivity of its employees.[43] The culture is a kind of 'mental programming' for an organization, which distinguishes it from its competitors.[44]

Your culture is the personality of your organization and the foundation on which your Conversation Company is built. Your staff and your customers make this culture tangible to others. This involves a method of reasoning that works from inside to outside. A traditional company is first and foremost interested in making its shareholders happy. Making customers happy only comes in the second place, with the staff a poor third. A Conversation Company turns this logic on its head. If the staff are happy, they will be pleased to make the customers happy; and if the customers are happy, profits will rise, so the shareholders will also be happy. The CEO of Southwest Airlines puts it like this: 'We take good care of our staff. Our staff take good care of our customers. And our customers take good care of our shareholders.'

CASE STUDY
The vision of HCL Technologies: employees first, customers second

When Vineet Nayar was appointed CEO of the Indian HCL Technologies in 2005, the staff were all under the impression that the company was a successful one. Everyone was in a party mood. However, the reality was less encouraging. HCL was evolving much more slowly than its major competitors. If the new CEO did not take action, the future was not looking very bright. Five years later, the company was one of the fastest growing IT organizations in the world. This transformation was achieved by injecting a new mentality into the company culture and by giving a new role to key members of staff. The new vision was summarized as 'employees first, customers second' – for further details see Vineet Nayar's book with the same title.[45] Nayar had concluded that the existing culture was not capable of meeting the challenges the company faced – and so he decided to work from inside to outside: first the staff, then the customers, then the shareholders.

The focus of the mentality change was concentrated on employees working in the value zone. The value zone is the place where employees and customers interact. The whole company was restructured to serve the needs of these key staff. The reasoning was as follows: if everyone does everything they can to help these staff, this must inevitably lead to satisfied customers. In this sense, the 'employees first, customers second' programme was more than just an HR plan; it was a general, company-wide strategy. The only way to make it succeed was to introduce a new company culture, in which open communication stood central.

This innovative philosophy was realized in four stages.

The first stage was known as 'mirror, mirror'. In this stage, the CEO wanted to make clear to everyone in the company just how serious the situation really was. It was time to face up to the facts – and to do something about them. This helped to create a broad consensus of approval for change. As a first step, the party mood had to go. While this prevailed, it would be difficult to adopt another approach. Nayar initiated a debate on this crucial subject in all departments and at all levels of the company. This debate pushed open the door to change – albeit only slightly.

The second phase was designed to build up trust through a process of transparent communication. All relevant details, including financial information, were made available to every member of staff. People were encouraged to ask questions. This was by no means easy in a company which had not previously been known for its open communication style. But it worked. Staff's confidence in managers increased. This was essential if the necessary structural changes were to be pushed through with any chance of success.

The third phase saw the implementation of these changes, and was by far the most radical. The entire hierarchical management pyramid was turned on its head. The supporting departments (such as HR, IT, finance) and the general managers were placed at the full disposal of staff working in the value zone. The basic premise was that staff in the value zone must receive maximum support from everyone in the company. This had far-reaching consequences. For example, if a member of staff had an IT request, it was ultimately the requester from the value zone who decided whether or not the proposed solution was 'acceptable'; previously this decision would have been made by the IT manager, whether the people in the value zone liked it or not. This had led to frustration in the past, since the value zone staff knew that many of the solutions they were being offered would not meet the needs of the customers.

The fourth and final phase was the development of a new role for the CEO and the other senior managers. Nayar saw himself as the facilitator of a never-ending process of change and improvement. A classic CEO is assumed to know all the right answers, whereas Nayer is more concerned to ask all the right questions. He monitors the continuing evolution of the company and its markets, and raises issues for discussion on the basis of what he sees. But the real decisions are taken and the real changes made by people working in the value zone. It is not the managers of a company who have a direct impact on the customers; it is the staff on the ground and in the field. The greater their commitment to the company, the greater their satisfaction will be – to the long-term benefit of everyone.

CASE STUDY

The Belgian Federal Department of Social Security – doing it for you

(Based on an interview in 2011 with Frank Van Massenhove, Chairman of the Belgian Federal Department of Social Security – FDSS.)

The Belgian FDSS is one of the most modern companies in Europe in terms of the new leadership philosophy. Under the guiding hand of Frank Van Massenhove, the FDSS has succeeded in significantly increasing the productivity and satisfaction levels of its staff. As a result, the customers – the ordinary citizens of Belgium – are also much happier with the service provided. The basis of this new target-oriented approach is that the staff are free to work wherever and whenever they like, as long as they reach their objectives. Should they want to work from home, 92 per cent have permission to do so. Only a relatively small number (reception personnel, cleaning teams, etc) need to be physically present in the FDSS offices, in order to provide a basic minimum service to visitors. Work is no longer allocated by the managers, but by the different teams themselves. In this sense, the management no longer manages; it facilitates, monitors and assesses the results.

The organization seeks to make things as easy as possible for staff by investing heavily in new technology. The FDSS is the first government department to digitalize all its activities fully. It is even forbidden in meetings to write with a pen and paper; everyone has their own digital notebook.

As a result of these drastic changes, some employees chose to leave the FDSS. The sharpening of a culture nearly always results in a process of natural selection. Those who remain are those who match the new culture. Once this point has been reached, increased efficiency rapidly follows. Moreover, the remaining employees are also very proud of the innovative attitude of their employer – and are happy to share this news with anyone and everyone who will listen. This has the added advantage that the FDSS now finds it much easier to attract top quality staff. Its excellent reputation is now known far and wide – and all thanks to the enthusiasm of its own people! In short, the FDSS has made full use of its conversation potential.

Our partner: social media

Social media are the mirror of society. All the conversations that previously took place offline are now amplified and expanded online. This means that every company can quickly discover what the world is thinking and saying. The transparency in consumer feedback has never been as great as it is today. This transparency means that it is no longer possible for companies to pull the wool over the individual consumer's eyes. Social media have forced companies to become more open and more honest.

The Conversation Company regards social media as a means, not as an end in themselves. They act as a kind of magnifying glass, which enlarges and accelerates the activities of the Conversation Company. Social media are in partnership with the Conversation Company. They are an extremely useful and important channel of communication to contact people in a more personal, more 'human' way. Through the use of social media, the Conversation Company is able to build up a group of strongly committed customers. These customers are then involved in a structural manner in the further development of the company as a whole.

In concrete terms, there are two aspects of particular importance. The first is reach. In social media, wide reach and narrow reach both have their uses. It is possible to do something good for a single individual, thereby creating value for both the individual and the company. This is an ideal approach, for example, for dealing with the problems of a particular customer. In this instance, narrow reach is important. But in some cases, you want to reach everyone, not just a single person. If you have a fun promotion stunt or a great YouTube film, you want the whole world to know! This too is possible via social media. Good content always spreads like wildfire.

The second aspect is developing structural relationships. Social media offer you the option of both loose and structural contact with the public. A fun action of limited duration may only result in a single positive interaction. But even this creates value for both the consumer and the company. However, it is also possible that this interaction may lead to a conversation. Social media then give you the possibility to work together with a wider group of people (staff, customers, suppliers, shareholders, etc) in a more structural manner.

The important thing to note is that both these options always result in value creation for both the consumer and the company. The Conversation Company exploits the possibilities offered by social media in all its many contexts and permutations: narrow reach and wide reach, loose relationships and structural relationships. In view of the fact, however, that the long-term aim is to secure the commitment of as many people as possible, wide reach combined with structural relationships is the preferred combination.

The social media figures

The figures associated with the use of social media continue to be impressive. An article was recently published that described just one minute of internet use.[46] The minute in question was in June 2011, and it comprised:

- 48 hours of video material uploaded on YouTube;
- 100 new Linkedin users;
- 320 new Twitter users;
- 1,500 blog posts going 'live';
- 6,000 photos uploaded on Flickr;
- 13,000 iPhone applications downloaded;
- 98,000 tweets sent;
- 370,000 people telephoned on Skype;
- 500,000 comments made on Facebook updates;
- 700,000 Facebook updates;
- 700,000 search enquiries on Google;
- 1,168,000 e-mails sent.

CASE STUDY
Twitter predicts stock market trends with 86.7 per cent accuracy

You don't believe that social media are a mirror on society? What do you think, then, of these figures? On the basis of the emotionality of Twitter updates, specialists can predict movements in the Dow Jones index with an accuracy rate of 86.7 per cent.[47] If the emotions on Twitter are negative, the market index will fall three days later. That is the simple but impressive conclusion of a research survey carried out by the Bloomington University of Indiana. Apparently, there is a strong correlation between the emotionality on Twitter and the emotionality of the population as a whole. These feelings are then reflected in the actions of investors. Using the same principles, the likely success of a film, book or song can be predicted with reasonable accuracy weeks before its actual launch.[48]

CASE STUDY Twelpforce is unique

The Best Buy retail chain uses social media in a unique manner. The focus of this use is concentrated on customer service and conversations. With this aim in mind, the company has set up a Twitter help desk. So what is so special about that, you might ask? Many other companies have Twitter help desks. True, but usually these are relatively small-scale affairs, run by a limited number of staff who have 'Twitter support' as one of their several core tasks. However, Best Buy has set up its own Twitter core team. In addition, there are another 2,500 Best Buy staff who actively help to run the Twitter service.[49] This means that at any one time there are literally hundreds, if not thousands, of Best Buy employees ready, willing and able to help customers with their questions and problems, 24 hours a day, 7 days a week. There is always someone who monitors conversations, to see when the company can usefully join in.

This powerful service team is known as Twelpforce (Helpforce on Twitter). All the staff attached to the team can tweet on the @twelpforce account. By adding #twelpforce to every tweet, all their other colleagues can follow or join in the conversation. This makes it easy to see which questions have already been dealt with and which have not.

When the programme was started in July 2009, the management team issued clear instructions to all its staff participants:

> The promise that we make to our customers from July onwards is a serious promise. Customers can ask us about their future purchases, our current range of products or our customer service. Via Twitter we are going to answer all these questions very quickly. Let us see what we can learn from these conversations.

> If you reply to a customer, remember that your tone is very important. Make sure that this tone is authentic and honest. Turn your contact into a conversation. Be yourself. Show respect but expect respect in return. Our aim is to help people. If you do not know the answer to a question, say that you will try to find out.[50]

The CEO of Best Buy, Brian Dunn, sees the Twelpforce as an important investment which will bring his company closer to its customers. In an interview in 2010 for the *Harvard Business Review* he said:

> Customers get free service and advice. In return, Best Buy gets free insights into the needs and concerns of those customers. Helping your customers in a genuine and authentic manner is the best possible investment in customer loyalty. In the long term, people will only choose the companies which show this kind of genuine interest in the consumer. Via Twelpforce, we are showing that Best Buy is already that kind of company.

FIGURE 3.2

The Conversation Company breaks through the paradox

This philosophy must form the basis of any attempt to optimize conversation potential. The Conversation Company succeeds in breaking through restrictive paradoxes. In this way, obstacles to conversations are removed, allowing staff and customers to work in unison to build a stronger company. Social media allow this staff–customer collaboration to be a close one and together these groups tell the rest of the world about the company of which they are both proud.

Every company has the potential to become a Conversation Company. This book will help you to find the route that is most suited to your organization's culture and strategy. Of course, a number of different starting points are possible. A company that profiles itself as a strong product leader (eg Apple) will choose a different approach from a low-cost player (eg Walmart or Ikea). A strong product leader might be more inclined to place the emphasis on co-creation and engagement with the customer for the development of new products. The content will focus on innovations and new designs for products. In contrast, a price-player will tell its customers about the cheaper sources of energy being introduced, in order to keep costs low. For much the same reason, this type of company might even farm out its service responsibilities to its own customers.

Many of the stories in conversation companies are about offering customer experience. This element is easiest to integrate for companies that have a strategy where the needs of the customer are paramount, for example Zappos.[51] Organizations permeated with this ethos usually provide excellent service, thereby ensuring that this is their most important conversation starter. Staff and customers work together to build up a stronger company. Via social media they are able to collaborate closely and they use these same media to tell the rest of the world what they – and their favourite company – are doing.

In short, there are routes enough and projects enough that will match the philosophy of your company to the philosophy of the Conversation Company.

In the following three chapters, we will be looking at the key component elements of the Conversation Company – culture, people and social media – in greater depth.

KEY CONVERSATION POINTS

Possible conversation starters

- Dare to embrace change with an open mind.
- 'The long term positioning of your company is determined by your culture' (CEO, Zappos).
- Your company culture is the conversation guide for your staff.
- People make culture tangible.
- Social media are a mirror on society and accelerate everything your company does.
- Via social media a Conversation Company builds up structural relationships with a large group of people, but without leaving narrow reach and loose contact opportunities unused.
- The Olympic minimum is getting tougher every day; don't delay change until it is too late.

Questions you must ask yourself

- How would you describe your company culture? Do you have a strong company culture?
- Can your company culture serve as a foundation to build a better company?
- How many of your staff (in percentage terms) fit well with your ideal culture?
- Do you know enough about social media to talk meaningfully about them?

Further information

Use these links for further interesting information on:

- Twelpforce in action: **http://twitter.com/#!/twelpforce;**
- the presentation by Rod Brooks of PEMCO, about the company's journey to become a Conversation Company: **www.slideshare.net/NW_Mktg_Guy/journey-to-an-engaged-enterprise-womma.**

Chapter Four
Company culture – the heart of the Conversation Company

The values of your company: empty words?

A short while ago I gave a workshop in a large organization in the financial sector on the role of company culture in conversation management. Before the workshop started, I was sitting in the lobby of the headquarters building, where the company values were proudly proclaimed on the wall. Its five key values were integrity, cooperation, quality, results and focus on the customer. During the workshop, I couldn't resist the temptation to try out a little experiment on the participants. I asked the 15 senior managers in attendance to write down a list of what they thought were the company's five key values. The results were startling. It was only after long discussions and much doubting that we finally arrived at the five correct values. And even then no one dared to bet money that they were 100 per cent correct.

In their 2008 book, Moenaert, Robben and Gouw[52] described the situation correctly. During the 1980s it was fashionable (and fun) to formulate a company mission and company values. Unfortunately, it soon became clear that this was not enough to guarantee financial success.[53] A mission statement is often an empty shell. Much the same is true of company values. Values will never have impact unless they form an active part of the company's day-to-day operations. They must shine through in every action. Sadly, most companies do very little to promote their values. They may send out a couple of circulars on the subject each year, but this is not enough. Values must be the very basis of your company culture. They need to be visible to those who come into contact with the company and you must manage them daily. Nordstrom, a company famed for its excellent service, makes its values 'live' by telling stories about them. Instead of giving its new staff long and complex lessons on the theory and processes of customer relations, it seeks to motivate them with inspiring and often moving examples from the company's past. It shows them how they, too, can help to give Nordstrom customers a 'wow' effect. This approach at least makes the values concrete, and is a hundred times better than a list of empty-sounding words in an impressive lobby.

The Conversation Company needs powerful values. Not to hang on a lobby wall, but to make them felt in every action and at every level of the organization. Values create a framework within which the company's employees know how they can or must behave. Whether they are old hands or new recruits, it offers a comforting degree of structure and security to their job. The Chairman of Levi Strauss expressed it in these terms in an article in the *Harvard Business Review* published in 1990: 'Our values determine our responsibilities and our behaviour. Our employees are given training in what these values mean. Each member of staff is evaluated, in order to assess their fit with the values. Management decisions are tested against them.' Companies with strong values generally have more motivated and more loyal personnel.[54]

In the Conversation Company, every employee is a potential spokesperson. A member of staff who does not know what the company values are or who is unable or unwilling to display them through his or her actions will never make a good spokesperson. Defining your values and letting them colour your operations at every organizational level is just step 1. Step 2 is to find and then cherish the members of staff who can communicate these values to others. The Conversation Company understands the art of applying its company culture consistently in each and every aspect of the company's life, almost to an extreme degree. The culture is seen as the conversation guide for the entire organization.

CASE STUDY Ekin: the extreme company culture of Nike[55]

Nike is a cool brand. It is a name that is synonymous with creative advertising. Have you ever seen the adverts with all the great heroes from the world of football? Then you know exactly what we mean. Nike is equally famous for its passion for innovation. With the Nike+ it radically changed the running experience for millions of joggers. By forging a link between running shoes and the iPod, it became possible for runners to keep their results in a systematic manner. Even better, it was possible to compare your results with the results of other runners from all around the world. All of a sudden the lonely jogger found that he or she was a member of a thriving jogging community! And Nike+ is just one example of the company's many trendsetting innovations.

As a result, Nike is the most talked about brand in its sector. According to Blogpulse April–July 2011, in comparison with brands such as Adidas and Reebok (its most important competitors), the number of Nike conversations is five to ten times greater (varying from period to period).

The basis of this success is a rock-solid company culture. Moreover, it is a culture that has existed ever since the company was first founded by Phil Knight, who for many years was also the CEO. The co-founder was Bill Bowerman, who had originally been Knight's coach as a middle distance runner. Both men had been inspired by Steve Prefontaine, another famous US athlete trained by Bowerman, who was convinced that better sporting material would lead to better sporting performance. Together, these three men laid the foundations for the Nike culture, and have done more for the company than all the other famous sporting names who have since endorsed its products. The culture is built around three core values:

- **Authenticity.** Nike is authentic in everything it does. Transparency is not a risk, it is a strength.

- **Athleticism.** Nike must be able to appeal to all athletes.

- **Performance.** Nike products must meet the very highest standards. Nike stands for success.

These three values are reflected fully in its most famous slogan: 'Just do it!' It is a philosophy Nike not only projects in the market place, but also within its own company. Its staff are also expected to 'just do it!'

Nike has built up its culture by using stories. Its leaders believe that the stories of yesteryear can help to shape the future. A number of the top managers have been charged with the task of telling stories about the past and the present of the company with the passion of true evangelists, not only to new staff, but to all their staff. Nelson Farris is the company's corporate storyteller. The tales that he tells are not tales of financial plans and sales figures. They are heroic tales about people and what they have been able to accomplish ('just do it!'). In this manner the stories pass into Nike legend, a legend that is carried and perpetuated by all the company's employees. One of the first and most well-known stories describes how coach Bowerman was dissatisfied with his running shoes. He wanted to design something better, and so when he went home he poured some liquid rubber onto a hot waffle iron, just to see what would happen – and so the waffle sole was born. It is a story that makes an innovative culture tangible.

When Nike was going through a difficult period financially, it became apparent that some of the staff no longer believed in preserving the old core values. But the company's founders held firm. It is above all in difficult times that you need to show your commitment to what you believe. The storm passed, and the future has proved that the founders were right.

To further strengthen its conviction, the company has also developed an extensive storytelling programme. The most extreme element in this programme are the 'Ekins' (Ekin is Nike spelt backwards). The Ekins are the company's official evangelists. Their task is to recount stories about Nike to both internal and external audiences. It is by no means simple to become an Ekin. The candidates have to undergo a nine-day bootcamp before they can be selected. They are trained with almost military discipline and precision at a location in Oregon, where the company's founders once trained as athletes. This is designed to make the Ekins feel part of the original history of Nike, allowing them an even better understanding of the rich heritage to which they now belong. At the end of the bootcamp, the Ekins must prove their ultimate commitment to Nike. This involves them having a tattoo on their ankle – a tattoo of the Nike logo in mirror image. Some might find this an extreme form of cultural management – nevertheless, there are already hundreds of Nike Ekins.

FIGURE 4.1

The story of Zappos, the online shoe-seller, is already widely known. In Chapter 1 we discussed the phenomenal growth the company has been able to realize, based on a flood of positive conversations. These conversations were based in turn on the excellent customer service for which Zappos is so rightly famous. The company's senior executives focus primarily on the management of this culture of excellence.

CASE STUDY
Zappos has 'just once' focus: the management of culture and values[56]

Senior executives at Zappos realize that the company's 'excellence' can only be maintained as long as the 'culture' part of the equation is also transparent and authentic. In a 2010 interview with the *Harvard Business Review*, Zappos's CEO Toni Hsieh said that this philosophy was first developed in 2004, when the company had already been in existence for five years. This was the point at which the founders realized that the provision of extreme service represented their best strategic choice. But to make this concept work, it was essential to have the right people. In this sense, the values of Zappos were first defined to help as selection criteria during recruitment interviews. Later, it became evident that they were also relevant to many of the company's daily activities and decisions. When Hsieh was first drawing up these values, he had in his mind (or so he admitted later) the perfect employee, the employee he would like to clone. This person's ideal personality was reflected in the values he selected. However, he wisely decided to consult with his staff about these values before casting everything in concrete. After all, it was vitally important that they, too, should believe in these values. Via an e-mail circular, he asked his employees to list the qualities which they most closely associated with Zappos. The result was a list of no fewer than 37 different values. This list was later refined to a list of just 10 core values, which encapsulated the essence of the Zappos approach. The whole process took more than a year to complete and even Hsieh was surprised that it took so long. But it was worth the effort: values must be honest and genuinely felt; otherwise they will fail to have impact. Hsieh wanted strong staff commitment to these values, since they were to be the leitmotif that would decide who was hired and fired, and how the customers were dealt with. Without this level of commitment, the whole exercise would have been nothing more than a costly waste of time.

The 10 values finally selected by Zappos were:

- Deliver 'wow' through service.

- Embrace and drive change.

- Create fun and a little weirdness.

- Be adventurous, creative and open minded.
- Pursue growth and learning.
- Build open and honest relationships with communication.
- Build a positive team and family spirit.
- Do more with less.
- Be passionate and determined.
- Be humble.

The company tries to maintain these values in everything that it does. The recruiting service has developed questions which test a candidate's compatibility with the values. The job description of every member of staff states explicitly that compliance with the values is an integral part of the job.

The Zappos approach is in many ways comparable with the theories of Collins and Porras.[57] They suggest that companies should imagine that they are making a rocket trip to Mars. The rocket only has room for seven passengers, and so the question is this: which seven employees do you take? The answer is simple: the seven employees whose personality most closely matches the values of the organization.

Culture must lead to identification with your company

The many workshops we have conducted with companies have suggested to us that the factors that prompt organizations to start with conversation management have little to do with company size or sector. The companies furthest along the conversation road have either had a social media crisis in recent years (Dell, Comcast) or have a very strong company culture (Zappos, Southwest Airlines). Research carried out for this book has confirmed these general impressions. Of the companies that already focus strongly on customer-oriented thinking, 82 per cent have clear and consistently applied company values, in comparison with 54 per cent of the companies that are at the start of their change process. Of the advanced companies

77 per cent think that culture is as important as strategy, against just 31 per cent of the starter companies.[58]

The same research shows that only 64 per cent of US and UK companies have clearly defined values. Just 56 per cent make efforts to manage these values actively; 45 per cent want to amend their values because of the increasing importance of social media.

Every company needs appropriate values. There is no point trying to introduce the values of Zappos into Ford, or vice versa. Your values have a great impact on the conversations about your company. If staff interact with people on the basis of these values, your company will speak with a single voice, even though it has a thousand different mouths. This uniform approach means that your customers will get a clear and consistent experience every time they come into contact with your organization. This leads to conversations that are appropriate for your company. Moreover, it ensures that the conversations are 'believable', and therefore have impact. If your company does not have clear values, each member of staff will be talking to your customers as an individual, not as the representative of a coherent whole. In this instance, the conversations will fly off in many different directions, and will not have the impact that the Conversation Company seeks.

Many companies have similar values. The four most frequently cited values are: result-oriented, customer-oriented, good service and integrity.[59] There is nothing wrong with these values, but they are hardly likely to excite your customers – at least, not expressed in this manner. If you read the 10 values of Zappos, you immediately get a 'feel' of what the company is like and what it stands for. Values must help you to differentiate your company. To such an extent, that after a while the outside world begins to describe your company in terms of your chosen values. Here at InSites Consulting, it gives us great pleasure if one of our customers tells us that he or she thinks that we are a passionate company. Passion is one of our core values. And if our customers are able to feel this passion and tell us that they have experienced it, this is a nice compliment – and shows that we are still on the right lines.

Our research[60] has also shown that the ability of your employees to identify with your company values is the key to a good company culture. The art when defining your values is therefore to ensure that people are able to recognize themselves in them. If staff are able to relate to the values of the company, a powerful mental and emotional

FIGURE 4.2

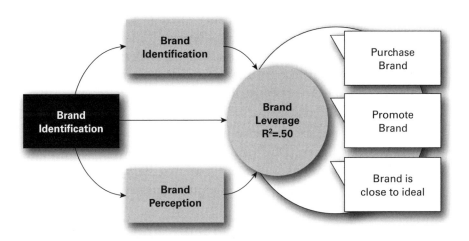

bond will be created.[61] This bond leads in turn to positive conversations. If your people feel good, they will converse enthusiastically about your company.

There are three values in particular that can help to ensure a strong identification with your culture, and so lead to positive conversations:[62]

- **Openness.** Nike describes this perfectly: 'transparency is a strength, not a threat.' The Conversation Company succeeds in communicating openly with its employees and customers. An open attitude leads to the development of trust. Clear and open communication always encourages trust between people, and trust is the basis of conversations that have impact. 'Open' can be interpreted in many different ways. You can be open to negative criticism. You can be open to collaboration with customers for the development of new products. You can be open to the creation of space for staff and customers who want to help your company. Our research[63] showed that the companies that are furthest advanced in terms of customer-oriented thinking are also the most open to the idea of giving trust to their employees.

- **Authenticity.** Being genuine and coming across to the public as genuine are crucial factors in ensuring the credibility of conversations. Van den Bergh and Mattias Behrer[64] argue that authenticity is one of the aspects that the brands of today must have, if they want to convince the new generation of consumers (generation Y). Being honest with your staff, honest with your customers and honest towards society are the key elements in acquiring this authenticity. Recent surveys have shown that marketeers regard authenticity as the most important trend in the years ahead.[65]

- **Happiness.** This factor is also mentioned by Van den Bergh and Mattias Behrer. Our own research[66] has shown that the modern consumer likes positive emotions. Being positive and making people feel good is an important conversation starter.

All three of these values form part of a strong culture. But it is not our intention that you should copy them literally! The art lays in using them as a source of inspiration when drawing up your own 'appropriate' set of values. Search for values that match your image and needs. Above all, search for values that you know you can make good. These values will determine the direction of everything that your company does: the recruitment of staff, the development of new products, the creation of new advertising campaigns, etc.

CASE STUDY   Ikea CEO remains true to the company values

Ingvar Feodor Kamprad is the founder and largest shareholder of Ikea. According to the Swedish press, he is the richest man in the world, with a fortune estimated at between 50 and 90 billion euros. Ikea works according to a very consistent principle: good design at cheap prices. Kamprad has remained true to this principle all his life. Notwithstanding his enormous wealth, he is still regularly to be seen eating cheap meals in Ikea restaurants. Some people even say that he buys his wrapping paper for the following Christmas in January, because that is when the paper is cheapest. If he stays in a hotel, he doesn't drink in the hotel bar but goes and buys what he wants from the local all-night store. Strong values are often coupled with the ideas of a founder. And continuing to cherish these values over a long period is a tremendous strength.

CASE STUDY
Studio 100 grows and grows on the basis of strong values

(Based on an interview with the former CEO of Studio 100, Dominic Stas, and commercial director, Tom Grymonprez in 2010.)

Studio 100 is a fast-growing Belgian company that looks set to become the Disney of Europe. The company has created numerous successful characters for children, such as Plop the Gnome, Maya the Bee, Pirate Pete and the House of Anubis. Its mission is to make children of all ages happy. It makes television programmes, films and musicals. In addition, it owns a number of theme parks in Europe, publishes magazines and books, and even has its own television channel. The story of Studio 100 is a story of unbroken success. In just 13 years, the company has generated an annual turnover in excess of 130 million euros and now employs more than 800 people. This success is built on a very strong company culture. Its values are: a 'we' feeling, result-orientation, mental flexibility (= open), open communication (= authenticity), enterprising and positive (= happiness). These values are a combination of the personalities of the founders and are complementary values. They integrate the three Conversation Company values in their own, passionate way.

The CEO, Dominic Stas, and the commercial director, Tom Grymonprez, see two key factors that have helped the company to achieve its meteoric rise. The first is the good quality and the good content of the product. The second is undoubtedly the strong company culture. A company like Studio 100, by its very nature, inevitably generates a huge number of conversations. The strong culture means that staff are also willing to add their own conversations that have impact. These employees seem to sense perfectly what they can say and what not. There is an unwritten law that the magic of the fictional characters should never be compromised – and it never is. Everyone is too proud of them for that. Nothing has ever appeared online that has given the management cause for concern. The culture is the perfect conversation guide.

The 'we' philosophy is translated into the remuneration strategy of the company. The bonuses for staff are group bonuses, which are determined by the total results of the company. This helps to eliminate internal competition between the company's salespeople. The individual is subordinated to the greater whole.

Thanks to this mentality, Studio 100 was able to launch a new digital television cooking channel in just 10 months. The time and money invested by the company was just a fraction of what its competitors would have needed to achieve the same results. Everything is managed with great efficiency. In particular, the mental aspect plays a positive role. Once a decision has been taken, everyone throws their weight 100 per cent behind it. This is the moment when the 'we' feeling has its strongest effect. Everyone is working for the same mission, so people dare to stick their necks out and accept the risks and responsibilities that are necessary to get the job done.

One of the problems with present-day company culture is that people always want to make perfect decisions that are right every time. For this reason, even the simplest decisions can be discussed for hours on end. Every possible scenario is examined in the greatest possible detail, to ensure that 'wrong' decisions are avoided. This method of working slows down the working of companies to a significant degree. And, of course, it still doesn't prevent bad decisions from being made! In setting up a Conversation Company, it will be necessary during an initial period to work on a number of projects for which you will have had little past experience. It is important to accept that you will make mistakes during this phase. Churchill was right when he said 'success is going from failure to failure without any loss of enthusiasm.' In this respect, we can all learn a lesson from Google.

CASE STUDY   Google encourages failure!

In less than 10 years, Google grew into a company that is worth 100 billion dollars. The Google culture encourages people to make mistakes.[67] Some of these mistakes even earn the perpetrator a pat on the shoulder from the big boss! Consider the story of Sheryl Sandberg, the vice-president of the company.[68] Sheryl is responsible for Google's automatic advertising system. This service accounts for more than 80 per cent of the turnover. At a certain point in time, Sheryl took a wrong decision, a decision that quickly cost Google several millions of dollars in lost revenue. 'I went too fast, didn't check my idea through, and so I wasted an awful lot of money,' she later admitted. Because the scale of her mistake was so massive, she went to apologize personally to Larry Page, one of the company's co-founders. Page accepted her apology, but surprised her with the comment: 'I am glad you have made this mistake. I would rather have a company where we do too many things too fast, than a company where we do too few things too slowly. The day when we stop making these kinds of mistakes is the day that we are not taking enough risks...'

Culture has an impact on every part of the Conversation Company

In the remainder of this book, we will be looking at the different steps that need to be taken in your transition to a Conversation Company. Your company culture will be the leitmotif running through each of these steps. Regard your culture as a guide. Allow it to tell you what you should and should not do. The Conversation Company manages its culture and manages its values in everything it says and does. This has consequences for the different departments in your organization.

HR implications

- Refer to the values in job vacancies.
- When recruiting staff, look first for a fit with your culture and only then at the person's other competencies and qualifications.
- Evaluate existing staff on the basis of their fit with your values.
- Be prepared to dismiss staff if they do not fit in with your culture.

Customer service implications

- The customer service department must work with the same values as the rest of the organization.
- Online conversation management must be conducted internally by true representatives of the brand.
- The values of the company must be projected through every channel of communication.

Marketing implications

- The values must be the same for both staff and customers.
- All communication must take account of the values of the company.
- Ensure that the different brands each adequately reflect the core values of the parent company.

CASE STUDY Southwest Airlines culture blog

In 2010, a difficult year for the air sector, Southwest Airlines booked profits of USD 143 million, making it the most successful airline company on the US market. Southwest is a company that owes much to its strong company culture. This culture is based on three fun values: have a warrior spirit, the heart of a servant and show a fun-LUVing attitude. There are even rumours that some stewards 'rap' the security instructions at the beginning of each flight! And the CEO occasionally comes on board to hand out bags of nuts to the passengers. The culture permeates every aspect of Southwest's operations. Already in 2006 it had started its 'Nuts about Southwest' blog. The idea was that staff could record any amusing or illustrative incidents that reflected the basic company values. Fun stories, interesting 'did-you-knows' and important company news were all shared via this blog – and this at a time when most companies had never even heard of a blog. In the meantime, the Southwest site has won the national award for best company blog in the United States three times. During the same period, the company has recruited its own small army of bloggers from its own staff. This means that new and interesting content, carefully planned to ensure sufficient variety, is added to the site on a regular basis. There is little doubt that it is Southwest's culture that sets it apart as a company from all its major competitors. And the blog ensures that the culture determines Southwest's conversation strategy.

FIGURE 4.3

CASE STUDY The Skittles brand book

Skittles is a new sweet. But there are already hundreds of different kinds of sweets in the shops. So how do your differentiate your brand? A new flavour? A new packaging? No, Skittles had other ideas. Instead, the company making Skittles played the culture card in full as the basis of its marketing strategy. Did it work? Boy, did it work! The brand already has millions of fans on Facebook. In the middle of 2011 the company even launched its own brand book, packed with funny quotes, colourful photos and whacky drawings. Just flicking through the book (**www.scibd.com/doc/32214928/Skittles-brand-book**) makes you happy! Ask yourself these questions: Can my image of Skittles be changed by looking at this book? Does it make me more positive in outlook? You don't need to tell me: I already know the answers. It proves beyond doubt that culture really can form the heart of a super-effective marketing strategy.

Help! My company doesn't have a Conversation Company culture

Do you have this feeling? Then you need to keep on reading. And don't worry: many other companies feel exactly the same, according to an article written in 2009 by Jeanne Meister on Harvard Business blog entitled 'When your company isn't ready for social media'. The following statements will help you to test just how close you are to having a Conversation Company culture.

- Our values are clear to everyone in the company.
- Our values permeate everything we do.
- New staff are only recruited if they match our values.
- We use at least one of the three Conversation Company values.
- Our internal and external values are the same.
- Our staff have access to social media at work.
- Our staff are allowed to talk about their work on social media.
- We encourage our staff to converse online with customers and consumers.
- If negative customer comments appear online, we do not remove these but seek to help the customer in question.

- If a member of staff says or writes something wrong, we coach him or her in better behaviour.

How did you score? If you managed 8 out of 10 or more, you are ready to make a rapid transition to a fully-fledged Conversation Company. If you scored less than 5, then you will need fundamentally to change your company culture. This is not impossible – but it will require a major effort from everyone in the organization.

In Part Four we will describe in concrete terms the steps that you need to take in order to turn yourself into a Conversation Company. One of the most important elements in this respect is the pilot projects. Pilot projects allow your company to become acquainted with the positive aspects of conversations. They can also be your first small steps in the direction of a new and better company culture. By defining your pilot projects cleverly, you can help to create a consensus for change within your company. Your total metamorphosis will take much longer than in companies which are already much further along the road – but at least you will have made a start. And remember: every journey, however long, starts with a single step.

KEY CONVERSATION POINTS

Possible conversation starters

- Many companies have no values or fail to display them consistently in their activities. Values are the guide of the Conversation Company. By communicating these values in a clear manner, it becomes easy for employees to start conversations about the company that will have impact.
- A good culture leads to identification with your company. This forms the basis for your staff's many enthusiastic conversations with each other and the public. It creates an emotional bond.
- The general values of openness, authenticity and happiness lead to self-identification. These values should form the basis for the selection of your own specific company values.
- Your culture will determine your conversation strategy – completely.

- If your culture is still far-removed from what it ideally should be, it is a good idea to start with a number of pilot projects (see Part Four).
- Stories about your company, its history and its values can make your culture tangible for both staff and the public alike.

Questions you must ask yourself

- What are the core values and the aspirational values of your company?
- Are these values recognizable and do they help to differentiate your company?
- Are the aspirational values compatible with conversion into a Conversation Company?
- Who are the heroes in your stories? Which stories typify your company culture?
- What is your score out of 10 for the Conversation Company culture test?

Further information

Use these links for further interesting information on:

- the Zappos values and how Toni Hsieh describes them: **http://about.zappos.com/our-unique-culture/zappos-core-value;**
- identification with brand and company values: **www.howcoolbrandsstathot.com;**
- the Southwest Airlines culture blog: **www.blogsouthwest.com.**

Chapter Five
People are your most important source of conversations

The power of people and new technology

The Arabian Spring

In the first half of 2011, a new spirit raced through the Arabian world. This was the Arabian Spring. First in Tunisia, next in Egypt and later in other lands throughout the Middle East, old regimes were put under increasing pressure by their local populations. For the first time in history, social media were an important factor and an accelerant of revolution. Some even talked of the 'Twitter revolutions'. People kept each other informed and encouraged each other to act through social media. For millions of people, Twitter has taken over the role previously played by CNN and other news services. The whole world was able to follow events in real time.

Most commentators agree that these revolutions would have occurred without the assistance of social media. The basic problem was caused by years of oppression at the hands of dictatorial regimes – and social media did nothing to alter or affect this fact. We must be careful not to overestimate the power of these media. Nor, however, should we underestimate their influence. Twitter and Facebook undoubtedly add a whole new dimension in situations of this kind. People now have tools at their disposal that offer them more resources and more impact than ever before.

For example, the millions of tweets relating to the unfolding events created a wave of sympathy for the rebels. People throughout the entire world were talking to each other about these momentous changes. Equally important, outside sympathizers were able to keep the rebels accurately informed about changing events and changing opinions. The rebels knew via social media that they were gaining increasing international support, and this not only influenced their strategy but also strengthened their determination. They were still able to listen to words of encouragement from President Obama, even though the local media were fully controlled by the dictator-ships. Such a thing would have been unthinkable just a few short years ago. Then, people were cut off from accurate information – but not any longer. During the revolution in Egypt, the regime tried to block this transparency, by pulling the plug on internet connections throughout the entire country. Even so, the people still found ways and means to send thousands of tweets to the outside world. Indi-viduals are far quicker, smarter and more flexible than regimes (and companies) when it comes to the use of social media.

The citizenry used the new media as their way of communicating with each other. Via various social networks (principally Twitter and Facebook, but others as well), they kept each other informed about the progress of the revolution. Notwithstanding the government's control of the television stations in Tunisia, news of the revolt spread throughout the country with amazing speed. This encouraged more and more people to take part in the protests, to such an extent that the regime was eventually toppled. Given this precedent, it is hardly surprising that the Egyptian government wanted to paralyse the internet as soon as the unrest started in Cairo.

This concept of 'power to the people' has had a radical impact on the work of journalists. Who makes the news today? The journalists or the people? Millions of Egyptians wrote their own story and told it to the world. Simply by typing #egypt, you could follow events on Twitter minute by minute. There were thousands of 'live' reporters in the streets. All they needed was a cellphone, preferably with a built-in camera. During the last week of January 2011, more than 1.3 million tweets were sent from Egypt.[69]

The inverted hierarchy: power to the people

The Arabian Spring demonstrated the power of the people in modern-day society. In the past, the social hierarchy was clear: the government was in charge and the people had to listen. The economic hierarchy was also clear: the companies were in charge and the consumers had to listen. This hierarchy has now been turned on its head. People –

and consumers – have become aware of the possibilities open to them. They have taken the power into their own hands. The CEO of Unilever is clear on this point, saying at a presentation during Cannes Lions: 'If they can bring the Egyptian government down in six weeks, they can bring us down in nanoseconds.'

When the retailer Gap proudly launched its new logo at the end of 2010, they were also confronted by this same inverted hierarchy.

CASE STUDY Gap's new logo[70]

FIGURE 5.1

On the day the new Gap logo was launched, there were no fewer than 2,000 negative reactions on the company's Facebook page. As a protest, a group of consumers opened their own Twitter account to fight the new logo. Within days they had more than 4,000 followers. But it didn't stop there. Another group of consumers started a 'design a new Gap logo' campaign. In less than two weeks, over 14,000 people had submitted entries, most of them parodying the new logo. The pressure on the company was growing all the time, to such an extent that it was finally forced to give in. A few days later the following message was posted on the Gap Facebook page: 'We have listened carefully to all the feedback from last week. It is clear that everyone feels passionately about our old logo. It is clear that everyone wants it back. And so we have decided to agree. Starting tomorrow, the old logo will be back in use.' In future, Gap plans to test all its proposed brand changes proactively against the reactions of its fan community.

Nor is it simply consumers who can exert pressure in this manner: staff can also get in on the act as well! More and more employees are prepared to use their impact if they feel that the company is not listening to them sufficiently. This is something that Nokia discovered to its cost in February 2011.[71] Shortly after Nokia had unveiled its new strategy, a website appeared on the internet under the name **www.nokiaplanb.com**. This site put forward an alternative strategy, drawn up by a number of dissatisfied employees. A few days later the site disappeared and the initiative came to an end. It was written off by the management as a prank perpetrated by a bored employee. In July 2011, BlackBerry was confronted with something similar. The company was going through a bad patch and had been hard hit by the successes of its rivals iPhone and Android. As a result, a senior member of staff decided to write an open letter to the management.[72] In both cases, it was clear that the employees in question had not been able to get their message across to their managers in any other way. And so they decided to take the initiative themselves.

Even politicians are starting to feel the power of the consumer. At the time of writing this book, the Belgian federal elections took place some 13 months ago, but the country still has no new government. The negotiations have proved to be extraordinarily difficult and little or no progress has been made. Angered at this situation, a group of citizens decided to take matters into their own hands. They set up G1000.[73] The idea is to bring together a thousand ordinary citizens, a perfect cross-section of the Belgian population, to work out ideas for a new kind of democracy. They will all meet up on 11 November 2011 in a large hall in Brussels. At 100 different tables they will discuss the great challenges facing our political system and will try to work out appropriate solutions.

CASE STUDY
How the reverse pyramid works at the softcat IT company[74]

The UK IT-service company, Softcat, applies the reverse pyramid to determine the level of the bonuses and salaries payable to its managers. The founder, Peter Kelly, believes in a democratic company. The staff are involved in all important management decisions. They even decide how much their bosses should be paid. The annual wage of the CEO is common knowledge in the company and every year the employees vote to see whether or not the CEO should get a pay rise. This vote counts as a decision! Unique, absolutely unique!

Internal and external communication form a perfect duo

Under the old management model, all power was vested in a company. This meant that all communication was guided by the wishes of the commercial department. This communication was also one directional: from inside to outside. *The Conversation Manager*[75] describes how this traditional style of communication is a finite process. To be effective, modern advertising must be the start of a good conversation, and the advertisers need to take part in that conversation. Dialogue thinking must triumph over the broadcast model.

The Conversation Company applies the concept of the total company. In other words, the Conversation Company knows how to deal sensitively with the inverted hierarchy and is able to deal respectfully with 'people power' both inside and outside the company. Its management model is designed to facilitate the conversations of both employees and customers, with the aim of generating as many positive conversations about the company as possible. These conversations will have impact. People – both inside and outside the company – are the most important source of conversations. When faced with this situation, a classic company behaves reactively and with suspicion; in contrast, a Conversation Company is proactive and positive.

Internal and external conversations are complementary. Your employees make your culture tangible. Everything that they say and do reflects what your company stands for. Customers converse about their experience of your company and your products. Both types of conversation influence public opinion and, consequently, your company results. For this reason, companies are becoming more and more aware of the power of the conversing customer. However, the role played by employees is still seriously undervalued.

By combining these two sources of conversations (internal and external), we can arrive at four different types of company:

- **Boring companies.** These are the companies that nobody talks about; largely because there is little or nothing to say. If you position your company in this quadrant, you are in serious trouble. In reality, this type of company does not exist in normal circumstances. It is all a question of what you make of it yourself. Every company has a story. The trick is to (want to) do something with it. Someone in the public service sector recently said to me that his sector belongs in this quadrant 'almost by definition'. This is not true. The inspiring case study of the FDSS (see Chapter 3, page 59) shows that government organizations can be found in any of the other three quadrants.

- **Proud companies.** In these companies, the employees form the most important source of conversations. Companies in a niche sector are often to be found in this quadrant. Advertising agencies are a good example. The staff are proud of their work. They make attractive-looking case videos of what they do. They then share them on the internet (and elsewhere) as a kind of reference. The managers and owners of advertising agencies are often influential figures who lead the conversations about their companies.

- **Worshipped companies.** The customers love these companies. The companies themselves don't say very much; they don't need to – the customers provide all the communication that is necessary. The most famous example in this quadrant is Apple. Apart from the late Steve Jobs, very few Apple employees engage in conversations. It sometimes has the appearance of a closed company, but it has one of the highest conversation totals in the entire business world. The fans are so convinced by the products that they promote the company non-stop.

- **Conversation companies.** These companies display the ideal combination between internal and external conversations. Companies such as Zappos, Best Buy and Southwest Airlines belong in this quadrant.

FIGURE 5.2

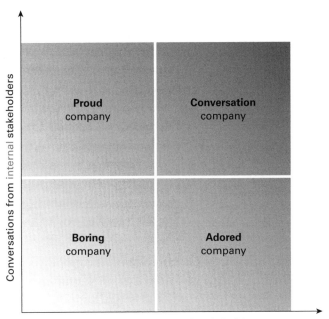

Conversations from external stakeholders

Scoring well on both sources of conversations offers a number of important advantages. Customers mainly talk about their experiences with your products and services. Your staff talk mainly about the culture and important events in your company. This combination ensures a good content mix. This increases the likelihood that potential new customers will easily find information about you on Google, since the search engine has recently adjusted its algorithm in favour of social conversations.[76] This means, for example, the Twitter messages now come higher in the order of search results. Moreover, information which is accessed in this way has a very high credibility rating.[77] In other words, it can be a huge help in finding you new customers.

During conversations, your staff and your customers will often come into contact with each other, which narrows the gap between the internal and the external world. This makes your company much more 'human' for your customers. Your anonymous organization suddenly acquires a face (or a voice, at least). This makes the company easier to approach. It also strengthens the emotional bond between your employees and your customers. In this way, the outside world will gradually gain more trust and confidence in you. This gives your own conversations even greater impact.

And the most important advantage? A McKinsey study has shown conclusively that companies whose internal and external worlds are closely linked grow fastest of all.[78]

Internal: every employee is a spokesperson

Each and every one of your employees is a potential source of conversations. Everybody talks offline about their job, whether at home or in the pub. But by allowing them to talk about their work online, you can reduce your unused conversation potential still further. There are plenty of your staff who would like to do this. Most people are proud of their jobs. And that pride forms the basis for their willingness to talk about their work. The Maslow Pyramid has proved this.[79] Nowadays, the majority of us have all we need in terms of basic necessities. We have enough to eat and drink. During the winter we are seldom cold. We also have few fears with regard to our safety, the second basic need. Similarly, the third need, for social contact, is also not normally a problem. All that remains are the fourth and fifth basic needs: recognition or appreciation and self-development. Our daily jobs help to satisfy these final two needs. And if people talk about their job, in part it is because they hope to get the recognition for which they crave.

To a certain degree, companies take advantage of this fact; for example, through their internal company magazines. You know the kind of thing we mean – the magazines that are produced monthly, quarterly or annually to keep staff in the picture and, when necessary, put them in the spotlight. These magazines do their job well. If someone is photographed on the cover, you can guarantee that they will show it to all their friends – whether they want to see it or not! Even so, magazines of this type do also have their downside; they cost a lot, appear with limited frequency and have an even more limited reach. Using the new media, however, it is possible to create the same effect as the magazine but to spread it on a much wider scale and with much greater frequency. Try this approach to make your staff proud of their job every day.

Regard every employee as a potential spokesperson. By allowing all employees to talk about their work, a much broader public will come into contact with your company in a less formal, more human manner. More and more research studies are showing that this approach also leads to an increase in creativity and effectiveness within your organization. The Stern Business School, linked to the University of New York, has looked closely at this phenomenon. Its conclusions were unambiguous: when staff converse online about their job, internal ambiance, internal communication, productivity and relations with customers all improve.[80]

It is necessary to add two important nuances to this general philosophy. First, the new approach does not signal the end of the traditional spokesperson. For certain official moments it is logical that there should still be a single point of contact. However, this classic job will be given a new dimension. Every member of staff needs to be made aware of the official standpoint of the company. Once they are online, they may receive all kinds of questions from many different sources, not all of them friendly. At this moment, the spokesperson must act as a conversation manager for his or her own staff. Act as a facilitator for your people, so that they know what to say and do. Second, the new approach does not mean that your staff will be spending hours each day playing on social media sites. It is more a question of responding to existing situations. Your staff will already be active in social media for at least some part of their working day. During this time there will no doubt be moments when opportunities spontaneously arise to launch a positive conversation about the company. Making effective use of available conversation potential at such times is what really makes the difference. But make sure that your employees have sufficient relevant content to share with their network. And trust them to use their own common sense with regard to the efficient use of their valuable time.

CASE STUDY The Ford story

(See also the *Contagious Magazine Special Report: Real-time marketing*, 2011.)

Scott Monty, the head of digital communication at Ford, has integrated social media into his company. To achieve this, Ford created a social media hub with the title 'The Ford story'. This site collects and concentrates all the social content about Ford. This is the place where you can find the Facebook page, Twitter account, YouTube channel and Flickr photographs. Ford's objective is that 1 per cent of its 200,000 employees should become active on social media, so that they can act as ambassadors for the Ford brand. To help make this possible, Ford allows considerable freedom with regard to the posting of photos and blogs online. Ford is, of course, a gigantic organization. By launching just a few thousand of its own workers into social media and by gathering all social content in a single location, it hopes to create a softer, more human image.

Don't control – facilitate!

It is normal for managers of some companies to feel nervous when they read this section. If your company culture is not yet strong enough, your staff may initiate conversations which turn out to be far from positive. Don't forget that your culture must be a guide to your conversational style. Make clear to your people exactly what they are allowed to say and what they are not allowed to say. If your culture is not yet adapted to the conversation era, this will increase the need for a well-defined conversation policy. It is always vital to give your employees the conversation support they need. The Conversation Company will provide an efficient and well-considered training programme which will make your staff feel more comfortable during their conversations (more about this in Chapter 13). If your company fails to manage these sources of conversation, you will be letting an important opportunity slip through your fingers, while at the same time maintaining the illusion that you have everything under control. But this is not the case. People will always do what they want. The only way to succeed is to facilitate the conversations of your staff proactively.

The Conversation Company facilitates the conversations of its employees at three levels:

- **Trust.** The employees are sometimes uncertain about what their employers will allow them to do. In these circumstances, they will usually prefer to do nothing, rather than make a mistake. This is a waste of their good intentions and their conversation potential. By providing strong values, clear guidelines and, above all, relevant training, the Conversation Company offers sufficient comfort to its staff, so that they can approach their online conversations with confidence. Kodak believes strongly in the power of its employees' conversational abilities, Tom Hoehn of Kodak confirmed in an interview in 2011. The company has more than 200 active bloggers amongst its own personnel. The activities of these bloggers are facilitated by a 'chief blogging officer'. This woman coordinates all content and ensures that the stories are in keeping with the culture and objectives of the company. The staff are encouraged to blog and are given the necessary training by Kodak, and the company also provides them with regular tips about possible interesting content for new blogs. In this way, the blog programme is invested with both a vision and an objective.

- **Content.** The Conversation Company instructs its employees in all matters of how to talk, what to talk about, how to respond to criticism, etc, and many more besides. In this way, it is possible to create a conversation comfort zone, in which the employees feel relaxed and confident to talk with others about their work. In later chapters we will be looking more closely at content strategy and planning.

- **Tools.** The Conversation Company provides the right software and hardware, so that its employees can participate easily and fluently in conversations. For example, in an interview in 2011, Jan-Willem De Waard, of the Dutch company Rabobank, said that the organization is prepared to provide staff with whatever hardware tools are necessary to do the job. If someone can show that they need an iPad to communicate effectively with customers, Rabobank will issue that person with an iPad.

CASE STUDY Companies such as Edelman and Altimeter Research invest in superstars

Some companies have their very own digital superstars. Digital superstars are people with a very wide reach (eg many Twitter followers). They are often seen as the 'face' of the company. Their dominance in both internal and external communication is considerable. In this respect, Edelman (a PR company) has played it clever. It pushes people such as David Armano and Steve Rubel to the forefront as the 'thought leaders' of the company. They are responsible for positioning Edelman as an expert in social media and for strengthening the image of the organization. This is done in a very open, personal and human way – and it is an approach that has impact.

Altimeter Research works in much the same manner. Jeremiah Owyang is its founder and a well-known 'face'. With his 75,000 Twitter followers, he is seen as one of the most trendsetting figures in social media. In mid-2011 Altimeter also took on Brian Solis, an even bigger superstar than Owyang. At that time, Solis had more than 90,000 Twitter followers and had just written a successful bestseller.[81] This is no doubt another smart investment. Digital superstars are an important conversation tactic for companies. It is worth thinking seriously about this option as a means to optimize your conversation potential. Check to see if there are digital superstars in your industry. If not, you have an excellent opportunity to become the first one!

Blocking social media sites is becoming increasingly pointless

Many companies block social media sites in the workplace because they are afraid of their own employees. They are worried that they might say the wrong thing, or do something that they shouldn't have done. This is something that you have to accept: sometimes they will say the wrong thing. Just as the CEO of BP said the wrong thing after the Deepwater Horizon disaster (eg 'I want my life back,' or 'There is enough water in the sea.'). You will not stop this kind of mistake simply by restricting access to social media sites in your company.

Besides, it has become almost impossible to block these sites. With the rapid growth of mobile internet, most of your employees probably now have Facebook in their handbag or jacket pocket. This means that via the iPhone they can use Facebook wherever and whenever they like. So what is the point of blocking the site on your company computers? What else can you do? Demand that all your staff hand in their iPhones when they enter the company's premises? That is hardly feasible, and not very good for your image (or your relations with your staff). No, nowadays the best option is to leave your company's access to social media sites unblocked. Instead, help your employees to use them wisely. They use these sites freely from the moment they get home, so the trick is to try and make them remember that even there, they are still (to some extent, at least) your employees – and should behave as such.

It is not the first time in recent years that we have had this kind of discussion. Fifty years ago, much the same thing was being said about the telephone. 'People should be working, not telephoning all day!' Fifteen years ago, the new problem was e-mails. 'People shouldn't be sending e-mails all day. It costs money and is not always secure.' At the time, of course, this may have been right, but in both cases (as history has proven) the technology was unstoppable – and is now unmissable. Ten years into the future, we will no doubt be thinking exactly the same about social media. Imagine how a talented, ambitious young graduate will feel about your company when that person hears that it doesn't allow access to Facebook...

External: your customers would love to help

Customers talk about your company. Both positive and negative experiences lead to numerous conversations, both online and offline. These are spontaneous conversations which arise because of the contact the customers have had with your company, and the impression that the contact has made on them. The Conversation Company focuses heavily on positive customer experiences within the framework of a clear company culture. In addition to these spontaneous conversations, you can also ask your customers for help. In this way you can broaden the conversations and better use your conversation potential.

Every year, the football programme in Northern Europe is disturbed by the arrival of unexpected periods of snow. When this happens, every effort is made to try and clear the pitch, so that the games can still be played. Many clubs appeal to their fans for help. They often turn up in hundreds, and within hours the pitch is ready for play. In a similar fashion, following the riots in the summer of 2011, the City of London appealed to its citizens to help in the clean-up operation. Thousands of people answered the call. Whoever you are and whatever you do, your customers want to help. They are full of goodwill.

If they have a positive relationship with a brand, they are pleased to make a contribution towards its success. All they are waiting for is a signal from you. So have you ever sent them one?

In 2009 the city of Boston launched its 'citizen connect' application for iPhone. The app offered local people the chance to inform the city authorities about all kinds of minor grievances. In this way, the city was asking its own citizens to help keep Boston safe and clean. The response was enthusiastic, with more than 4,000 downloads during the first 12 weeks (search 'Boston Citizen Connect' on Google for full details). A defective traffic light, a pothole in the road, new graffiti on a wall: within just a few months 6 per cent of all damage and service enquiries directed to the city authorities were made via the app. The city had asked for help and the citizens had shown that they were pleased to provide it. In effect, the city is actually sharing part of its work with its iPhone respondents (ie, its customers).

CASE STUDY
Thank your customers: examples – Heineken and Porsche

If your customers help you, it pays to say 'thank you' – because then they will be prepared to do even more for you. When Heineken passed the magic milestone of 1 million fans, they dispatched a number of attractive (and scantily dressed)

FIGURE 5.3

young women out into the bars of Amsterdam, to give 1 million hugs to as many of these Heineken fans as they could find (as reported in an article entitled 'One million Heineken hugs' published in *The Dutch Daily News* on 15 February 2011).

Porsche went even further.[82] To celebrate its 1 million fans, it stuck the names of 27,000 of these fans to the bodywork of a Porsche GT3 Hybrid. The car was displayed in the Porsche Museum, so that proud fans could rush along to see if their name had been selected. It is a perfect example of how to make maximum use of conversation potential.

The customer in the boardroom

The Conversation Company goes further than just facilitating the conversations of its employees and its customers. The ultimate goal is to develop a structural collaboration between your company and the market. The positive conversations of your employees and customers serve to provide a lever effect. Together, you can reach further and achieve more. If you can succeed in making your customers talk in the 'we' form of address, you are well on the way to success. This is a clear expression of the customers' complete identification with the culture of the company; in fact, it is conclusive proof of their commitment to your brand. It is generally to be expected that your staff will automatically refer to the company in the 'we' form. If they don't, it is obvious that their thoughts are somewhere else.

In this respect, your company can play a pioneering role. If you are the first company in your market to address your customers in the 'we' form, they will follow you. Take the initiative, and push the door open for your customers. You will be surprised how quickly they want to come in! Lady Gaga does this brilliantly. She still speaks to her most loyal fans as 'my little monsters'. One of her many tattoos is specifically dedicated to these monsters. In this way, she underlines her commitment to her most faithful followers. This creates a strong emotional bond. It is always a good idea to communicate in this clever manner, if you can. Not all your customers will be open to the idea. But those who are prepared to play their part in your story will become your most important ambassadors.

The Conversation Company involves its customers in all aspects of company life. All important strategic choices are made the subject of prior consultation with the fans. In this way, it is almost as if the customers and fans are present in the boardroom. The 'customer in the boardroom' is a metaphor for the successful bridging (or even closing) of the gap between the internal and external worlds of your company. The consumer, customer or fan is integrated fully into the decision-making processes of your organization. Structural collaboration of this kind reduces the risk of making wrong choices. It strengthens your internal and external basis of support. Above all, it is the ideal breeding ground for conversations that have impact.

CASE STUDY Mobile Vikings: customers who go through hell and high water for the brand

(Based on an interview in 2011 with Chris De Meyere and Hans Similon of Mobile Vikings.)

Mobile Vikings is a challenger company in the Belgian telecom market. The company focuses on the market in mobile internet and telephonics. It is fighting with limited resources against three much larger competitors. Even so, it manages to attract a thousand new customers each week. As the Belgian market consists of some 10 million consumers, this means that it is winning 1 per cent of this market every three months. It is a company that lives off the conversations of its customers. And the percentage of fans among these customers is high. The company addresses the customers as 'Vikings'. All its communication attempts to create a 'we' feeling. As a result, many of the customers are prepared to help other customers with their questions and problems. They even develop handy new apps for each other. The really dedicated ones have even created new websites, specifically designed to help the company.

How has the company managed to achieve this? In large measure, as a result of its excellent culture. Each and every member of staff feels a strong emotional bond with the company. The internal communication is extremely transparent. As a result, the employees feel a strong sense of personal responsibility to provide outstanding customer service. Their product offer is equally transparent. If there are likely to be technical problems, they make sure that this is announced well in advance and they do everything they can to limit the impact for customers. If people know what is going on and see efforts to put things right, they are more willing to be understanding. The company's conversation manager, Chris De Meyer, follows Twitter until the early hours of the morning and even on his days off. He is able to help his customers at all hours of the day – and night. Chris doesn't mind doing this and the customers think it is fantastic to be offered help in this way, almost 24/7.

Customers are also involved in the further development of products and services. Via Facebook Mobile Vikings periodically asks its customers what they do not like about the company. The objective is to implement this feedback as quickly as possible. Some matters are arranged within a week, others over a period of just months. In all cases, the communication is transparent – even if the news is not good. Again, the customers think that this is great: first to be asked their opinion by the company, and then to see that something is actually done about it!

Let the consumer co-manage

You can even go a step further. The true Conversation Company 'sub-contracts' a part of its management functions to the customers. If the commitment of the individual customer increases, the emotional bond between consumers in general and the company will also become stronger. This can offer numerous advantages to the company. If your customers are involved in the development of new products, this increases the likelihood that your products will be a success. If your customers act as a kind of secondary helpdesk for other consumers, the costs for your company will fall and its credibility will rise. Customers who not only recommend your brand but actively defend it are the best possible form of advertising there is.

More and more companies are seeing the wisdom of delegating part of their management tasks to their customers.

CASE STUDY   Delegation: four case study examples

Moxie is an online clothing company, which delegates the ordering of its new collection to its customers. Not so long ago, it discovered through a relatively simple Facebook competition that its customers have a very good idea of what will sell well and what will sell poorly. The company therefore decided to involve a number of these customers structurally in the purchase of its new designs. The customers were chosen on the basis of their existing relationship with the company and their commitment to the brand on Twitter and Facebook. They were even given the official title of 'junior buyer', and, as thanks for their efforts, receive a number of free clothing vouchers. The CEO of Moxie sees this as the future of professional buying: 'We can more or less fully attune our sales to the input of our customers.'

Lego involves its customers structurally in the development of its new products. Every customer is free to design his or her own box of Lego fun on the site 'Designed by me'. In this way, customers can build and buy their own dream Lego kit. Lego fans love this type of co-creation. The site also offers the possibility to design your own packaging. Other users are given the chance to look at designs of their fellow Lego fans. They can even buy them, if they want to. Lego then considers whether to offer the most popular kits for commercial sale through traditional channels. By analysing these individual boxes, the company is able to identify potentially interesting trends in the market. This increases the likelihood of success for its new products.

Danone recently allowed it customers to help in choosing its new online advertising agency. The company engaged various agencies to draw up a campaign based on a number of different concepts. In the Dutch market, Danone has a very active fan community. And so in this market the Danone community, rather than the Danone management team, was allowed to choose the winning concept. Danone also gave the agencies access to the online opinions of the fan community. In this way, the agencies' proposals could reflect the up-to-date input of that community. This transparency offered benefits to all concerned.

Apple fans spontaneously get together to help the company. The most important helpdesk for Apple users is other Apple users. This saves the company a great deal of time, effort and money. The consumers are such great fans of the brand that they regard helping Apple as a kind of hobby.

The Conversation Company fully trusts and relies on people. By showing confidence in and giving clear instructions to its employees, it helps to create positive conversations. Conversing employees make the company seem more human and approachable. This narrows the gap with the customers. The Conversation Company also allows its customers to help in the co-management of its activities. By allowing the customer into the boardroom, it bridges the gulf between the company and the market. This leads to an open company culture. As a Conversation Company, you will be regarded as a company with a very personal approach. This is something that consumers appreciate. In this chapter, we hope that we have made clear that social media are an important partner – but not an end in themselves – in the managing of conversations with consumers. They act as a conversation lever for both your culture and your people. In the next chapter, we will be looking at the ways in which you can best make use of these tools.

KEY CONVERSATION POINTS

Possible conversation starters

- The classic hierarchical pyramid has been inverted. Ordinary people now have a much greater impact on company policy and on society as a whole.

- The Conversation Company facilitates the conversations of its employees and its customers. The combination of internal and external conversations offers numerous commercial and financial advantages.

- The Conversation Company involves its customers in all levels of decision making. The customer is present in the boardroom. This bridges the gap between the company and the market.

- The Conversation Company develops structural collaboration between its staff and the market.

- Customers want to help you. They can ensure that your conversation potential is fully used. Don't forget to thank them from time to time.

- Customers can assume a number of functions previously reserved for managers.

- Conversing employees make your company seem more human. Customers like this.

Questions you must ask yourself

- Is your company a boring, proud, worshipped or conversing company?

- What can you do to help your staff conduct conversations that have a lot of impact?

- Do you have any digital superstars in your company? If not, how can you attract them? If so, how can you make better use of them?

- What do your customers want to help you with?

- Which management tasks can you delegate to your customers?

Further information

For more about the use of superstars, look at the presentation:
**www.slideshare.net/stevenvanbelleghem/
best-employer-of-the-year-superstar-company.**

It is also interesting to follow the Twitter messages of **@briansolis,**
@jowyang, **@armano** and **@steverubel.**

FIGURE 5.4

Chapter Six
Social media – the ideal partner for the Conversation Company

Social media bind your staff, your customers and your company to each other

For the Conversation Company social media are a means, not an end. Social media are the ideal partner for the Conversation Company. The advantages are obvious: speed, a wide potential reach, a human method of communicating, no hierarchy, full transparency, the creation of communities, etc. It is the only channel where feedback from the outside world is transparent and so direct. Social media force companies to be more honest, quicker and clearer in their communication. This trend has allowed companies to develop in the direction of genuine customer-orientation.

The checklist mentality which some companies use when dealing with social media is not the right way to maximize your conversation potential. Regarding Facebook pages and Twitter accounts as some kind of magic trick will only lead to disappointment. The reality is that, with a few exceptions (such as Charlie Sheen), nobody is likely to have a million fans on the first day. For the vast majority of companies, it takes time and effort to build up a community of fans and followers. Besides, wide reach on social media is only one of the important criteria. Building up a strong relationship with the customer is just as important.

In Chapter 5 we discussed the important role played by your employees in helping to make your culture tangible. In this chapter we will be showing how social media are the ideal way to spread your culture and stories about your company on a wide scale. In addition, social media are also the ideal place to conduct structural collaboration with your customers. The Conversation Company seeks to exploit these possibilities and to integrate social media into all aspects of its organization.

In recent years, social media have built up a huge following of users, with an enormous potential reach. In July 2011 there were 1.2 billion social media users worldwide; 96 per cent of people have heard of Facebook and 62 per cent are users; 80 per cent know of Twitter and 16 per cent are users. In addition, more and more people are using social network sites to link themselves to particular brands. More than half (600 million people) follow at least one brand via social media. In Europe 51 per cent of social media users are linked to a brand; the figure for the United States is 57 per cent and in India a massive 70 per cent. Media, fashion, food and retailing are the most popular sectors to follow. People expect information about products, promotions, invitations to events, etc. They want to give feedback and are keen to collaborate on the development of new ideas.[83] These are all opportunities that companies need to exploit.

Mobile internet quickens the pace

The growth of social media is already happening at a tremendous pace. The arrival and development of mobile internet applications is set to further double the intensity of social media use. In 2011 in Europe, 28 per cent of people already possessed a smartphone with mobile internet. This rises to 34 per cent in the United States, 38 per cent in India and 41 per cent in China.[84] This makes mobile internet the fastest penetrating technology in the history of mankind. And it is a trend that has huge implications for companies.

The arrival of mobile internet has fully democratized the worldwide web. Yesterday's non-internet users now only need a second-hand smartphone and a location with free wifi access (eg a McDonald's) in order to go online. In the past, you needed a workplace, a computer and an internet subscription, which was too expensive for many people. But this barrier has now disappeared. The situation in the United States proves this beyond doubt. The highest smartphone penetration levels are to be found in the poorer Hispanic and Asiatic sections of the community. In 2011 research company Nielsen found that in the traditionally more affluent white community only 27 per cent currently have a smartphone. These figures are the reverse of what you would 'rationally' expect, and they mean that all target groups in all social classes will soon be approachable on a large scale via social media.

As a company, this means that you can expect real-time feedback on everything you do. If you launch a new product, within days you will know what the market thinks of it. In the past, you needed to wait at least six weeks before the first market research figures were available. By then the damage had already been done. Real-time feedback applies to everyone and everything. When a number of armed men attempted to seize the offices of the Discovery Channel, the employees responded by reaching for their own weapons: their smartphones.[85] Photos of the attackers were soon being beamed around the world on the internet. Interviews with the victims were watched by millions. Even the emergency services could watch 'live' what was happening inside the building.

The impact of these developments on the purchasing behaviour of consumers has been immense. In the United States 27 per cent of smartphone users use their phone while they are out shopping, to find out more about the products they are thinking of buying. They also compare prices and look for promotion offers in other stores. From now on, people always have the internet with them, wherever they go and whatever they do. In other words, they have instant access to all the information in the world. The impact for the retail industry is phenomenal.

The combination of internal and external conversations (see Chapter 5) is well suited to take advantage of the changes ushered in by mobile internet. If your staff make greater use of online media, they will be ready and waiting to pick up customer feedback, so that they can avoid or solve possible problems and fully exploit conversation potential. If your company culture and service are good, this will result in positive conversations. Consumers who are looking for online information while they are out shopping will find these conversations in their search results and will be influenced by them. The fact that the internet has been democratized means that companies now have no other option: they must integrate the use of social media into all their activities, if they wish to survive.

Two dimensions: reach and a structural relationship

The Conversation Company manages social media on the basis of two dimensions.

Dimension 1: Building up reach

Via social media, it is possible to look at everything your company does through a magnifying glass. Companies that have many fans on Facebook and Twitter have the luxury of being able to spread their stories, content and campaigns on a massive scale. Social media allow the reach of every action you take to be multiplied both directly and indirectly. The built-up reach of your own social media channels is the ideal way to communicate directly with your fans and followers. Coca-Cola makes excellent use of these opportunities. Its 'Happiness machine' films are spread exclusively via its social channels. In this advertising gimmick, the traditional drinks machine is transformed into a box full of surprises. Every time someone orders a can of Coke, they get an extra surprise. This can vary from a second can of Coke to a giant pizza or even 50 free bottles of their favourite drink. The actual machine is only physically 'available' to a handful of people, but Coca-Cola films the machine and distributes the video to its 26 million Facebook fans worldwide.

In addition to the direct effects of a wide social reach, there are also a number of indirect effects. When the Belgian entrepreneur Walter Torfs posted a tweet in which he asked for people interested in working in his local chain of shoe shops, many pundits thought that he was wasting his time. 'The target group he is searching for might not be on Twitter,' said the critics. However, the tweet brought Torfs a number of interesting indirect benefits. The next day there was a full page article about his tweet in one of Belgium's best-read daily newspapers. And, thanks to all this free publicity, just a few days later all his vacancies were filled.

Although a wide reach is important, social media also offer interesting short reach possibilities. Helping individual customers can mean a serious added value for both the person concerned and for your company. The numerous webcare teams in companies such as ING, Delta Airlines, Comcast, Dell, Gatorade, etc show the value that leading companies attach to this enhanced form of customer service. No single conversation is left unanswered. And by helping individual consumers, you are maximizing your conversation potential.

Dimension 2: Building up structural collaboration with the market

For the very first time, companies now have the opportunity to build up a structural relationship with a large group of people. Customers want to be involved with your company. In Chapter 5 we mentioned how the Conversation Company tries to create a 'we' feeling between itself and its consumers. The structural involvement of customers in your management processes is a part of this approach. And social media offer a framework that is ideally suited for this purpose. Dunkin Donuts regularly asks the help of its fans to think up new product concepts and the fans do indeed regularly submit fresh ideas for new doughnuts. Sometimes this collaboration goes further than simple product development. Last summer the brand asked for help in compiling a list of summer songs that fitted well with the tastes of its ice smoothies. Before Dunkin Donuts takes action, it always consults the opinion of its fans.[86]

Notwithstanding the fact that structural relationships are the objective, loose individual contacts can also create added value. If a customer accidentally comes across interesting content from your company, this may immediately result in the sale of a product. Long-term structural relationships often start with this kind of chance internet encounter. And the more of these encounters you can transform into lasting partnerships, the greater the impact of social media on your company will become. In this manner, the quantitative contacts of the first dimension (reach) will be transformed into qualitative contacts via the second dimension (collaboration).

Every company dreams of having a large number of qualitative contacts. This is something that the Conversation Company also wishes to achieve, but without losing sight of the value of individual, one-off contacts. This is the unique aspect of social media: wide or narrow reach, structural collaboration or one-off contact – they all have their value. Every type of conversation is valuable both for the customer (who is helped) and the company (which benefits from positive conversations).

FIGURE 6.1

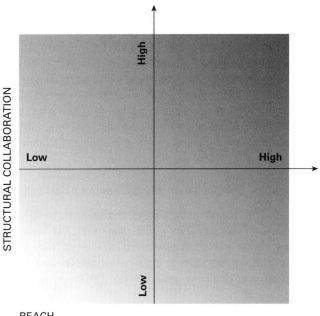

CASE STUDY
How KLM translates the two dimensions into four strategies

CASE STUDY
How KLM translates the two dimensions into four strategies

By combining the two dimensions – reach and structural collaboration – it is possible to create four quadrants. Each of these four quadrants requires a different strategy. KLM has managed to implement effective social media use into each of the four quadrants, thereby developing a fully integrated approach.

Quadrant 1: Low reach and low levels of collaboration – KLM webcare

KLM took its first steps into webcare during a crisis. When an ash cloud from the now notorious Icelandic volcano with the unpronounceable name – Eyjafjallajökull – grounded air traffic throughout Europe, KLM attempted to help its passengers via Twitter, Facebook and Hyves.[87] KLM had noticed that customers were asking questions via these channels with increasing frequency. The company decided to move from listening to participation in these conversations.[88] Every contact is one to one and therefore by definition low reach. Nor is the 'collaboration' structural: it is loose, with a specific short-term purpose. Even so, these contacts are very useful for the individual customers.

During the crisis many passengers expressed their gratitude to KLM for this new service.

Since July 2011 KLM has been providing a 24/7 online service of this kind – the first major airline company to do so. Followers and fans can ask questions (in English or Dutch) about every aspect of a plane journey: baggage, seat reservations, online booking of tickets, etc. The questioners get an answer within an hour and there is a commitment to solve problems within 24 hours. To answer the questions properly, KLM decided not to set up its own dedicated webcare team, but to delegate the task to a number of internal KLM ambassadors. These members of staff are employed in different countries and different departments, so that there is a sufficiently broad range of knowledge and experience to make good their promises, all day, every day.

Quadrant 2: High reach and low levels of collaboration – KLM campaigns

In recent years, KLM has developed a number of highly influential campaigns via social media. Campaigns are activities with a wide reach, but based on many different individual contacts. A good example is its 'Tile and Inspire' campaign. In April 2011 the company invited everyone to make their own Delft Blue tile, based on an inspiring photo and an equally inspiring text. The company worked 4,000 of

FIGURE 6.2

the best tiles into the fuselage of a real Boeing 747. 'The energy of "Tile and Inspire" fits perfectly with the brand positioning of KLM: reliable, inspirational, Dutch and open,' according to Frank Houben, the airline's director of communications and corporate identity. 'The campaign united people from all over the world – just like Facebook. And with this unique approach we were able to seamlessly combine online and offline elements. People were given the opportunity through a virtual channel to get their portrait on a real plane'.[89] The tiles that were not among the chosen 4,000 were still shared with the KLM community via social media. The results were truly impressive. During the campaign more than 120,000 tiles were made, of which 77,000 were submitted as entries for the competition. The campaign was also responsible for adding 50,000 new 'likes' on Facebook in 154 different countries. In other words, with this single campaign KLM generated one fifth of its total number of 'likes'. There were also more than 3,000 messages about the campaign on other social media outlets (Twitter, blogs, videos, forums). Add to this more than 440,000 YouTube views and more than 600,000 campaign site visits, and you can safely conclude that on this occasion KLM got the very best out of its conversation potential.

Quadrant 3: Low reach and high levels of structural collaboration – the KLM community

By adding the second dimension of 'structural collaboration' to its strategy, KLM has intensified its relationship with customers. Behind the scenes, KLM has a closed 'in-touch' community with which it is in almost daily contact. This is a small group of customers with whom the airline works very closely. The purpose of this community is to offer the company a continuous sounding board in the market for its ideas (see the case study: **www.communispace.com/air-france-klm**).

Charles Hageman, Research Manager at KLM, involves the members of this community in the company's decision making, as reported on the communispace blog in 2009. 'These consumers give non-stop feedback about everything that KLM does. In addition, they are encouraged to take part in the development of new products and service concepts. All communication takes place via an open dialogue between the members of the community and KLM. These small, closed communities can be of great value to companies. They offer the chance to involve customers in strategic projects in a secure and trustworthy environment.' In this instance, the customer really is being taken into the boardroom, before any decisions are made.

Quadrant 4: High reach and high levels of structural collaboration – co-creation of a new Facebook page

Finally, KLM also seeks to build up structural collaboration with a much wider group of customers. Its chosen channel is Facebook. KLM already has more than 250,000 fans on Facebook. KLM has also made a separate 'bright ideas' page. It uses this page to ask consumers for feedback about possible new products and concepts. The consumers also have the opportunity to put forward 'bright ideas' of their own. In other words, company and customers combine to provide better service for the benefit of everyone.

In recent years KLM has invested heavily in its social media strategy. The company tries to remain 'conversation-worthy' all year round. It is important for an airline company to think in this manner. A satisfied customer will usually not have access to mobile internet at the moment when he or she is enjoying his positive KLM experience. For example, the sharing of good experiences while you are actually on board an aeroplane is not possible. This helps to explain why so many conversations about airlines are negative: the problems occur when the passenger is back on the ground – where he or she does have access to mobile internet. KLM's four-pronged conversation strategy helps to limit this effect through the maximization of its positive conversation potential.

FIGURE 6.3

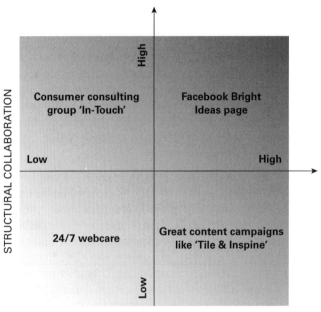

CASE STUDY
Heineken surprises Champions League fans and charms the world

For football fans, every match is important. But some matches are more important than others. A match between Real Madrid and AC Milan comes into this category. A real fan will count off the days before such a game. But what do you do if your partner, boss or professor asks you to attend a classical concert on precisely that same evening? Believe it or not, the majority of football fans 'give in' and go to the concert, albeit reluctantly. During the concert, which really is very boring, the orchestra suddenly strikes up the Champions League hymn. At the same time, a large screen drops down, showing the teams as they come out onto the pitch. A message also appears on the screen: 'It's hard to say no to your partner, isn't it? And it's hard to say no to your boss and your professor, too. But we have some good news for you. We are now all going to watch the big game between AC Milan and Real Madrid – an entertainment brought to you by courtesy of Heineken.' In just seconds, an audience of bored concert-goers is transformed into an audience of 1,000 cheering football fans. This was a tremendous publicity stunt, but it was no easy task to get 1,000 football fanatics to a single location in secret, more or less against their will. It required the collaboration of the aforementioned partners, bosses and professors. Some of the conversations necessary to persuade the fans to attend the 'concert' were even recorded on hidden cameras. Is this not all a bit excessive; a bit too much effort to go to, simply to please a relatively limited number of fans? No, not at all. Via social media the interest in the stunt was magnified many times over. The results were impressive. More than 1.5 million people saw fragments live on Sky TV, 10 million saw it reported in television news programmes and no fewer than 5 million unique visitors viewed the campaign page on the Heineken website.[90] Social media offer every company the chance to transform something small into something big. Something very big indeed.

CASE STUDY Harvard increases its reach via social media

Harvard, one of the world's trendsetting universities, is well on the way to becoming a Conversation Company. In recent years, the university has made great efforts to integrate social media into its communication. This plan must further strengthen its perfectionist and strongly content-based culture. Moreover, it is a plan that offers benefits for both professors and students alike.

The university is moving away from traditional methods for communicating with its students and the professional community. Harvard has decided that this communication can be made quicker, more efficient and more interactive through the use of blogs. The *Harvard Gazette* is an internal blog network in which content by and for the students is distributed and shared (see **www.slideshare.net/harvardwww/analytics-and-social-tools-in-practice**). The blogs are both content-related (new management insights) and practical (details of where lectures are taking place). All the content can be consulted online and there is also a user-friendly mobile application. Every student has the possibility to share the content further via social media, an option that is facilitated by the simple, easy-to-use 'like' function.

The communication with Harvard's management public has also moved more from offline to online. Of course, the legendary *Harvard Business Review* has been retained, but Harvard has also created a number of impressive new blog sites. Opinion makers from various industries are keen to act as guest bloggers. Four or five new articles with high level content appear each day. More than 500,000 people follow these articles via Twitter. More than 50 Harvard professors are also active Twitter users.[91] They spread relevant content and are available for conversations with (potential) students.

Finally, Harvard decided with effect from 2010 to scrap the classic direct marketing approach for its management training courses. Harvard had lived in a culture for many years where direct mailings had had the largest marketing return on investment. The majority of course participants had replied to a brochure that had been sent to them by letter. The disadvantage of this method was the huge cost associated with printing and dispatching 400,000 brochures each year. When the idea was put forward to replace this classic way of working with the new possibilities offered by online marketing, many people thought it was a bad idea: the majority of its turnover was being generated by these direct mailings. Nevertheless, the decision was taken and implemented. What transpired? Suddenly it was possible to reach many more potential customers. In recent years, the same mailing list had been used time after time. By using social media wisely, it was now possible to increase the total average number of participants per course and also to increase the profitability of the different programmes.[92]

Harvard's efforts in social media in all these various fields has revolutionized its marketing philosophy. The university was wise enough not to approach the new media with a checklist mentality. Instead, it opted for the well-reasoned creation and spreading of content in a way which allowed the strengths of all the different channels to be exploited to the full.

CASE STUDY Wizard Istanbul

If you are planning a city trip to Istanbul, be sure to take a look at the following site: wizardistanbul.com. This site offers answers to all the most frequently asked questions about the city. The site was set up by the Turkish national tourist board. Nothing new in that, you might think. But you would be wrong. The content on the site has been provided exclusively by consumers who are fans of Istanbul. These people love the city so much that they are prepared to make the necessary effort to help others discover its many charms.

Four Cs: customer experience, conversation, content, collaboration

In order optimally to manage the two basic dimensions – building up reach and building up structural relationships – the Conversation Company makes use of an approach that is based on four key pillars (the four Cs): customer experience, conversation, content and collaboration. Why these four? Our research[93] has shown that the companies that use these four pillars grow more quickly than the companies that do not. Moreover, these four aspects lay at the basis of much unused conversation potential.

Customer experience

There are still far too few companies that supplement their traditional offline customer service channels with the new online possibilities offered by social media. At the end of 2010 just 6.5 per cent of companies offered online services to their customers. The Conversation Company believes in a total philosophy towards customer experience. The role of social media within this philosophy is to react in real time to people's problems and complaints. The examples of KLM and Twelpforce demonstrate perfectly how this pillar fits in to the overall picture. Other companies, such as Dell, build mission control centres. These centres are manned 24/7 by staff who answer the online questions put by customers and prospects. No single conversation is left without a response; everyone is helped.

Conversation

The Conversation Company manages online conversations in three stages: observing, facilitating and participating.[94] It starts simply by listening to consumer conversations, adding a few relevant comments where necessary. At the same time, the company prepares its content in such a way that it can easily be shared with other interested parties. Clever companies combine these online conversations with their offline activities. The Heineken Champions League stunt makes clear that the effect of small offline events can be magnified many times by social media. Heineken facilitated this process by providing the right content in the right form. Some time ago Kraft had the idea of integrating customer tweets into its offline adverts. People quickly caught on to this idea and were super-keen to get their quotes in the adverts. As a result, more than 1.5 million tweets were sent to Kraft in the course of the campaign.[95]

Content

Companies should no longer be concerned with the planning of one-off advertising campaigns, but with the global planning and management of their content. Your company must learn to think like the publisher of a newspaper. The paper with the most interesting content is the paper that is read the most. Good content is the ideal way to increase your reach. Here are two case study examples.

CASE STUDY The MacLaren Formula 1 team and Gatorade

The MacLaren Formula 1 team

(For more information see *Contagious Magazine Special Report: Real-time marketing*, 2011.)

The website of the MacLaren Formula 1 team broadcasts live reports of each race and it is possible to chat online with the people who work in the pits. On occasions, the team's star drivers, Lewis Hamilton and Jenson Button, also chat to the fans. The purpose of the site is to supplement live action with added value extras. And it works perfectly: during each race an average of 100,000 fans view the site's extra content and there are options for the fans to spread this content via their own social media.

Gatorade

(For more information see *Utalkmarketing.com*, 2010.)

Gatorade also demonstrated its ability with regard to content when planning the Gatorade replay campaign. The aim was to use this story to engage Gatorade's customers more fully in the culture of the brand. The company wanted to convince consumers of the reason for its existence: to give extra energy to athletes. The concept was based on the assumption that every great sportsman has at least one race or game that he or she would like to replay, to try and change the result (perhaps because the sportsperson narrowly lost). Gatorade selected two college football teams who had played out a tight 7–7 draw in 1993. The very same players were trained by Gatorade specialists for 90 days to prepare for the rematch. Gatorade used this time to spread content relating to the story. The highlight was the reply itself, which enjoyed huge public interest. A documentary has also been made about the event, which has since been seen by more than 90 million people. Hundreds of teams have submitted their candidature for a possible rerun of this event. Gatorade replay continues to live a life of its own – all to the benefit of the brand.

Collaboration

The Conversation Company collaborates structurally with its customers. This increases the average level of consumer commitment. It is possible to be fairly creative within this pillar.

CASE STUDY 4Food and Procter & Gamble

4Food

This successful hamburger outlet in Manhattan draws up a new menu every day with the help of its own customers. Using a series of tablets left on the tables, the diners can put together their own recipe for the 'perfect' hamburger. Every new concept put on display for the other customers and 4Food's best-selling burgers are promoted via Twitter and Facebook. For each burger sold, the recipe maker receives 25 cents.

Procter & Gamble

In a similar vein, Procter and Gamble (P&G) has developed Vocalpoint, a community in which 350,000 mothers help to develop new product ideas for the P&G brand. These mothers are also the first users of the new products during the development phase, so that they can provide feedback with regard to possible problems or weaknesses before the product is finally launched on the market.

And now? Implementation

In this second part of the book, you have learned about the philosophy of the Conversation Company. The basis is a strong company culture. This culture is the conversation guide for your staff and your customers. Your people make your culture tangible. At the same time, the Conversation Company also seeks to develop structural collaboration with consumers. Some consumers will even be involved in the management of the company. Via social media, the bond between company and customer is strengthened at all levels. Social media can also magnify aspects of your culture and the experiences of both customers and staff alike. This creates a positive lever. The Conversation Company maximizes conversation potential on the basis of four pillars (the four Cs): customer experience, conversation, content and collaboration.

In the remainder of the book, we will be looking in more depth at the following two subjects.

First, how can you continue to manage the four pillars of customer experience, conversation, content and collaboration successfully?

Second, how can you integrate conversation thinking fully into your company?

Your company will need to undergo three separate phases of change and implement 10 internal strategic projects before it can truly be regarded as a Conversation Company. Part Four of this book must therefore be regarded as a handbook. It is a detailed step-by-step plan based on the vision contained in the first three parts.

KEY CONVERSATION POINTS

Possible conversation starters

- Social media are not an end in themselves; they are simply a means to strengthen your connection with the consumer.

- Fifty per cent of people follow at least one brand on social media. Mobile internet will quickly increase the necessity for all companies to use social media, but will also increase the conversation opportunities available to these companies.

- The Conversation Company manages social media on two dimensions: the build up of reach and the build up of structural relationships with customers.

- The checklist mentality does not work. To use social media effectively, they must be integrated into every aspect of your company.

- The four pillars to manage a Conversation Company are customer experience, conversation, content and collaboration.

Questions you must ask yourself

- Which social media do your target group use? Where are they active and what are their expectations?

- What is the profile of your fans? Do you know your fans? Do you work together with your fans?

- How can you persuade a number of your customers to enter into a structural collaboration with the company?

- How wide is your social reach and how can you increase its range?

- What are your strategies relating to customer experience, conversation, content and collaboration? For which of these four pillars do you score best? And worst?

Further information

Use these links for further interesting information on:

- the KLM Facebook page: **www.facebook.com/KLM** – take a look at the 'bright ideas' section;
- the Heineken Champions League case: **http://youtube.com/watch?v=iK-deK6B9g4.**

Part Three
The four Cs for the management of the Conversation Company

Chapter Seven
Customer experience, conversation, content and collaboration

Why these four components?

It should by now be clear that the philosophy of the Conversation Company is not compatible with the old style of marketing. A recent survey of the professional literature suggests that everyone (or almost everyone) is moving away from the old way of doing things. Jaffe[96] argues that we need to turn the AIDA model back to front. This means investing more in your most loyal existing customers in order to attract new ones. According to Jaffe 'Retention is the best form of acquisition.' Hsieh[97] pleads for the ultimate customer experience. Solis[98] promises us companies who dare to take on the conversation challenge with the consumer and organize all their activities on this basis. Mainwaring goes even a step further. He promises that greater collaboration between brands and the consumer will actually lead to a better world.[99] The importance of employees in conversations is underlined by Bernoff and Shadler.[100] All these opinion makers (and many more besides) are turning to the new methods to try and woo the consumer.

The Conversation Company makes use of four new disciplines (the four Cs): Customer experience, conversation, content and collaboration. These have not been chosen without careful consideration. A survey of 400 marketeers has shown that companies grow more quickly than their sector rivals when they use these four components in unison.[101]

The largest portion of underused conversation potential is also to be found in association with these same four components. By managing them actively, you can optimize that potential. In their different ways, each of the four Cs can help us to eliminate the paradoxes we discussed in Chapter 2. These four pillars will help to build a conversation lever for both your employees and your customers. And this will all take place in keeping with your company culture and company values.

The first pillar, customer experience, is the most important conversation starter. If your employees and your customers feel well treated, they will talk to each other about this fact. By managing customer experience, you are investing in word of mouth. You are developing a focus for staff and consumer satisfaction. In this way, service will no longer be seen as a cost, but as an investment in conversations.

Managing the conversations themselves is the second pillar. This involves observing, facilitating and participating in conversations. Your participation in conversations in social media will make your company seem less distant, more human. By asking and answering questions, the interaction between the company and the market will increase.

In addition to the reactive answering of questions, the Conversation Company adopts an active strategy with regard to content. This strategy is the third pillar. Your content proves that you are an expert in your field. Your company moves away from campaign-based thinking and towards the planning of conversation-generating content that will have great impact.

The final pillar is the pillar of structural collaboration between your company and the market. The customer wants to help you and you will be happy to accept this help. The Conversation Company builds various communities of customers, which help to determine the future of the organization.

CASE STUDY   Ben & Jerry's work hard at every C

Ben & Jerry's is a very conversation-worthy brand. In our opinion, this has much to do with the attitude of the two founders. Right from the very beginning Ben & Jerry's was keen to project a very positive company culture, which wanted to do its best for its customers. This is always a profitable approach. The brand was criticized when it joined forces with the giant Unilever conglomerate, but was nevertheless still able to maximize the use of its conversation potential. Why? Because an analysis of its approach shows that it is an expert at each of our four Cs.

The customer experience of the company's end users is in keeping with its culture (do good and have fun). The Ben & Jerry's sales points, the company's website and packaging all exude the same atmosphere. The behaviour and attitudes of the co-founders undoubtedly form the basis of this approach. Their famous 'free cone' day also fits in perfectly with this philosophy. On this day, the company gives each of its customers a free ice cream, to thank them for their loyalty and custom. In short, the Ben & Jerry's experience is a consistent experience that makes people feel good.

But this is not all. Ben & Jerry's is also very active in conversations. The clever trick discussed in Chapter 2 is a perfect example of the way the company operates. Its Facebook pages for different countries reflect regional sensibilities and are all highly interactive. All its offline events are widely publicized through its online channels. Fans can communicate with the company directly and will always be given an answer, if one is necessary.

Ben & Jerry's is convinced that a company must do good for society and help to generate fun. These values are clearly reflected in Ben & Jerry's content. This makes what it says sound credible. In March 2011, the brand organized a Twitter content action on the theme of fair trade, a subject that is close to the company's heart. Twitter users could download an application which made it possible that their unused Twitter space (a tweet has a maximum of 140 characters, but can, of course, be shorter) could be filled up with content about fair trade. In other words, if someone sent a tweet of just 50 characters, the remaining 90 characters would be used to add a message about fair trade. This action met with an enthusiastic response from the Ben & Jerry fans. In total, more than 500,000 characters were 'given away' in this manner. The campaign was also praised on more than 1,000 blogs.[102] By continually returning to the same themes, the impact and credibility of the company increases significantly. Even so, there is still room for improvement, particularly with regard to the offering of relevant daily content to the fans. The emphasis is still focused too heavily on creative campaigns. More use could be made of blogs and social media to optimize the content strategy.

Finally, Ben & Jerry's is a strong believer in collaboration, both in the large-scale public forums and in smaller, closed fan communities. During the summer of 2011, the brand asked an open forum of consumers to choose a name for one of its new flavours. Nothing special in that, you might think: plenty of other companies do much the same. True, but this action was framed in such a way that it was perfectly in keeping with (and therefore further strengthened) the Ben & Jerry's culture. The winner received no prize, but was allowed to donate 10,000 dollars to the charity of his or her choice. The brand regularly organizes activities of this kind with a similar theme, in order to cement the involvement and commitment of its customers. In addition, the company also has fan communities in many countries, including Belgium and the Netherlands.[103] This group consists of just 200 fans, but the entire Ben & Jerry's conversation and company strategy has been discussed with them. Moreover, at the conclusion of the discussions they wrote a complete social media communication plan for use by the company's managers. The managers felt able to implement this plan in full, and one of the most visible results of this co-creation is the new Facebook page.

FIGURE 7.1

In presenting this case study we are not saying that Ben & Jerry's approach to the four Cs is perfect in every respect. But we are saying that the company is consciously attempting to manage each of the Cs. Thanks to the company's willingness to learn and to invest further in its conversation strategy, Ben & Jerry's conversation value is increasing day by day.

CASE STUDY The unique story of a bicycle seller

The Dutch cycle company Vanmoof was founded as recently as 2009. Its purpose is to sell high-level design bicycles. Right from the very beginning, the co-founders, the brothers Taco and Ties Carlier, had a very conversation-worthy objective: they wanted to help ambitious, urban career people throughout the world to cycle in style. To a large extent they have achieved this objective: they now sell something like one thousand bicycles each month in 34 different countries. And they have never invested a single euro in marketing. Everything is based on conversations. The CEO, Jasmijn Rijcken, commented in an interview in 2011: 'It is other people who say that we are a cool brand; you will never hear us say it.' The company's conversation strategy relies heavily on the four Cs.

The design of Vanmoof's first bicycle was immediately an example of collaboration. The founders asked 100 of their friends what the perfect city bike should look like. This feedback was sometimes surprising. Urban cyclists are not always on the look-out for the latest technological trends. They want an attractive-looking bike that is rain-proof and (as far as realistically possible) vandal-proof. Vanmoof continues to keep a close watch on customer feedback via social media. At one particular time many customers expressed a desire for a baggage carrier on the back of the bicycle. Vanmoof listened to what its fans were saying and a carrier has been added to the most recent models. Rijcken sums it up nicely: 'Our customers are the fifth member of our board of directors.'

Content is an important part of Vanmoof's strategy. The company tells its customers what is happening in the factory on a daily basis. The R&D team is constantly working on new bike designs. These plans are shared online. Members of the team also share photographs and videos which show the progress they are making. They are not worried by the fact that the competition might also be looking. In fact, they do not regard other cycle manufacturers as competitors. Their competitors are public transport, walking and the motor car. In addition to information about its bikes, the company also seeks to inspire cyclists with the experiences, tips and photos of other cyclists. It has an advantage in that its home market is the Netherlands, a typical cycling country – but this is not the case everywhere it operates. By finding and sharing photos of cyclists on Vanmoof bikes in the middle of the busy streets of New York, the company hopes to encourage more people to take to two wheels.

FIGURE 7.2

Conversation with Vanmoof's target group is built into the company's DNA. It does not attach so much value to the quantity of its online followers, but rather to the level of interaction with them. In the summer of 2011 its Facebook page had just 4,000 fans, which is not a huge number for a global brand. But the level of activity is high. The customers and staff of Vanmoof talk with each other daily about bicycles, new designs and a thousand and one other things. And they talk to each other like they talk to their friends. Never for a second does the company lose contact with its fans and followers.

As a small company, Vanmoof sees customer experience as a top priority. A bike has more than 150 different components, so that something can always go wrong. Everyone associated with the company is responsible for ensuring that the customer has a good experience. If customers phone, it can sometimes happen that they will actually get one of the co-founders on the line. And in the event of problems, every Vanmoof user can come along to the Amsterdam showroom to pick up a reserve bike. Vanmoof regards this type of service as the best way to bring its company culture to life.

Vanmoof is by nature a Conversation Company. It uses the four Cs in a natural and spontaneous manner – and in so doing has turned the company into a success story.

How do you score on each component?

To give this book a little colour, a number of interesting and instructive case studies have been discussed. Some of these – such as KLM and Ben & Jerry's – score well on all the Cs. Others shine with regard to one particular C, but still need to do better with the rest. For example, during our conversation with Rod Brooks of PEMCO he made clear that his company still invests too little in content. With its available resources, it has opted for a more active focus on customer experience and conversations.

You can make this kind of analysis for your own company. How do you score on each of the four Cs? Using the following self-test, you can see how you are currently performing for each discipline. This will show you where you still need to make more progress and also (more encouragingly) where you are already on the road to success. Answer each of the questions yes or no.

Customer experience

1 Does your company attempt to be conversation-worthy in every phase of the purchase process?

2 (a) Does your company manage expectations? (b) Do you deliver slightly more than you promise?

3 Does your company offer the same service both online and offline?

4 Are all your staff trained to give good service?

5 Do all your staff know how to react to both satisfied and dissatisfied customers?

6 Does your company manage every touchpoint as a conversation starter?

7 Does your company innovate sufficiently in terms of customer service?

8 Can your customers choose their own preferred channel of communication to put their questions?

9 In the event of problems, does your company always opt for a solution that benefits the customer?

10 Are more than 80 per cent of the comments about your company positive?

Conversation

1 Does your company observe the conversations of consumers?
2 Are the conclusions of these observations shared throughout the entire company?
3 Does your company participate in online conversations?
4 If a consumer asks your company a question, do you always answer?
5 Do your staff participate in conversations?
6 Does your company sometimes put questions to public forums to gain input and feedback from consumers?
7 If your company makes a mistake, do you admit it and apologize?
8 Does your company offer objective, added value in dealing with commercial questions from consumers?
9 Does your company use the real names of the people who administer your Twitter accounts?
10 Does your company manage its conversations itself?

Content

1 Does your company have a content plan?
2 Does your company have employees who can create content?
3 Does your company have the right online channels to spread content effectively?
4 Does your company have a good knowledge of the other channels which exist to spread content, other than those you are currently using?
5 Does your company have bloggers among its employees?
6 Does your company have a kind of editor, who can plan and organize your content?
7 Does your company have the right software to process content efficiently?
8 Does your company know in which content areas it wishes to focus its efforts?

9 Does your company have a plan to convert content into leads?

10 Does your company facilitate the sharing of content?

Collaboration

1 Has your company already taken decisions in conjunction with its customers?

2 Does your company have a small, closed fan community with whom it consults?

3 Does your company have a large, open fan community with whom it consults?

4 Does your company have a staff community?

5 Does your company involve customers in the development of new products?

6 Does your company involve customers in the development of new service possibilities?

7 Does your company involve customers in the launching of new products?

8 Does your company involve customers in the choosing of new suppliers?

9 Does your company actively manage its relationships with fans and ambassadors?

10 Does your company take more than 50 per cent of its decisions in collaboration with staff and/or customers?

For each category, a score of 5 or less out of 10 means that you still have a very long way to go. Scores of 5, 6 or 7 out of 10 means that you have built up some initial experience, but that there are still a number of necessary steps you need to take. If you have scored 8, 9 or 10, you are an example to be followed in that particular discipline. If you have scored high for every dimension, you are already worthy of the title of a Conversation Company – and you can pass this book on to a less fortunate friend!

In the following four chapters, we will be looking at each of the Cs in more detail. This will reveal to you the different points you still need to work on.

KEY CONVERSATION POINTS

Possible conversation starters

- The principles of marketing are not compatible with the principles of the Conversation Company. As a result, we must say farewell to the concept of marketing, a philosophy from a previous century.

- The four Ps of marketing have been replaced by the four Cs.

- Companies that manage the four Cs – customer experience, conversation, content and collaboration – grow faster than companies that do not.

- The management of the four Cs creates a conversation lever for your internal and external people.

- The management of the four Cs takes place within the framework of a clearly defined company culture and values.

Questions you must ask yourself

- How does your company score on each of the four Cs?

- In which areas are you well on the way to success and in which areas do you still have a long way to go?

Further information

Take a look at the Vanmoof website: **www.vanmoof.com**.

Chapter Eight
Customer experience

Customers are more than the sum total of your turnover

Most companies give better service to their loyal customers than to their occasional customers. Someone who frequently flies by plane will be given access to the pre-flight lounge and will need to queue less at the different control posts. A regular visitor to a restaurant will more readily be given a drink 'on the house' than a first-time diner. This approach is both logical and correct. It is based on the classic principle of 'you scratch my back, and I'll scratch yours'.

Unfortunately, the producers of consumer goods (eg foodstuffs manufacturers) tend to have a much poorer focus on the top 20 per cent of their consumers. Often, they don't really know who they are. Nevertheless, the same principle holds good in their market. For example, let's take Coca-Cola.

CASE STUDY
Relatively few customers generate massive turnover for Coca-Cola

Surprisingly, 80 per cent of Coca-Cola's massive turnover is generated by just 12 per cent of its customers. For Cola-Light and Coke-Zero the figures are even more extreme: 6.5 per cent of Cola-Light buyers generate 80 per cent of turnover and for Coke-Zero it is just 3 per cent.[104]

Coca-Cola makes a real effort to get to know these people. It is one of the very few food and drink producers that has an online loyalty programme: 'My Coke Rewards'. Every item of Coke packaging has a code. This code can be entered into the company's website. In this way, customers can save up points which can be cashed in for special reductions or fun gifts. This allows Coca-Cola to identify the large-scale repeat buyers of its products.

Most companies are familiar with this Pareto principle, which states that 20 per cent of customers generate 80 per cent of turnover. A clever company will make sure that it looks after this top 20 per cent – and looks after them very well. Identifying your best customers and linking this to specific actions or campaigns is the classic way to manage a customer portfolio.

The Conversation Company is also concerned with the financial value of its customers, but also adds a second, equally important dimension: their conversation value. In addition to providing income, every customer is also a source of conversation potential. This means that someone who buys relatively few products can be influential for the company by means of the positive comments the person gives about those products. For example, a famous businessman only needs to fly on your airline once to generate considerable conversation value; the leader of a youth movement who tries out a new brand of breakfast cereal has a similar conversation value.

According to an article by Kumar, Petersen and Leone,[105] there is not always a strong correlation between a high frequency of purchase and a high willingness to recommend. Their research has shown that people who buy relatively little can still have a relatively high conversation value. In their study, the group of recommending frequent buyers was precisely the same size as the group of recommending infrequent buyers: 29 per cent of the total customer population.

Your absolute top priority customers are the ones who combine significant financial value with significant conversation value. Go in search of influential people among your loyal customers, but also do the same among your occasional customers. The objective is to optimize the conversation potential of both groups. To achieve this objective, every interaction with a touchpoint of your company must be conversation-worthy.

Does this mean that every customer is not equally important? No, not at all. The Conversation Company treats every customer in a conversation-worthy manner. Even if individual customers have little conversation potential, the experience must be perfect. However, when you are spreading your content and setting up your structural collaboration, the most conversation-worthy customers will naturally be your primary focus.

Conversation-worthy in every phase

Do you like planning journeys? Personally, I love it. I can amuse myself for hours, searching for fun hotels and interesting places to visit. When I was booking a hotel for my last holiday, I was struck by the fact that this also offers a conversation potential. For me, the booking of a hotel is always something of a high spot, but all you get in return is a boring confirmation of your reservation. Yet it would be very easy to make this purchasing phase conversation-worthy. After all, this is the phase on which the travel sector concentrates most heavily, since it is during this phase that customers are won or lost. And this is not only the case in the travel sector. All marketeers are trained to approach the customer during the decision-making process that precedes purchase.

This philosophy is no longer valid in our modern conversation-driven world. Consumers expect a good experience at every phase of the purchasing process: before, during and after sale. Besides, you optimize your conversation potential precisely by making every interaction with the customer conversation-worthy.

McKinsey investigated the buying behaviour of 20,000 people and came to the conclusion that consumers are always in one 'consideration' phase or another of the purchasing process.[106] In the first phase, they consider a number of brands. This list is drawn up on the basis of their past experiences. Even if they are not in a purchasing phase, they will still from time to time come into contact with the touchpoints of your company. These contacts will determine whether or not you are on their shortlist. The second phase is an active evaluation of these shortlisted companies. In the third phase, the actual purchase will be made. After the purchase – the fourth phase – they evaluate what they will do in the event that a further purchase needs to be made in future. The number of positive conversations and the future buying intentions are determined on the basis of their interactions with touchpoints after the purchase.

FIGURE 8.1

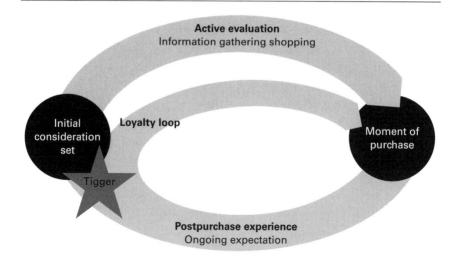

In the light of this new way of buying, it is important for the Conversation Company to map out all its touchpoints carefully. Make an analysis of every place, both online and offline, where your target public can come into contact with your company. It helps to divide these touchpoints into four categories[107]:

- **Messages.** These are one-way communications sent out by the company. This might include mass-media advertising, press releases or the packaging of your products.
- **Interactions.** These are all the places where an interaction can take place between a potential customer and the company. Examples include sales points, telephone calls, face-to-face conversations, reactions on a blog and conversations on social media.
- **Products.** Their experience of your product is an important touchpoint for customers. This determines the extent to which your product will live up to their expectations, or not. This includes the moments when the customers are given an opportunity to test your product.
- **Products being used by someone else.** Potential customers often first come into contact with your product when they see it being used by someone else. This can be in the house of a friend, but also in films and television programmes (product placement).

To create a top customer experience, it is necessary to look at all the touchpoints in all the different phases of the purchasing process. Remember that these experiences are the most important conversation starters for your customers. And a good experience will always lead to a positive conversation. By thinking carefully about every touchpoint in every phase of the purchasing process, you will get a better overall picture of your weak and strong points.

Ask yourself the following questions:

- What can you do to make every touchpoint conversation-worthy? Which touchpoints are already generating positive conversations? Which ones are not?
- Are your touchpoints designed to meet customer expectations?
- Do all your touchpoints provide a consistent experience?
- Is the online and offline experience provided by your company identical?
- Are there certain touchpoints which regularly cause potential customers to withdraw from the purchasing process? If so, why?

Investing your different touchpoints with the same strong conversation value will only be possible if you work within a structure where everyone has the same objective – namely, to make the customer happy. In the silo structure, different departments are responsible for different touchpoints, so that the consistency of the experience cannot be guaranteed. For example, 12 per cent of consumers think that there are major differences between the online and offline experience of a brand.[108] Departments must work together closely across the different touchpoints, to ensure the same conversation-worthy approach throughout the company.

CASE STUDY The Ralph Lauren iPad app

Clothing manufacturer Ralph Lauren has launched an interactive iPad app to promote a new line of sportswear. The possibilities offered by this app are unique. Users can colour in the clothes with their fingers! In this way, a black-and-white photograph can be transformed by the user into a multi-coloured outfit. And the models in the photographs can be made to assume different positions, so that you can see how the outfit looks from every angle. But the application goes much further than the simple modelling of new clothes. Users can immediately order or purchase the clothes they like. And the promotion of the clothes through sharing on various social media, such as Facebook and Twitter, is also an option.

This app is a specially developed touchpoint designed to support the launching of a new line. It brings all the different phases of the customer's decision-making process together in one 'place'. Users can admire their clothes, buy their clothes and share the experience with their friends – all at the touch of their iPad buttons.

Learn to manage expectations

Apple succeeds repeatedly in making all its touchpoints conversation-worthy. A visit to one of its stores is a unique experience. What strikes me most is the packaging of its products. Many Apple users really look forward to the launch of a new product from their favourite company. And once you finally get the product in your hands, you are first pleasantly surprised by the design of the packaging. Everything is so elegant and so compact that the simple process of taking your new toy out of the box gives you your first 'wow' feeling. This shows how Apple gives careful thought to making every phase of the purchasing process conversation-worthy.

Every company dreams of giving its customers a 'wow' experience. To develop the right mentality, the Conversation Company makes use of the number of 'highly satisfied customers' as a success indicator. Only a score of 10 out of 10 is regarded as satisfactory. If members of your team are aware of this norm, they clearly know what you expect of them. At first glance, this may seem to be an extreme position, but in reality you can manage this situation more easily than you might think. To a large extent, managing customer experience is a matter of managing expectations.

The company always decides for itself how high it wants to raise the bar. The secret is always to do just a little bit more than you had actually promised. Most people have a natural inclination to do this the other way around: to promise slightly more than they are actually able to deliver. How often have you heard a company promise that someone will ring back in the morning, only to be contacted late the following afternoon or even the next day. This is not a disaster, but it is still doing less than the company promised – and so it will not result in a positive conversation. The management of expectations can lead to one of four situations[109]:

- Your company does less than it promised. It has not been able to do the things it said it would do. The customer is understandably disappointed. This is a possible reason for a negative conversation.

- Your company does exactly what it promised. You have done exactly what you said you would do, no more and no less. This will satisfy the customer, but he or she is unlikely to give you 10 out of 10. The resulting conversations will tend to be limited.

- Your company does slightly more than it promised. You do more than you said you would do, perhaps quicker than promised or with a super-friendly attitude. This will result in a 10 out of 10 score – and plenty of positive conversations. And it doesn't take much extra to get this maximum, examples are: sending a document more promptly than you said, the use of clever packaging (Apple), the washing of a car during its maintenance check-up, serving an extra hors d'oeuvre that wasn't on the menu, solving problems with a smile...

- Your company does much more than it promised. This might seem like the best scenario of all, but in reality it is not such a good idea. First, you might not even make a sale, because the customer thinks you undersold the product in the first place. Second, it can sometimes give the customer a funny feeling. For example, if you are invited to dinner by the big boss of the company immediately after you have made your first (modest) purchase, you might find this a little odd, almost an overreaction. To generate positive customer conversations, it is not necessary to go to extremes. This can even lead to negative conversations of the 'what's behind all this?' kind. The only exception to this general rule is the 'one-off' surprise. If you do something out of the ordinary but make clear that it is unlikely to be repeated, you can sometimes create a very satisfied customer indeed. A typical example is the upgrading of a seat from economy to business class on a plane. The customer realizes that this isn't going to happen every time, but is nonetheless delighted by the gesture – and won't forget it.

The Conversation Company succeeds in ensuring that every inter-action provides just a little bit more than the customer expected. This practice must be implemented consistently at every touchpoint throughout the organization.

CASE STUDY
Carglass manages expectations and doubles turnover

(Based on an interview with Jean-Paul Teyssen, CEO of Carglass Belgium, and Caroline Ameloot, Sales and Marketing Directeur, Carglass Belgium.)

Carglass repairs and replaces damaged car windows. It is a market in which it is difficult to differentiate your company. Consumers see the replacement of a car window as a necessary evil and therefore usually base their purchasing decision on price. Or so you would think. But in recent years Carglass has shown that this hypothesis is not necessarily true. In a difficult market, the company succeeded in doubling its turnover in the years between 2005 and 2010. How did it achieve this remarkable success? Since 2004 Carglass has focused exclusively on providing excellent customer service. The company was not prepared to accept anything less than 10 out of 10 for customer satisfaction. This extreme focus laid the foundations for its amazing financial turnaround.

The change process within the company was approached structurally. According to its CEO, Jean-Paul Teyssen, there were three main pillars on which this process was based:

> The management of the company determines 50 per cent of the culture and the culture determines 50 per cent of the financial result. The first step in the change process was therefore to force the management to take a hard look in the mirror. We analysed our leadership style and decided that we definitely needed to change a number of things. So we started with ourselves first! Secondly, we created a circle of 'success'. The basic idea was that satisfied staff would lead to satisfied customers, and satisfied customers would lead to satisfied shareholders. And if the shareholders are satisfied, there is automatically more scope to make the staff even more satisfied, and so it goes on – a kind of positive vicious circle. Thirdly, we decided to measure everything we do. The satisfaction levels of customers and staff were noted meticulously. We were able to draw up an accurate picture of what our customers felt about every phase of contact with the company. This helped us to further evolve step by step towards even more extreme levels of customer satisfaction.

As a result of the company's positive, customer-based culture on the one hand and the huge amounts of data relating to its touchpoints on the other hand, Carglass gradually became a master in managing the expectations of its customers. In every phase of contact, the customers were offered slightly more than they had been promised. This led to the generation not just of a single 'wow' moment, but of a whole series of 'wow' moments.

It all begins with the making of an appointment. After the customer has filled in the necessary form online, he or she receives an e-mail confirmation. This states that a Carglass employee will contact the customer within four hours to confirm all the details. Nothing so special in that, you might say. But there is: because the large majority of customers are phoned within the first hour. In other words, their expectations have already been exceeded for a first time. Carglass could just as easily say that its staff will call within one hour, and in 95 per cent of cases this would be true. But it also means that in 5 per cent of cases the customer would be disappointed – with possible negative conversations as a result. So why make things difficult for yourself? By setting a time limit of four hours, you make everyone happy! Remember: you always decide for yourself how high you want to set the bar.

And so it continues throughout the rest of the purchasing process. When the Carglass operatives are on their way to the rendezvous, they telephone 20 minutes before arrival, so that the customer knows exactly what is going on and doesn't need to waste any time unnecessarily.

Finally, the operatives not only repair or replace the damaged window, but ensure that the car is left in generally good condition. They will remove any rubbish (kids' empty Cola bottles and sweet wrappers) and will even give the interior a quick vacuum, if required. These are only small details, which cost little in terms of time and money, but can have a huge positive impact. Every touchpoint has been carefully considered and for every one of them a way has been found to offer customers slightly more than they were expecting. And they love it!

This approach has led to extremely satisfied customers. Carglass ask: 'Would you recommend our company to your family and friends?' The net promoter score for Carglass is the percentage of customers who give a score of 9 or 10 out of 10, minus the number of customers who give a score of between 0 and 6 out of 10, with a minimum score of –100 and a maximum score of +100. Carglass scores +71. According to net promoter score theory,[110] a company will grow faster than the market if it achieves a score higher than zero. So with a score of +71... we hardly need to paint a picture.

CASE STUDY
Check in, pay with Amex – and get a 5 dollar discount

American Express works together with Foursquare to promote the use of its credit cards with consumers and shopkeepers. In March 2011, the company started a pilot scheme in Austin, Texas. Companies such as Starbucks, Whole Foods and Starwood Hotels agreed to take part. The project gave consumers the chance to earn a 5 dollar discount if they checked in via Foursquare while they were in one of the shops in question and then paid with an American Express card. Foursquare and Amex ensure that the discount is deducted from the customers' monthly account settlement. The shopkeeper doesn't need to do anything. In other words, this is a three-double win situation. The shops in question get free word-of-mouth advertising via the customer check-in. Foursquare gains in visibility and the Amex discount is a prime conversation starter.

CASE STUDY Allianz rewards customers for a healthy lifestyle

The price of your car insurance is determined in part by the way you drive and your accident record. The fewer the accidents and the lower the levels of damage, the less you pay. Allianz has now decided to apply the same principle to its life and hospital insurance policies. In this venture, it has collaborated with Nike on Nike+, which is a project linking Nike running shoes with Apple software to monitor the personal performance of joggers via the internet. Allianz uses these popular apps to set the premiums for its insurance policies. The more people exercise, the less they will be asked to pay. In this way, Nike, Allianz and the consumers are working together to ensure the better general health of society at large.

This represents a new touchpoint focused on a positive, interactive after-sales relationship. In effect, the customers can manage their own relationship with the insurance company. If they want to live healthily, they can reduce their annual insurance bill. This is a very clever move by Allianz. Insurance companies find it notoriously difficult to generate after-sales conversations. This again proves that, with a little creativity, conversation potential can be created in all the purchase phases of every sector.

Organize your company for customer experience

Customer experience is relevant to everything your company does. Every action of every member of staff contributes to the experience of your customers. The Conversation Company takes account of the following matters in its attempt to ensure high-quality customer satisfaction:

- *Compile a touchpoint scorecard.* To evaluate a touchpoint accurately, you need information relating to several important dimensions. Reach, conversation worthiness, customer satisfaction and staff satisfaction are the four most important factors in managing the conversation potential of these touchpoints. Draw up a scorecard that assesses all these factors for all your touchpoints.

- *Every member of staff has a responsibility.* By now you will realize that your own staff are the most important conversation starters in your company. However, not every employee is aware of his or her potential impact on customer experience. Make sure that everyone in the company understands their role in the customer relationship.

- *Include customer experience in your training programme.* Your employees influence your customers' experience of your company. These employees are doubtless filled with good intentions, but not everyone knows the best way to make a customer happy. For this reason, ensure that all your staff receive proper training in the creation of positive customer experiences.

- *Measuring is necessary.* It is likely that every touchpoint has unused conversation potential. However, it is important in this respect that there should be consistency across all the different touchpoints. To achieve this consistency and encourage optimization of the conversation potential, it is necessary to have concrete and reliable data. Measure the experience and the conversation value of every touchpoint. This will allow you to draw up an action plan.

- *Do something extra for conversation-worthy customers.* Your company probably already offers extra incentives to its most financially lucrative customers. The Conversation Company does the same for its most conversation-worthy customers or fans.

CASE STUDY Cadillac learns from the Ritz Hotel

Cadillac has made immense strides forward in customer experience during the period 2009–11.[111] In large part, this was due to the ability of the luxury car manufacturer to hire in the customer service trainers of the Ritz-Carlton hotel chain. The Ritz Hotel provides a unique experience, and one which exceeds its customers' expectations every day. Cadillac wanted to provide a similar experience for its own customers and decided to learn the tricks of the trade from the very best experts in the field. It is often a smart move to learn from experts in other industries.

KEY CONVERSATION POINTS

Possible conversation starters

- The financial value of customers is obviously important, but do not forget to attach similar importance to the conversation value of customers as part of your customer management process.
- Their experience of your touchpoints is the most important conversation starter for customers.
- Consumers are always in a purchasing phase.
- Every step in the purchase cycle must be conversation-worthy.
- Ensure a consistent level of experience at all your touchpoints.
- Your ability to manage expectations determines the number of conversations about your company. The Conversation Company always does slightly more than it initially promised.
- Every single person in your company is responsible for customer satisfaction.
- To measure is to know. Carefully chart the conversation value of each touchpoint: this is the only way to optimize your customer experience.

Questions you must ask yourself

- Who are your most important customers in financial terms and what do you do for them?
- Who are your most important customers in terms of conversation-worthiness and what do you do for them?
- Which of your company touchpoints are conversation-worthy and which are not?
- How do you manage customer expectations at each of these touchpoints?
- Does your company have sufficient data for each touchpoint, so that you can evaluate them all accurately?
- Do you provide your staff with proper training in customer experience?

Further information

Use these links for further interesting information on:

- the Guillaume Van der Stighelen blog post: **http://guillaumevds.posterous.comhink-before-you-promise**;
- the Allianz campaign: **http://vimeo.com/23406453**.

Chapter Nine
Conversation

Participating; reactive and proactive

The managing of conversations was covered extensively in *The Conversation Manager*.[112] In short, the methodology of the conversation manager is as follows: he or she observes conversations as a manager, facilitates conversations as a brand and participates in conversations as himself or herself. These are the three steps for managing conversations, which each require a very different approach if success is to be achieved. In this chapter, we will be focusing on participation in conversations.

Responding to questions and complaints is reactive conversation. This obviously makes up a large and important part of your overall conversation potential. If people ask you a question, they (quite rightly) expect an answer. If you can succeed in providing a satisfactory answer, these people will get a happy feeling. At the same time, your company wins their growing trust and confidence. Unfortunately, participating is still regarded too narrowly by too many companies. The majority equate managing conversations with the setting up of a webcare team. In reality, however, participating in conversations involves much more than dealing with the complaints of dissatisfied customers. For example, when someone recommends your company to others, you can thank them for their efforts. Answering fans and positive people is just as much a part of reactive conversing as answering your critics.

Of course, you can also converse proactively with consumers. If customers are talking about a subject about which you are a specialist, you may be able to provide them with relevant and interesting content. This is how Gary Vaynerchuk achieved worldwide fame. Gary is a wine merchant in New York, with more than 900,000 Twitter followers. Every day he visits online communities where consumers are discussing wine. During these discussions, Gary answers any questions that the participants might have. He helps them, but without attaching any commercial message. Kodak uses much the same approach. If it sees an online discussion between consumers about the merits of different digital cameras, it will try to bring added value to these discussions by suggesting that the participants read certain (impartial) magazine articles. These are examples of proactive conversing at its best.

Of course, the content strategy to be discussed in the next chapter is also an important element in the proactive management of conversations. Giving people something to talk about is an ideal way to facilitate conversations about your brand.

The conversation manager observes, facilitates and participates

Since not everyone will have read *The Conversation Manager*, I will briefly describe the three basic steps to manage conversations.

The first step is the observation of conversations on social media. The most frequently asked question in workshops about online conversation management is: 'How can we take part in customer conversations?' We usually answer this with another question: 'How long have you already been observing the conversations of your customers?' They look surprised for a moment, but then the penny drops. They suddenly realize that they haven't even got this far! The managing of conversations begins with a long period of observation to find out what your customers are actually talking about. One of the key objectives is to understand the language of the customers, to learn how they speak about your brand.

The second step is to think of ways in which you can facilitate these conversations. It is useful to have tools at your disposal that will allow you to talk efficiently to customers. Your aim is to make things as easy as possible for these customers to share information and experiences relating to your brand. These tools can sometimes be relatively simple things, such as the addition of a 'share' button on the information page of your website. It is also necessary to ensure a regular supply of fresh and relevant content that is conversation-worthy (see below). Another way to facilitate conversations is through your own customer communities (also described later in the book).

It is only during the third and final step that you actually start conversing with customers. It is best to join in these conversations as

TABLE 9.1

As a manager	As a brand	As a peer
Observe	Facilitate	Join

a person (or peer), not as a representative of 'the brand'. Modern consumers are not interested in impersonal, standardized messages from companies; they want to speak to real people, who will listen to what they have to say and do something with their feedback.[113]

This, then, is a short summary of how you can manage conversations on social media: you observe the conversations as a manager, you facilitate the conversations as a brand and you participate in the conversations as yourself. Each phase requires a different approach, but you need to combine them all if you wish to achieve success. The worst mistake you can make is to participate in conversations as a manager. If you don't speak to the customers in their own language, they will leave you in droves. All you will be left with for your efforts is a very nasty boomerang effect.

Each profile requires a different conversation approach

Remember that not all customers have the same relationship with your company. Their emotions can be very different in this respect. Some will be real fans of what you do, whereas others might hate you. Between these two extremes, there are three nuanced gradations of emotion: positive, neutral and negative. Each of these emotions will elicit a different reaction to your brand and requires a different approach in response from your staff. But be careful: do not forget that these emotions are based on the customer's relationship with your company, not on particular positive or negative incidents. For example, a fan may occasionally have a bad experience of your company, but still remain a fan. The emotions reflect the general feeling of the customer towards the company. This being the case, it is useful to define your response to these different sentiments in advance.

Fans: give them content to share

These people think that everything you do is brilliant. They will seldom (if ever) say anything negative about your company. And everything that you say to them, they will be happy to pass on to others. The only thing you need to do is to give these people sufficient content to share. Your content strategy (see Chapter 10) is very important for them. If you give them nothing, you are effectively creating unused conversation potential. It goes without saying that you must regularly thank these fans for their enthusiastic support. Occasionally, you should also express your gratitude in a more concrete form (a small gift, special discount, etc). The biggest mistake you can make is not talking to these fans. Do not assume that they will remain positive for ever. Regard them – and treat them – as an important conversation partner. Invite them to collaborate with your plans for the future of the company.

Positives: involve them

This is a very interesting and useful group. As far as your company is concerned, these people are positive towards the outside world. They share your updates and success stories with their own networks. Behind the scenes (via e-mail, telephone or a Twitter message) they give you feedback about things that could be improved. This is how you recognize the people in this category: they are full of praise to their friends and constructively critical in their contacts with you. They want to help you to make your company better. Consequently, you should also invite these people to take part in a structural collaboration process. Involve them in the development of new products and new content. They will offer you their opinions with pleasure. They are healthily sceptical, but understand where your company is trying to go.

Neutrals: activate them

Your company leaves these consumers neither hot nor cold. If you want to activate these people, there has to be something in it for them. For example, they may well react to competitions or free offers. They will only spread your content if, in their eyes, it is sufficiently newsworthy and relevant.

Negatives: listen and talk to them

These people often spread negative information about your company. They feel that it must get better (as opposed to the positives, who think that it can get better). Enter into dialogue with this group. Listen to their feedback. Perhaps they are right on some matters: if you admit this and act, your company will rise in their esteem. Ensure that you deal with their negative comments in a positive and sympathetic manner. Even if these people are not positive, your own positivism will neutralize their negative conversation.

Haters: ignore but understand where the hate comes from

Members of this group have lost all confidence in your company. They believe that you are not capable of doing better. Everything you say, they take the wrong way. They shudder at the thought of having anything to do with your products. Even if you enter into dialogue with them, you are unlikely to change their opinions. In this sense, there is little point in reacting to their negative comments: this will simply be adding fuel to the fire. You cannot win the discussion with these people. 'Take no notice of trolls (negative people). Let their negative content stand, but ignore their comments. If you give them any form of attention, they will feel that they have succeeded in their mission to annoy you,' says Willaerts, a social media expert.[114] The only thing worth listening to is the reasons why they have this hatred of your company. Perhaps you can learn from the past to avoid these kinds of feelings developing in other customers in the future.

If you use this system wisely, you will plant many new seeds and put out many existing fires. This should improve your relations with almost everyone, positives and negatives alike. It will isolate the only people with whom your relations can never improve – the haters. You can approach fans and positive people both proactively and reactively with your stories. Negative people are not expecting to hear from you: deal with them reactively, as the circumstances dictate. Answer their questions politely and correctly, and use your own questions to gently probe the reasons for their negativity towards your company. But do not overdo it: this will only work against you.

Twitter is just like a pub

Many companies still do not really know the best way to behave on Twitter. Every expert stresses the importance of coming across with a 'human face', but what exactly does this mean in concrete terms? What kind of language should you use? Have you anything meaningful to say? Is Twitter a part of your communication mix? You have probably already asked yourself these questions – or heard them from others.

To make the discussion easier, I compare Twitter with a giant pub. (In contrast to Twitter, this is an environment in which most marketeers feel perfectly at home!)

Just like in a pub, on Twitter a wide variety of people talk about a wide variety of subjects. And these subjects can change in just a fraction of a second. The really good, juicy stories fly around the pub in an instant.

As a company, it is interesting for you to mingle with this crowd of people. Try to make friends with some of them. Listen to what they have to say, and say something relevant in reply. Buy a round of drinks when it is your turn. If one of your friends has done something special or is celebrating something special, give them a small present: it really can work wonders for your relationship. But this is all people expect in a pub: a friendly chat, a kind word and occasionally a helping hand on their way through life. Sometimes, just sometimes, they may even find the love (or the company) of their life. You shouldn't overestimate the chances of this happening – but to underestimate it would be an even bigger mistake.

You know what really irritates me in a pub? You have probably experienced it yourself: those punters who barge in with their bunches of wilting roses, which they then try to sell to you with their intrusive sales techniques. Just when your conversation was getting interesting, they come along and interrupt you. Most annoying! And it is the same with companies on Twitter: once you start using aggressive sales techniques, you will soon see your public disappear!

Something that I learnt from my student years is that you need to pop along to the pub regularly, if you want to belong to a particular group. People who only came along once every three months never really seemed to fit in. And if they attempted to compensate for this by trying to make a big impression, they soon had the same effect as the rose sellers: everyone disappeared. Again, it is the same on Twitter. Some companies build up a nice group of fans, but only send them a tweet when there is some really big, important news to announce. To make matters worse, the companies are sometimes so preoccupied with their own news that they don't bother to answer the questions of their followers. This is no way to keep your friends.

The popular people in the pub tend to be the positive people, the people with an interesting view of the world, who know how to amuse and entertain others. Most of us go to the pub to be with our friends, to listen to their stories, to enjoy ourselves. People with a negative outlook do not normally make interesting conversation partners. So when you are twittering for your company, try to be positive and enthusiastic. Personally, I think that it is great that all those 'investments' I made during my student years are now beginning to pay off. And believe me: life on Twitter and life in a pub are much more similar than you might think.

Of course, there is a technological side to Twitter that you will not find in your average pub. This something you need to bear in mind. For example, Google remembers what you twittered and who you twittered it to (which is not something that you can always say after an evening in the pub!). This means that weeks later you may be confronted with a statement that you once made in a moment of weakness or enthusiasm. In addition – and again unlike a pub – there are lots of people outside your little circle of friends who are also examining every word you say. This makes all the tips mentioned above doubly important.

CASE STUDY   Conversing with cows? Yes, you can!

See also the *Contagious Magazine Special Report: Real time marketing*, 2011.)

If you ask a group of 15–25-year-olds to name their favourite brand, you might imagine that very few of them would immediately think of dairy products. But you would be wrong – at least in Norway. There, the Litago company has succeeded in making milk interesting for this traditionally difficult target group. The key to this success story: conversing with cows via a GPS transmitter! Litago promised young people that, together with the cows, they would be able to choose a new milk flavour. The company set up a live-stream video of a meadow, which was divided into different compartments. Each compartment represented a new flavour option. The compartment where most cows spent most time would determine which of these options was actually marketed. Consumers could influence the behaviour of the cows in different ways. For example, it was possible to place a brass band in one of the compartments, so that the cows would move away in disgust to the other side of the meadow. You could even become the friend of an individual cow on Facebook, in the hope of persuading her (and her fellow bovines) to move to the compartment of your choice. Hundreds of consumers actively conversed each day with the different cows in the meadow! In the meantime, the new flavour has been launched and is now the fourth best-selling drink in Norway, after Coca-Cola, Cola Light and Pepsi Max.

FIGURE 9.1

CASE STUDY Watch out for the F-bomb!

In March 2011 an unusual tweet appeared on the official Chrysler Twitter account. It read as follows: 'I find it ironic that Detroit is known as the #motor city#, and yet no one knows how to f**king drive.' Shortly thereafter, the tweet was removed, but the damage was done. Many Twitterers had already sent the provocative text to their followers. A few hours later, a blog post appeared apologizing on behalf of the brand. This blog contained a message almost as remarkable as the original tweet. The person responsible for the tweet worked for Chrysler's PR bureau, and was instantly sacked. What had happened? The unlucky man managed Twitter accounts for a number of different brands. The tweet that he wanted to send was destined for his personal account, but by accident he selected the Chrysler account! A clearer structure and a better organization can help to avoid human errors of this kind.

Organizing for your participation in conversations

Conversations are managed in real time. To meet the expectations of the market, you need to be well organized. The following points are worth bearing in mind when you are setting up your organization.

- Decide whether to delegate or not. Many companies decide to delegate the management of their online conversations to a specialized outside agency. At a congress, the marketing VP of a major foodstuffs producer once explained to me his company's motives for sub-contracting out this task. The first reason was cost-related: the company simply wanted fewer permanent members of staff on its books. In bad times, any dismissal costs would then have to be borne by the agency. The second reason was related to flexibility: some questions need to be answered late at night or during the weekends. It is easier to 'force' external staff to work these unsociable hours than to persuade your own staff – said the VP. As far as I am concerned, however, these 'advantages' do not compare with the even greater real advantages to be obtained from managing your own conversations. It is important that these conversations live and breathe the culture of your company. It is equally important that these conversations should give your company a human face. Both these things are easier to achieve with your own employees. An agency can never have the same identification with your culture as your own people. The consumers will quickly feel the difference between a passionate member of staff and hired help.
- Define the role of the conversation manager. The conversation manager is ultimately the person responsible for your conversation strategy. This does not, of course, mean that he or

she will conduct every conversation in person (although in companies with a limited number of conversations this may sometimes be the case). If the number of conversations is high, there will be a need for one or more community managers (see the next point). If your company is in a sector where a high number of questions and complaints can be expected, it is probably a good idea to embed the team responsible for answering these questions and complaints within your customer service team. Online complaint response is an additional channel, alongside e-mail and the telephone.

- Appoint community managers. In contrast to conversation managers, community managers are responsible for the operational managing of your conversations.

- Draw up a conversation flow chart. Assess and describe the different types of questions you will need to answer. Agree different scenarios in advance: who will decide what in any given situation. If the majority of your employees take part in online conversations, there is need for additional clarity with regard to who will deal with what types of question. Also agree who will manage the Twitter and Facebook accounts. If you have a community manager, he or she will be the logical choice for this latter task. Leave no room for misunderstandings. Make clear to everyone to whom they should send relevant conversations for handling.

- Remember that training is important. This is where the training implemented during the first phase of your transformation into a Conversation Company now comes into its own. Make sure that all staff have had the training they need before they start to participate in conversations in your name. In particular, it is recommended to give specific training in the conducting of positive online conversations that will have a lot of impact.

- As far as possible, address people in their home language. If they contact you in English, then it is acceptable to answer them in English, even if you know that this is not their home language. Most people, however, will seek to contact you in their own language. Make use of your employees who can deal with situations of this kind. Search in each country where you operate for someone who can assume the role of community manager.

- Provide the right software. To manage conversations professionally, you need to provide your staff with the right software.
- Draw up a crisis plan. Sooner or later, something in your company will go seriously wrong (it happens everywhere). Plan in advance how you will deal with this crisis online. By thinking proactively about this, you will be able to take better decisions when the critical moment finally arrives.

Three golden rules for online conversations

These three golden rules have been devised so that they are easy to understand and easy to apply – for everyone. Of course, to some extent these rules simplify the complexity inherent in most conversations, but you may nonetheless find the tips useful when you are not certain how to react to a difficult question.

Be positive

Whatever happens, be positive! The moment a company starts to behave in a defensive manner, the online community will immediately smell blood. Being positive does not mean that you need to exaggerate your company's virtues. It is more a question of the words that you use and your tone of voice. Saying something positive about someone or something in a positive manner can only help to give everyone a warm feeling for your company.

Sorry, how can we do better?

We all make mistakes. The easiest way to help in this situation is by apologizing. In many cases, this is all most complainants are looking for: recognition that there has been a mistake and an acceptance of responsibility for that mistake. Saying 'Sorry, this time we got it wrong' can often work wonders in this situation. Of course, it is even better to take things a step further, by trying to find out what you can do to put things right for next time. 'How can we improve things?' or 'How can we help you further?' are simple sentences that will allow you to continue the conversation in a constructive manner.

Thank you

This may seem like a matter of common courtesy, but saying 'thank you' is not always as evident or as simple as it seems. For example, many people nowadays seem to think that it is cool not to say 'thank you'. On other occasions, you may simply be too busy and forget. This is a bad mistake. You can perhaps compare it with certain traffic situations. When you give someone priority at a crossroads, the least you expect to see is a hand raised in acknowledgement by the other driver. And if that doesn't happen, you will most likely get cross, sometimes very cross indeed. It is the same with customers who are kind enough to recommend your products. All they want is some signal of recognition and gratitude. After all, they know for certain that you will have seen their conversation online – so why don't you say something?

Direct and indirect sales through conversations

Conversations and selling – there are two points of view about this combination. Some companies see their Twitter and Facebook friends as a kind of gigantic database, to whom they can shoot off all different kinds of offers and promotions. Others find that conversations and sales do not mix well together.

The truth is somewhere in between. Conversations and word of mouth do indeed have a direct effect on your company results. In this respect, there is nothing wrong in launching specific sales actions as part of your online relationship with commercial customers. The US food retailer, Whole Foods, seeks to combine the two approaches.[115] The greater part of its conversations are reactive. Many consumers ask questions and these questions are answered. A smaller proportion of the conversations are, however, proactive. In these conversations the company shares relevant content about itself and the sector. Only 5 per cent of the conversations are linked to sales and refer to promotional offers. This seldom results in criticism. The company's pull activities (answering questions) are so large scale that its push activities (commercial promotions) are accepted as part of the total package. As long as the right balance is maintained, problems do not arise.

This means that conversations can lead both directly and indirectly to sales. See the clever thinking of de Maagt.[116] The commercial initiative may come from your company, but it is just as likely to come from the consumers themselves. There are four different ways in which a conversation can lead to sales.

- Your brand communicates a commercial message (direct sale with initiation by the brand). A limited number of your messages during conversations will be overtly commercial. On these occasions, there is a direct link between conversations and sales. Some companies provide a specific sales channel for interested parties. For example, Dell has a Twitter outlet channel, where it sells older and cheaper models of its computers. Consumers who follow these conversations are looking for a good deal.

- Your content strategy indirectly maintains interest in your brand (indirect sale with initiation by the brand). In addition to communicating with your fans, this strategy also has advantages to offer when you are looking to attract new customers. A company with plenty of content is more likely to be found during search enquiries on Google by potential customers. The limited nature of the commercial information in this content will allow these searchers to come into contact with the company in a manner that increases its credibility. This can help to create leads and possible new customers.

- A customer shows interest in your products (direct sale with initiation by the customer). Your customer opens a conversation which shows that he or she is possibly interested in one of your products. You can convert these people by giving them something which adds value to their search. Have objective information available which you can provide to them (see the Kodak example above). In this way, you facilitate their purchase process in a (relatively) impartial manner.

- Positive conversations take place without concrete action (indirect sale with initiation by the customer). Here results are achieved by the effect that positive conversations about your products between consumers may have on purchasing decisions. This word of mouth may lead indirectly to sales, but it is almost impossible to quantify.

CASE STUDY Heinz and Delta Airlines

Heinz sell new flavour via Facebook

(Based on Hall, 2011.)[117]

Heinz launched a new ketchup flavour onto the UK market: ketchup with balsamico. The first bottles were distributed to the public via Facebook. The first 3,000 'likers' were each given a bottle. In addition, Heinz also sent 57 bottles to well-known bloggers in the sector. After this launch, other interested parties were able to order a bottle via the Heinz fan page. The number of fans increased by 54,000 as a result. Over a million bottles of the new flavour were produced. Within three days they were all sold out.

Delta Airlines opens webshop on Facebook

Delta Airlines has a webshop on Facebook. Via the company's fan page, it is possible to buy air tickets online. You don't need to leave Facebook to complete the transaction: everything can be arranged on the same platform. Delta's motto is 'Go where the customer is!' This is a wise strategy. Getting customers to come to you can be a very expensive business; it is much cheaper if you go to them. Sales via Facebook have the advantage that ticket buyers are likely to share the news with their friends – perhaps encouraging them to book tickets of their own. This is not possible with tickets purchased on an e-commerce site.

KEY CONVERSATION POINTS

Possible conversation starters

- The conversation manager manages conversations as follows: he or she observes conversations as a manager, facilitates conversations as a brand and participates in conversations as himself or herself.

- Participation in conversations is more than just answering questions and complaints. You can also conduct proactive conversations with consumers, providing them with relevant content.

- Your content strategy is also a form of proactive participation in conversations.

- Every customer emotion requires a different conversational approach. You must converse differently with fans, a positivist, someone neutral, a negativist and a hater.

- Prepare for your participation in online conversations thoroughly. Do not delegate this task to an external agency. Instead, draw up your own conversation plan.

- Proactive conversations can lead to immediate online sales.

Questions you must ask yourself

- What is your conversation flow?

- Who is responsible for your company's participation in online conversations?

- Do you have the possibility to convert some of your online conversations into immediate sales?

Further information

To look at the Facebook shop of Delta Airlines go to: **www.facebook.com/delta**. Read my first book *The Conversation Manager* to learn all about managing the conversation with your clients.

Chapter Ten
Content

Purpose of a content strategy

Social media are forcing companies to move away from campaign-based thinking. If your company is satisfied to share content on your Twitter and Facebook pages just twice per year, the level of inter-action is likely to be very low. People will soon forget your company and Facebook searches will show you less frequently than more active pages: that is the way their system works. In addition, the impact of traditional advertising is decreasing every day, so that your offline, campaign-based way of thinking is coming under pressure from all sides. For this reason, the Conversation Company has converted to the idea of content management.

The content strategy of the Conversation Company has various objectives:

- Being recognized as an expert in your field. Strong and relevant contact will enhance the positioning of your company, show that you are aware of the latest trends and that you are interested in innovation. This will help you to be seen as an expert in your field and will increase general awareness of your brand.

- Maintaining relations with the customer in a positive manner. Share new content at regular intervals. This will encourage your customers to keep in touch with your brand. Do not bother them with new offers every five minutes, but provide them with information that is interesting and useful. If you offer them relevant content of value, this will make it more acceptable to launch a promotion with a strong storyline every once in a while.

- Attracting new customers. Your content is shared with existing customers and fans. If the content is strong enough, they will share it with their family and friends. This is how the Conversation Company comes into contact with new people. Relevant content can arouse the curiosity of new prospects, so that they may want to discover more about your brand.

- Increasing social media reach. Finally, good content will automatically ensure that your company has a wider reach on social media. This will increase support for your content and heighten its impact. A wider reach also makes it easier to achieve the first three objectives.

Choose your subjects wisely

Our world is awash with information. It has even been contended that the information added to the internet in a single day is equivalent to all the information in all the libraries in the world. Whether this is true or not, the Conversation Company must make its content stand out among this huge mass of data. And the only way to do this is to develop a clear and well-considered content strategy.

Bearing this situation in mind, it is essential that your company only offers relevant content. The choice of the fields on which you wish to concentrate will determine whether you are successful or not. In order to make the right decision, you must carry out both an internal analysis (what you can do and what can make you different) and an external analysis (what the market is looking for).

First and foremost, look for areas where your company can offer unique content. Of course, this content must be in keeping with your company's culture and values. Examine your own expertise and focus on the things that could make you outstanding in your sector. Also look carefully at what the market wants. What topics are of particular interest to your target group? You can track these topics down by conducting a netnographic investigation or a detailed online search. Combine all these elements together into a coherent content strategy. For example, if you are a company in the home nursing sector, offer content about the care of people with illnesses in which you specialize and look for subjects where online information is currently lacking, for which people have expressed an interest via their search enquiries. In this way, you can almost guarantee yourself an interested public.

By combining the internal dimension (the extent to which you are unique) and the external dimension (what people are looking for), it is possible to create four main content categories:

- **To be avoided.** This is content in which you are not unique and for which there is little demand. In other words, a waste of time and money. This category must form 0 per cent of your total content.

- **Competitive.** This is content that interests the market, but in which you are not unique. In view of the level of market demand, you will occasionally, perhaps even regularly, need to make use of content of this kind. Bear in mind that your competitors will also be sharing this kind of content, so limit your efforts to a maximum of 25 per cent of your total content.

- **Niche.** There are not a huge number of people interested in this content, but it does differentiate you in the market. Invest where necessary, but limit your efforts to 15 per cent of your total content.

FIGURE 10.1

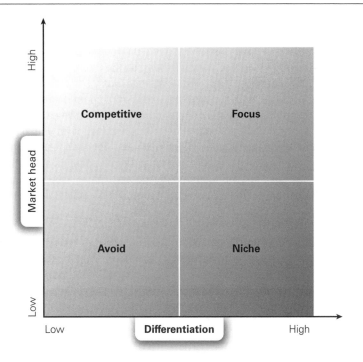

- **Focus.** This is the content where you can really make a difference. There is market interest, but your competitors are not able to satisfy this interest. Make sure that 60 per cent of your total content falls into this category.

The concrete implementation of your content strategy can take place at many different levels. Talk about your industry in general. Show that you know in which direction the sector is moving. Mention new trends and fashionable insights that will confirm your expert status in the field. Your customers will be interested in sharing specific content about your company. Facts, figures and 'did-you-knows' can all be very useful. Furthermore, you will also be able to generate large amounts of informal content through your own staff. Make your culture tangible. Tell 'human-interest' stories about your activities. And, last but not least, remember to talk about your products. You can even use content that compares your products with those of your competitors, as long as you do so in an objective manner.

CASE STUDY Converse: Domaination

The popular shoe brand Converse has used these ideas to perfection. Its most important target group is teenagers. To build its content strategy, it first investigated the most popular search requests on Google for this age category. This allowed Converse to invest in topics that failed to interest other brands. This had a double advantage. First, it was virgin territory – there were no other serious competitors. Second, it meant that it was very cheap to buy Google adwords to promote these unused content domains. In this way, Converse was able to 'claim' a dozen or so topics that were highly relevant for young people. These topics included: 'the first day of the holidays', 'tips for a first kiss' and 'how do I talk to a beautiful girl?'. For each topic, Converse made a mini-site, some of which even set 'missions' for their young viewers. These missions usually required the teenagers to find a new search term, which would give them access to the next mini-site. In this way, Google was transformed from an advertising tool into an interactive game. The content on the mini-sites was never commercial. There was no promotion of shoes, just a small brand logo at the bottom of each site. Everything was geared to meeting the content requirement of the target group. The investment in the mini-sites and the Google adwords cost around USD 100,000. The number of new visitors to the Converse website exceeded 600,000. This is an impact level 2,600 per cent greater than traditional marketing.

The golden question: which content is conversation-worthy?

What type of content do people share? That is the golden, 1 million dollar question that many internet experts are asking themselves today. To provide them with an answer, we conducted a unique study as part of the preparation for this book. We collected all the conversations from a thousand or so Facebook pages of 200 global brands.[118] In total, we analysed some 770,000 conversations about these brands. We did a similar exercise for Twitter. In this instance, we selected a week at random in June 2011 and analysed the tweets for 300 brands. This gave us some 246,000 conversations. Our insights with regard to the most frequently shared material were gleaned from the data-mining of these million brand-related conversations.

Our first conclusion is that both Twitter and Facebook are relevant for every company in every sector. Even the least conversation-worthy brands had at least one mention each day on both networks. The most interactive brands had an average of 37 mentions per day on their Facebook fan page. On Twitter the level of conversation is even more intense. The most interactive brand had an average of 225 mentions per day in tweets. The brands that scored well in the study include the BBC, NBC, Pepsi, Starbucks, American Express, Disney, Red Bull and Canon.

A more startling conclusion, perhaps, is that there is no correlation between the number of interactions and the number of fans. This means, for example, that there are some fan pages with many fans but very little interaction. In other words, numerous fans do not necessarily guarantee you good conversation potential. Above all, it is the content of your company that determines the level of interaction.

A third important conclusion is that the content people share is not the same on Facebook and Twitter. True, there are some similarities, but the differences are even more striking. This is what people share:

- **Experience with your products and/or services** – (people leave feedback about their experience). It is noticeable that there are more conversations about specific products than about brands. This is particularly the case for media companies and the food industry.

- **Experience with offline touchpoints.** Offline customer experience is an important online conversation starter.

The customer-friendliness of employees in a sales point is the most important conversation starter.

- **Competitions and games.** Content with a games or competitive element produces many conversations. In addition to interaction, 'gamification' results in many 'likes'.

- **Free material.** Free always works. If people think that they can get something for nothing, they will talk about it to everyone! This is not only true of free products, but also of free content.

- **Interest in collaborating.** If you involve people in your decision-making, they like to tell others about it. If their engagement increases, so too will the number of conversations. This does not need to be complicated. Simply asking your fans a question can be enough to generate plenty of interaction. In addition, the customers can also show their enthusiasm through their 'likes'.

- **Aspects of lifestyle.** Even if this does not immediately relate to your products, people like to talk about music, eating out, sport, etc, and again show their enthusiasm for this content through their 'likes'.

- **Positive messages.** This is the value of happiness. There are more interactions as a result of the sharing of something positive than of something negative. Consumers like happy stories and positive messages generate plenty of 'likes'.

- **News.** Your fans like to share news about your company, and like to be kept informed about the developments relating to their favourite brand.

- **Advertising.** There are a lot of conversations on Twitter about advertising. This is probably related to the presence of the high penetration media and numerous advertising professionals on this network. Complete reviews of advertising campaigns are sometimes shared.

- **Social media news.** There are plenty of conversations on Twitter about the latest iPhone and iPad apps.

- **Employee stories.** Company employees share considerable amounts of informal content via Twitter. They talk about where they work and give their followers a glimpse of what goes on behind the scenes. This content is re-tweeted at higher than the average rate.

People share plenty of content about brands. One out of every six tweets about brands is re-tweeted. And there are a number of ways that you can increase the chance of a re-tweet. Tweets with a #tag are more likely to be shared. Actively asking for a re-tweet can double impact. Updates on Foursquare (a social network site that allows you to let people know where you are) get the lowest level of reaction. Only 2 per cent of Foursquare check-ins result in interaction.

If you produce content, you would be wise to take account of these conclusions. Make sure that there is enough variety in your content. Organize a competition every now and then. Include a games element in your stories. Make sure that your news is newsworthy. And keep it positive!

This last point is crucial. Our extensive study proves that the overwhelming majority of people make and share positive content. Only 10 per cent of the comments on Facebook fan pages and 14 per cent of tweets are negative. It is very difficult even to find hate pages about brands on Facebook. Protest pages with a clear objective do exist and sometimes win support. But out-and-out hate campaigns are seldom popular with the broader public. People are put off by the negative attitude; they prefer to share positive messages.

Content planning: projects, updates and campaigns

After agreeing the topics you want to focus on, the next step is to plan your content. To do this, you should make use of three content streams: content updates, content projects and content campaigns.

Updates

Updates are short messages that you send with a certain degree of regularity. Updates are usually a combination of formal content (facts and figures, news, recruitments, etc) and informal content (culture, staff news and events, a look behind the scenes, etc). These are content pin-pricks that allow your fans and followers to keep abreast of all the important and not-so-important developments in their favourite company. Updates are usually shared via social media. They keep your company in the thoughts of your customers.

Projects

Projects run over a longer period and are usually related to a particular theme. For example, a project might be a product launch, the opening of a new department, an important research study, a major customer event or a recruitment drive. The company develops content relating to the theme on a regular basis over a longer period, varying from between one week to three months. Projects work towards a specific objective, and the content is planned in relation to that objective. This content (regular small and large pin-pricks) is primarily shared via online channels, but can be supplemented by offline media. A project can also be supported by means of a campaign (see below). Projects focus the spotlight on a certain aspect of your company.

Campaigns

Campaigns are shorter and more intensive than projects, and are frequently supported with offline media. This content is designed to increase awareness of your company or to announce important news (eg a new product). All available media are employed to force a specific short-term result (usually increased visibility and sales).

Creating this framework and ensuring the smooth flow of the three different streams is not an exact science. They do, however, give you a solid basis for action. Try to think in terms of these three streams and draw up a content plan based on your company-specific objectives. The easiest and most practical way to do this is by preparing an Excel spreadsheet in which you fill in for each stream and each quarter the details of the things you want to talk about and the resulting content that will need to be created. In concrete terms, for example, an update might consist of a daily blog post, a Facebook update or a number of Twitter messages. A project might cover the Christmas period, if this is important for your company (eg if you are a food and drink manufacturer). During this period, you must provide content relevant to the theme on a daily basis. Your company may need to manage different projects consecutively (eg one for whisky and one for champagne). A campaign might be the launching of a new product, where you want to see results as quickly as possible and consequently deploy every means at your disposal.

TABLE 10.1

	Updates	Projects	Campaigns
Objective	Maintaining relations in a frequent manner	Mid to long-term realization of objectives	Short-term realization of objectives (awareness, sales)
Duration	Continuous	1 week to 3 months	Average: 1 month
Frequency of new content creation	High (almost daily)	High: during the project new content is almost continuously shared	Low: the same content (advert, games) is used repeatedly throughout the campaign
Intensity	Low	Average	High
Media pressure	Low	Average	High
Target group	Interested parties, fans and accidental passers-by	People interested in the theme, fans and accidental passers-by	The wider public
Media choice	Primarily online channels (Facebook, Twitter, blog)	Primarily online channels, supported by suitable offline media	Targeted offline media pressure, supplemented with all own online channels
Type of content	Formal and informal 'did-you-knows', news, a glimpse behind the scenes	Content in function of project objectives	Commercial content

The combination of these three streams will gradually result in the widening of your reach and engagement. The updates will ensure a steady influx of newly interested parties. The campaigns will boost your reach dramatically for a short period. Because campaigns are expensive, you need to think carefully how you use them. Organize them at the right time and in the right place. Uses updates and projects to maintain customer interest usefully in the periods between campaigns. In this way, you will keep in touch with the people who are interested in your company all year round.

CASE STUDY
Book launch for Jay-Z uses unique content planning

Microsoft wanted to increase awareness and use of its search engine, Bing. At the same time (mid-2010), the famous rapper Jay-Z was on the point of launching his biography, *Decoded*. He wanted to turn the book into a bestseller, and so Bing and the rapper joined forces to devise a brilliant content campaign that would allow them both to realize their objectives.

Every page from the book was 'hidden' in a different public place. In 13 cities inside and outside the United States, fans could search for the pages. These pages were not just placed anywhere. Each location was carefully chosen on the basis of the content of that page. Sometimes posters were used; sometimes the texts were put in places where you wouldn't usually expect to find advertising. There were also a number of ingenious surprise locations: on a specially designed Gucci coat, on the bottom of a swimming pool, on the packaging of a hamburger, etc.

Via social media, Bing communicated the general location of the next page. On the basis of the accompanying photos and clues, the fans could put the book together digitally before it was even published. More than 5 million people took part in this national search event.

As a result, Jay-Z's book immediately rocketed into the Top-10 bestsellers list. During the same period, the number of Bing users increased by 12 per cent, so that the site entered its own Top-10 list: the list of most frequently visited websites. In total, this content campaign resulted in 1.1 billion hits for the search engine. There was just one small downside to this magnificent success story: without the gigantic budget of USD 11 million, none of it would have been possible!

CASE STUDY Blendtec shows what it can do

(See also the article in the *New York Times* by Rob Walker, published on 22 August 2008, entitled 'Mixing it up'.)

Showing what you can do is fine, but why not do it in an amusing manner? Blendtec claims to be the world reference in the field of food mixers. Its motto is: 'You can mix anything with Blendtec mixers'. The legendary YouTube films in which the company's CEO tossed his iPhone or iPad into a Blendtec blender proved this point beyond doubt. These films always ask the question: 'But will it blend?' After this, the mixer pulverizes everything that is fed into it. Throughout the years, the company has made more than 100 of these films. Among the items blended to a pulp were a full four-course dinner, marbles and even golf balls. One of the most recent hits destroyed a complete set of Justin Bieber gadgets! The films have been watched over 150 million times. Can you imagine what it would have cost to achieve the same impact with traditional advertising? No one could afford it. And its effect? In recent years the sales of the company have risen by 600 per cent. Case closed.

Advertising is also conversation-worthy content

Of course, during campaigns use is still made of offline media. InSites Consulting, *Pub Magazine* and the Flemish Media Company carried out a test survey of almost every television commercial that was broadcast on the Belgian channels VTM and 2B in 2010.[119] The viewers evaluated more than 1,300 different commercials. The research focus was twofold: first, what was the conversation value of the adverts and, second, what were the purchasing intentions of the viewers after they had seen the different campaigns? The most remarkable conclusion was that purchasing intent increased by 44 per cent following the viewing of a conversation-worthy commercial, in comparison with a commercial of average conversation worthiness.

In *The Conversation Manager* I defined advertising as the start of a good conversation.[120] This study confirms my definition. If the message of the advert is strong enough, people will talk about it. Above all, it is the content – the story – that gets the conversations started. The majority of conversations about spots of this kind are offline. The online reactions are nowhere near as numerous.

There are two types of conversation possible following the viewing of a TV commercial. There will be conversations about the commercial itself and there will be conversations about the brand it represents. The impact of the brand conversations is three to four times greater than the impact of the commercial conversations. If people talk about the advert, that's fine – but the real conversation potential is generated by discussions about the brand. The objective of the advertisers is therefore clear: to make adverts that focus attention on the brand message rather than on the means of its communication.

The great trap to be avoided in television advertising is controversy. There is sometimes a tendency to think that a controversial advert must lead to more conversations. But this is not necessarily the case. Of course, if the advert's story is well-framed and recognizable, controversy may act as an additional stimulus. However, controversial adverts without a clear storyline lead to fewer conversations. Moreover, most of these conversations are about the advert and not about the brand. This is therefore self-defeating.

We want to emphasize that the Conversation Company still believes in the power of advertising in the mass media. Adverts fit perfectly into a content strategy. But the condition must be that the advertising is conversation-worthy and that it matches the culture of your company. The difference with traditional marketing is that these campaign are not central, they are not the main focus of your activities. They are just a part of a much broader strategy focused on conversations.

Organizing your content management

Content management is a time-consuming and therefore expensive operation. Nevertheless, it is vital to prepare your content management thoroughly and well in advance, so that the process can unfold efficiently and with impact.

You need to take account of the following:

- Who is the editor-in-chief? This person is responsible for the overall compilation of your content planning. He or she facilitates the creation of content and makes sure that the planning is respected. This role may be allocated to the conversation manager as part of his or her duties. After all, content is a proactive manner to encourage conversations.

- Who creates the content? The editor-in-chief cannot be expected to make all the content. It is advisable to appoint a number of other employees to assist in this task. Campaigns are usually farmed out to advertising agencies, as are certain parts of most projects. However, much of the content for these projects will still need to be created within the company. Make clear who is in charge for each project. Routine content updates are best carried out in-house, since this is both cheaper and more flexible.

- What does the planning look like? Make a clear and practical planning, in which updates, projects and campaigns are all included. Specify who is responsible for the creation and spreading of content for each element. A quarterly planning is probably the most relevant. A year plan is not sufficiently 'agile' and will reduce your ability to react to changing circumstances. Successful content exploits current trends and events.

- Always take account of the context. The atmosphere, place or manner in which your film or advert is viewed will determine to a large extent whether it is appreciated or not. Even the best food loses its taste in bad company or a grotty restaurant. Try to take account of the context of your target group. If they are likely to view your material on a mobile application, take account of this when putting together your story line. The better you are able to manage the context, the greater the impact of your content will be.

- Do you have in-house writing or video talent? Content scores heavily if it is well written and well presented. Do you have employees who show talent in these directions? If so, they can be useful partners for your content creation. If you don't have natural talents, try to encourage the most suitable members of your team to help, providing extra training as necessary.

- Don't forget outside content. You don't need to make all the content yourself. There are hundreds of interesting articles, reports and videos already in existence, many of which may fit your story perfectly. If you come across information of this kind, share it with members of your target group. It will confirm their impression that you are an expert in the field. Install a number of practical tools, such as Google Reader, to help you with your content selection.

CASE STUDY   Foursquare begs for content

(See also Lee, 2011[121])

Since the middle of 2011, Foursquare has more than 10 million users. Via this social network, the users can 'check in' to let people know that they are at a particular location. This allows them, for example, to let their friends know where they are. When they check in, Foursquare provides them with tips and information about interesting things in their vicinity.

During the summer of 2011, Foursquare also appealed to its users to write more content during their check-ins. It is good that people check in (that, after all, is the point of the system), but the site wanted more stories and tips. The company understands that this content can attract both visitors and businesses to the location – and this is where Foursquare's commercial potential rests. Without content, the system is nothing more than a fun gimmick for social network fans. With content, it can offer an added value that will interest many members of the wider general public.

CASE STUDY   Hubspot: from zero to hero in just two years – thanks to content planning

Hubspot is a US software company. Its software helps companies to establish new leads via various different channels, such as social media, but also via Google and other websites. The company was founded in 2004, but enjoyed its most spectacular growth between 2009 and 2011. During those two years, the number of its customers rose from 1,400 to 3,600 (see **http://en.wikipedia.org/wiki/HubSpot**).

Hubspot's philosophy is very close to that of a Conversation Company. The Hubspot culture is very open and authentic. The company believes in the power of conversations between staff and consumers to support its growth. In 2010, the company was chosen as 'the best employer in Boston'.[122]

Hubspot invests in a very smart content strategy.[123] The company has three objectives. First, it wants to be seen as the opinion leader in its domain. Second, it wants to become more 'findable' in Google searches. Third, it wants to build up its reach on social media. With these aims in mind, it publishes new content every day on its blog, on YouTube, on other blogs, on Slideshare, etc. Within a relatively short period of time, it scored as the best company in its sector for all three of its objectives. The figures for its blog are particularly impressive – 10 per cent of all visitors to the blog subsequently find their way to the company website. Between 10 and 20 per cent of these people become leads.[124] The company thinks like a publisher or newspaper editor: it must have an interesting article every day. And until now, it continues to find them! This allows Hubspot to build up greater online reach that it can instantly convert into sales.

Conversion: from content to leads

As Hubspot shows, the ultimate purpose of a content strategy is to attract new customers or persuade existing customers to re-buy. To achieve this, you will need to draw up a touchpoint content plan. Include in this plan all touchpoints where a (potential) customer can come into contact with your content. Then decide at which of these touchpoints conversion to sales is likely to occur. In the case of Hubspot, the converting touchpoint is its website. One in five (20 per cent) of all visitors to the website go on to contact the company for more information. Hubspot's blog is the touchpoint that leads people from the content area to the sales area. Its social media accounts ensure that there is sufficient daily traffic to the blog.

In an interview in 2011, Jan-Willem De Waard of Rabobank commented that this company has a similar plan. One of its target groups is starting entrepreneurs. To offer useful free advice to these people, Rabobank has created a content site: 'I'm going to start!' (**www.ikgastarten.nl**). Starters who are impressed by the information on this site can follow a link to the main Rabobank site, where the actual conversation takes place.

For companies working in the knowledge sector, Slideshare can be used as a useful converting touchpoint. Slideshare is a social network site where people can share presentations (PowerPoint, etc). This is the ideal place to show what you can do and what you have to offer. In this way, it is often possible to directly convert a reader into a sales lead.

The compilation of a content plan can perhaps best be compared with putting together a football team. Your ultimate objective is to score. To do this, you need to get the ball to your strikers. Some teams play a long ball game, so that the ball is played quickly and directly to your forward players. Other teams play a passing game, with lots of short combinations before finally whacking the ball into the goal. This is the tactic adopted by Converse: the customers first visit a number of preliminary mini-sites, before they finally find their way to the main Converse site. But no matter how you do it, getting the ball into the back of the net is the only thing that counts. You are the trainer of the team, so it is for you to decide the best route to goal. Every strategy has its advantages and its disadvantages, but one thing is certain: if you don't have a strategy, you are going to win nothing at all.

KEY CONVERSATION POINTS

Possible conversation starters

- Content planning requires campaign planning.
- Choose content domains that you want to claim for your own on the basis of the extent to which you can offer unique content which differentiates your company and satisfies market needs.
- Your content strategy must lead to you being seen as an expert in your field; must maintain your good relations with existing customers in a relevant manner; must attract new customers; and must extend your social network reach.
- People share content about their offline experiences with your products and/or services, games, free products or content, news, information about lifestyle, advertisements, positive messages and your requests for collaboration.
- If an advertisement generates brand activation, its impact will be four times greater than a spot that generates no brand activation. If an advertisement is a starting point for a conversation, it still has a valid place in your content strategy.
- Content planning consists of three different elements: updates, projects and campaigns.
- Organize your company for content management.
- Identify the golden touchpoint that will increase the conversion rate from content to sales.

Questions you must ask yourself

- What content domains do you want to claim?
- Is your organization ready to start with content management? If not, what do you still need to do before you can start?
- Are your current campaigns conversation starters?
- Are you capable of planning your content on the basis of the three conversation streams: updates, projects and campaigns?
- How can you increase your content-to-sales conversion rate?

Further information

Use these links for further interesting information on:

- the Converse Domaination case video: **http://vimeo.com/8254341**;
- all our research into television adverts: **http://slideshare.net/stevenvanbelleghem/ tv-advertising-brand-activation-sales-impact**;
- the Jay-Z book launch case video: **www.youtube.com/watch?v=GekFwQKlEqk**;
- the Blendtec videos: **www.youtube.com/blendtec**.

Chapter Eleven
Collaboration

Co-creation scores in the checklist mentality

Co-creation is hot. In recent years, the world has been witness to a whole host of successful co-creation cases. Doritos allowed its fans to develop an advert to be shown during the Superbowl. Lays Crisps asked its customers to help choose a new flavour and snack manufacturer Mora produced a new croquette in collaboration with its consumers. Co-creation stands high on the checklist of the majority of today's marketeers. It is seen as a smart move to experiment with this new way of working. And, of course, there is nothing wrong with this – providing it goes further than just a marketing campaign. That was the problem with all the above examples: they were all 'one-offs'.

Currently, 3 per cent of companies have experience of new developing products and services with their consumers. In most cases this collaboration starts with a pilot project.[125] If the test is successful, the collaboration can gradually be built up in a structural manner.

This is what happened at Vitamin Water. To begin with, its managers saw co-creation as just another item on their checklist to tick off. However, they gradually evolved towards a more structural form of collaboration with their customers.[126]

CASE STUDY Vitamin Water

As a first step, Vitamin Water decided to appeal to its fans on Facebook for help in developing a new flavour. It added a sub-page called 'the taste creation lab'. Here fans could put forward their ideas and other fans could vote on them. The winning flavour was put into production and sold in the shops. The fan who first suggested the flavour was rewarded with a cash prize of USD 5,000. The brand discovered that fans were super-enthusiastic about this type of project and so it decided to take further, more structural steps in the same direction. Fans were next allowed to help design the packaging and choose the name for the new flavour. Perhaps in part for these reasons, the new product was a big success. Moreover, during the co-creation period the number of Vitamin Water fans on Facebook doubled to 1.3 million. The company was now convinced: since then, it has developed a number of other products in collaboration with fans, working in large, open communities. What began as a one-off campaign has become part of its philosophy.

CASE STUDY
Unilever: the consumer becomes a member of the R&D team

(Based on De Ruyck et al, 2011.)[127]

Unilever is one of the trendsetters in the field of consumer collaboration. At the beginning of 2011, the Unilever R&D team wanted to bring its personnel even closer to the consumers. The dry figures produced by traditional market research were no longer deemed to be enough. We at InSites Consulting were fortunate enough to be involved in the phased project that was designed to put this right.

To begin with, Unilever staff were encouraged to find out more about the daily lives of consumers by playing a series of online games, based on all available data from previous market research. The better the employee scored in these games, the more merit badges he or she earned. This was preparatory to the next step, when the R&D employees were allowed to follow the behaviour of consumers within the framework of a three-week long community, specially created for this purpose. Here 100 consumers shared information about their daily habits and customs. Every Unilever employee could follow a particular consumer in detail to get an even deeper insight into how he or she actually lived.

This first phase allowed the staff to get to know their consumers better. This not only led to greater understanding, but also to more questions. For this reason, we organized a second community which could look more deeply at the issues raised by the first. To do this, we decided to regard the consumers as temporary R&D personnel. During this phase we again used a games element, since we assessed that this would help to maintain the freshness and enthusiasm on both sides. Different teams were made, with both consumers and staff in the same team. These teams competed against each other to draw as many lessons as possible from the community.

During both phases, a dedicated website was available on which staff from the entire Unilever R&D division (more than 1,000 employees) could follow the activities and results of the communities. New consumer facts, stories and 'did-you-knows' were added each day.

After the second community came to an end, the R&D staff who had been involved met to discuss their findings. This resulted in the compilation of a concrete action plan with a list of ideas to be implemented. In short, the consumer had become a part of the Unilever R&D decision-making process. But this project resulted in more than just a number of good ideas; it also changed the culture of the R&D team. The staff learnt to appreciate the value of the consumers for their work. In this way, a solid basis has been laid for the structural involvement of consumers in innovation development.

FIGURE 11.1

The customer enters the boardroom

Just 8 per cent of the companies who co-create with their customers use this collaboration for the launching of new products.
The focus of co-creation is mainly fixed on the initiation of new
ideas.[128] But even if consumers are more or less continually involved
in the process of dreaming up new ideas, this is still not necessarily
enough to be able to speak of 'structural collaboration'. Structural
collaboration means that the customer is involved in all aspects of
your company's life. Of course, this does involve the development
of new ideas, but it must be extended to include matters such as
the identification of new consumer trends, the launching of new
products, the drawing up of a content strategy, the enhancement
of touchpoint conversation-worthiness, the planning of advertising
campaigns and even the setting of prices. Cook[129] claimed that companies are better able to solve all their main business problems if
they collaborate closely with their consumers. For example, when
Heinz wanted ideas for a new range of cold sauces, the company
immediately decided to make use of its community. The ideas put
forward by the community were not only processed and interpreted
by the Heinz management team, but also by the other members of the
community. Of the concepts finally put into practice, 20 per cent
were the result of this consumer analysis. In other words, if Heinz
had not involved its consumers, it would have missed one fifth of
the important insights necessary to implement its innovation project
successfully.[130]

Recent research carried out at the University of Wageningen[131]
has demonstrated that products with packaging labelled 'co-created
with consumers' sell significantly better than equivalent products
that are not labelled in this way. In other words, consumers have
more confidence in each other's judgement than in the judgement of
the company.

To integrate market input into its activities in a structural manner,
the Conversation Company makes use of the following resources:

- **A listening culture.** As part of your transformation into
  a Conversation Company, you will have already developed
  a listening culture. The feedback from your observation of
  conversations is valuable when decisions need to be made.

If you still have further questions following your observations, do not be afraid to put them to your community. The people there will be happy to answer them.

- **An ongoing closed community for employees.** It is useful for your employees to have a continually available platform where they can converse with each other and exchange knowledge and ideas. Many of your staff are extremely knowledgeable about their work and will often have some very good ideas. By grouping this creativity in a single community, you will increase the level and efficiency of interaction between your own people. It is the ideal place to work out new ideas together. In the Conversation Company, every employee has a contribution to make towards future growth and success. Having your own open staff platform will facilitate this process.

- **Large, ongoing open communities for consumers.** These communities are accessible for everyone. The most well-known example is the Facebook fan page. In addition to the main page, there are options that allow you to add sub-pages, where you can co-create with your fans. In this way, you discuss your plans openly and everyone can be involved.

- **Smaller, ongoing, closed communities for fans of the company.** You can create enormous opportunities by bringing together between 50 and 150 of your fans in a closed community. You can involve them (and would be strongly advised to) in the co-creation of new products, new advertising and many of your company's other strategic decisions. The advantage of such a community rests in the commitment of its participants. These people know that they have impact. Moreover, a closed community means that the competition cannot look over your shoulder to see what you are doing. If you are working on a trail-blazing innovation, it is essential that your community can talk (as it were) within the virtual closed walls of your own company. The conversations will then have the necessary depth to bring real added value to your activities. Professor Rudy Moenaert calls these communities 'strategy squads':

small, strategic teams of customers whose continuous and intense collaboration with the company can significantly reduce the duration of the strategic planning timetable.

- **Short-term communities.** This type of community can be useful for working intensely with selected groups of consumers for a short period on a specific project or campaign. You can ask fans from your large, open community to take part in these smaller work groups.

All communities can either be short-term or long-running. As mentioned, communities can be set up for a specific project (eg a product launch) or as part of your structural decision-making process (eg content management). You can compare it with the difference between a travelling fun fair and a theme park (and thanks go to Tom De Ruyck for this metaphor). A fun fair (equivalent to a short-term community) is certainly fun, but a theme park is even more fun – and also more interesting in terms of price per attraction. Having said this, the running of a theme park costs a lot more time and money – so bear this in mind. If you are planning to start an ongoing community, decide in advance what topics you wish to discuss with your customers. To begin with, discussion about the four Cs and new products should be sufficient to keep things going for a while. And if things become quieter or you no longer have any questions (for the time being), let your community members take a break. After all, most theme parks also close their doors during low season.

As a consequence of this intense collaboration between your company and the market, your decisions will no longer be imposed from above. And when the majority of your decisions are taken in this manner, following consultation with the market, then you can truly speak of structural collaboration. In this way, the consumers really are represented in the boardroom. Their voice can be heard in every part of your company, a voice that is every bit as loud as the voice of managers and staff. You may even want to consider actually appointing a consumer as an honorary member of your board. In many football clubs supporters' representatives attend board meetings. So why not in your company?

CASE STUDY Wrong assessment of its target group costs Tropicana 20 per cent of turnover

(See McCracken, 2009.)[132]

In 2008, PepsiCo wanted to give its Tropicana brand a new image. The management team considered that the traditional packaging was no longer 'hip' enough and decided that it was time for a change. To bring this change about, the managers decided to call on the services of Peter Arnell, a top designer for brands such as Tommy Hilfiger, Samsung and Home Depot. The new packaging was launched in 2009 – with dramatic consequences. Sales immediately fell by 20 per cent. Six weeks later, the old packaging was back on the shelves. So what went wrong? The new packaging was certainly hip: that was not the problem. Unfortunately, it did not sufficiently reflect traditional US culture. It just wasn't 'stars and stripes' enough! The loyal Tropicana drinkers were attached to this old, 'classic' packaging. It was fun and reminded them of the good things in life (in the United States). Most Tropicana fans are married with two children, but sometimes struggle to make ends meet. Even so, they want to offer something healthy and wholesome to their children. This mindset has nothing in common with the glitzy new packaging that Arnell produced. The average US consumer does not work in an advertising bureau or a trendy fashion house. If PepsiCo had taken the trouble to discuss its plans with its fan community, this costly mistake would never have been made.

CASE STUDY Clothing company sets prices via Twitter

(See also *Contagious Magazine Special Report*, 2011b)[133]

The Japanese clothing manufacturer Uniqlo allowed its customers to set the price for its best-selling articles via Twitter. Every tweet that mentioned an article of Uniqlo clothing resulted in a price reduction of one cent for that article. The action ran for a week. Consumers were able to follow the evolution of the prices in real time. It was also possible to buy the price-reduced items via the company's website. In total, some 5,500 tweets were sent. The resulting discounts ranged from 25 per cent to 70 per cent, which is comparable with other sales actions. But the total turnover broke all Uniqlo records – and all because the customer had been allowed to set the price.

CASE STUDY
Heinz builds a wall of fame for community members

InSites Consulting runs a fan community for Heinz. This is a small, closed community, made up of people who share a common interest in new products and new advertising campaigns in the food industry. They discuss the trends prevalent in this industry, and are regarded by Heinz managers as their eyes and ears in the sector as a whole. The community is very enthusiastic and proud to help one of the largest and most well-known food brands in the world. To thank its community members for their efforts, Heinz recently decided to set up a community 'wall of fame'. This consists of a virtual display of all the projects and campaigns in which the community has been involved. Saying 'thank you' and showing respect for your community's input is the very least you can do. The community members really appreciate the gesture and it motivates them to carry on.

Choosing the right people

Of the three types of community we have mentioned, the staff community and the large open community tend to develop organically. You have little direct control over who joins in and who doesn't. The members come together more or less spontaneously to discuss particular subjects that interest them. Your role with regard to these people is simply to listen. This will allow you to discover a series of unfulfilled market needs, which may eventually lead to new products and services. Of course, you are also free to ask them questions, but you must always remember that these are open communities – so anyone might be listening to their answers.

If you want to solve a specific management problem, it is better to discuss possible solutions with a smaller, closed group of people. There are two ways you can do this. You may opt to build sub-groups into your large, open community. Alternatively, you may prefer to set up a new, closed group of between 50 and 150 of your most ardent fans, fans who you have carefully vetted and selected yourself. The second option has the major advantage that you have everything in your own hands – and this is advisable when you don't want the whole world to know what decisions are being taken and how they are being reached.

The listening culture you have built up will give you a full picture of the feedback from all your different customers. However, it is important to remember that not every customer will be able – or is suitable – to help you solve management problems. To give your company access to the right advice on a daily basis, you need to listen to the right (and relevant) people. For its communities, the Conversation Company seeks to attract people who can offer an added value. The minimum condition is that they must have a clear commitment to the company and what it stands for. They might be an expert in the sector, or a knowledgeable and enthusiastic amateur in the sector or just a big fan of your brand. Research by De Ruyck and Schillewaert[134] has shown that without this kind of emotional commitment people seldom have enough interest to contribute effectively to an online community. In other words, you need to talk to people who are keen to talk back. If this natural motivation is missing, your community will not achieve what you want it to achieve.

If you really want to progress to co-creation with your community, you need to add the following two dimensions to your selection criteria. You need **people with innovative vision and social independence.** Members of this group formulate their vision about innovation in an independent manner. They base this vision exclusively on their own experience and opinions, without taking account of what might be 'popular'. This results in very pure ideas. They like trying out new things and generally have more extreme views than the 'average' customer. As a result, they can sometimes come up with revolutionary ideas.

You also need **social influencers.** These people discuss innovations while taking account of what their social environment thinks. They are regarded by this environment as creative specialists, who are quick to see the advantages of new innovations. Consequently, their opinions about such innovations are frequently asked – and followed. They like to be occupied creatively with new products and think that it is important that others also approve of the products they like to use. They converse with others proactively on these matters. It is therefore clear that this is a very relevant group for collaborative purposes. It is also a group with significant conversation potential. This means that the members not only help with the initiation and development of new ideas, but that they also start conversations during the implementation of these ideas. They have a sixth sense for the innovations that will catch on and those that will not. In this respect, they filter the ideas of the first group.

CASE STUDY
Intuit: a three-year process to embrace structural collaboration

(Based on Cook, 2008.)[135]

Intuit, a producer of financial software, needed three years to fully develop a programme of structural collaboration with its customers. When a number of enthusiastic employees gave feedback to customers in online forums, the management was amazed at the response. This unplanned action resulted in a huge number of positive conversations, forcing Intuit to realize that helping its customers could perhaps offer the company a significant added value. Intuit cautiously decided to take things a step further and began to think about ways in which customers might be able to make a structural contribution towards its business activities. During a management meeting in 2005, Scott Cook, the CEO of Intuit, asked his 300 top managers a simple question: 'How can we gain an advantage from the contribution of our customers?'

The first idea was a wiki on which all the most frequently asked questions relating to the completion of tax forms were discussed. People could also ask their own specific questions and would be given answers. The wiki was launched just 33 days after the management meeting. Three years later the site already contained a massive 170,000 pages of advice for and by consumers on tax-related matters. More than 400,000 people made (and still make) use of this accumulated knowledge.

Notwithstanding this success, at this stage there was still no question of structural collaboration with the market in the rest of the company. This was largely due to the failure of a second initiative. In late 2005 Intuit launched a second website for which consumers were also asked to provide content. This was a review site for local traders, linked to the financial software of the company. However, the market failed to grasp the link between the reviews and the software, so that the website never reached a critical mass. The project was cancelled after just a few months.

Fortunately, at the end of 2008 one of Intuit's engineers came forward with another idea that had the potential to lead to true structural collaboration. He suggested the addition of a users' forum to every page of Intuit's software package. This would allow users to ask questions and give feedback about that particular page. The questions could be answered by both Intuit staff and other Intuit customers. At the same time, the company would also receive detailed feedback on every aspect of its programme, which could be used to improve its performance further. These insights proved to be extremely valuable to the company and persuaded it to go full out for greater customer collaboration at all levels of the organization.

FIGURE 11.2

Why should customers help you?

According to Pink,[136] the old principles of customer motivation are no longer valid. The 'carrot and stick' approach firmly belongs to the past. People are now motivated by autonomy (being able to take matters into their own hands), knowledge (getting better at something) and a higher purpose (contributing to something greater than themselves). In other words, people want to help from a sense of intrinsic motivation. This explains why 53 per cent of internet users are willing to help the brands they like.[137] Financial incentives are no longer necessary, provided you can show to people that they are creating an added value. The only people who need a financial inducement are those who are not really committed to your company.[138]

Professor Dr Niels Schillewaert has expressed it in the following terms[139]: 'The manner in which you approach and engage people is as important as the questions you ask them.' You can add to the intrinsic motivation of your community by giving attention to the following (relatively small) matters, which often meet a symbolic need.

You should also remember that differentiation in these symbolic needs is a new and potentially potent form of differentiation:

- Add social statistics. If a member of the community makes a greater than average contribution in terms of content, make sure that this can be seen in the profile of that person. Some people like this kind of social status. It makes them feel good and encourages them to do even more in future. You can also introduce a games element that rewards people for their activity.

- Give social rewards. When a member of the community does something important (eg suggests a brilliant new product idea), you can reward this person with a form of social recognition. This might, for example, be a digital merit badge. Once again, communities love this kind of 'game' element. It builds up their online profile and stimulates them to yet greater efforts on your behalf.

- Show the results of members' input. If a new product is actually manufactured as a result of an idea from a community member, show this product on your community site. Give credit where credit is due. The more the members of the community are able to see that your decisions are based on their input, the greater their motivation will become.

- Remember the importance of conversations: Don't regard your community as just a place where customers contribute feedback and ideas, while the company remains a passive spectator. Community members think that it is fantastic when company staff join in their conversations. A video message from your CEO can work wonders. Two-way communication is not only more satisfying, but also yields content of higher added value.

- Offer personal added value. The provision of added value must also be a two-way process. It is not just a question of your customers helping you; you must help them as well. If they can learn something useful from the company or another customer, this is very positive for their motivation.

- Make offline contact. Invite the members of your community to visit your offices or factory or organize some other customer event. Let them get to know your staff: it can only help to strengthen their ties to your company.

Your role: moderator and participator

A community can only succeed if it is an active, living community. It is the task of the Conversation Company to guide and lead the community in a motivating manner. What you must avoid at all costs is your community becoming a kind of ghost town, a forum with 200 members but just three messages, none of which are answered.

The key to success is finding the right balance between normal conversation and generation or extraction of valuable input. In a small, closed community it is necessary that someone should act as a moderator for the discussions. After all, the company wants input in response to specific management questions. The community manager will usually play this moderating role, taking into account the following principles:

- Have no hierarchy. Everyone has the same right to talk or remain silent. In a community, there is no hierarchy to govern the relations between the community manager, the fans and the staff of the company. All are equal.

- Intervene only when necessary: A community manager will always be present in the community, organizing the discussions, but should not be too noticeable. Like the best waiters in a quality restaurant, they should be there when you need them and invisible when you don't.

- Encourage the community members: The community manager must stimulate community members to take part in the discussions, but without being too pushy. By asking the right questions, he or she can nudge the members into action, so that the group remains vibrant, fun and useful to the company.

- Be neutral and objective. The community manager has no opinion and always finds the opinions of others equally valid.

- Be a fan. The community manager must also have a keen personal interest in the subject(s) under discussion.

- Summarize and ask for feedback. In order to be certain that the company has correctly understood the input from its fans, the community manager must occasionally summarize the various conclusions of the discussions and ask for feedback that confirms this summary.

- Be quick. We live in a world of real-time feedback and communication. The community manager must respond quickly to the questions and comments of community members.

- Be firm when necessary. In extreme circumstances – comments involving racism, bad language, deliberate disruptiveness, etc – the community manager must dare to put the offender in his or her place.

- Say thank you. The community manager is grateful for the time and effort spent by the community members on behalf of the company and should express this gratitude on a regular basis.

You can compare the role of a community manager with that of a DJ. A DJ needs to get people onto the dance floor – and keep them there. This means that he or she needs to create a pleasant atmosphere and select the right music to satisfy a wide variety of different tastes. And a good DJ also remembers to keep up to date with the latest record releases: being trendy never did anybody any harm!

CASE STUDY Ducati builds the company on collaboration

(See also Sawhney, Verona and Prandelli, 2005.)[140]

In the motor sport industry, competitive advantage is often the result of smart technological development, linked to a culture that reflects the life style of the customers you hope to keep faithful to your brand. Ducati is an Italian producer of top-quality sports cars and was one of the first companies in the sector to connect with its fans via online communities. As early as 2004 Ducati already had a large, open community in which more than 160,000 people participated. Since then, the words 'marketing' and 'customer' have been replaced in the Ducati vocabulary by the terms 'community management' and 'fan'. For Ducati, its fans are an important company asset.

The fans are involved in almost every commercial decision. The choice of events, promotional actions and sponsor deals are all decided after consultation with and feedback from the community. In addition, Ducati also observes all conversations between its fans about lifestyle. These conversations provide direct input that is taken into account when designing new products. The members of the community are well aware of their impact and, because of their love for the brand, they are highly active. Ducati receives on average 200 reactions per day from its fans.

The development of a new motor engine is a complex matter. Even if you are a fan of Ducati, this does not necessarily mean that you are able to contribute anything meaningful in this highly technical field. Having said this, some members of the Ducati community do have a high level of technical expertise. Many like to maintain their own engines in their spare time and so know, for example, when a particular part is difficult to reach. To learn from the experience of these people, the company started its own online tech-café. This is a smaller community within the large, open forum, specifically for these techno-wizards. Some of them have even put forward designs for the next generation of Ducati motorbikes.

The CEO of Ducati wants the whole company at all levels to appreciate the value of fan input. With this aim in mind, he has tasked every Ducati employee to interview a fan of his or her choice periodically. This creates a tighter bond between the staff and the community, and increases respect and understanding on both sides.

Ducati genuinely sees its fans as part of the company. The majority of the decisions relating to product management, R&D, new design and commercial management are only taken after consultation with the fans via the online communities.

Impact through market research

(See also De Ruyck *et al*, 2011.)[141]

How and why does market research have an impact on a company's decision makers? It is not a question of representation or a strong methodology. No, company leaders want market research that inspires them. They want to see, feel and hear how their customers live and how they relate to their products. In short, the research must be worth talking about, must be conversation-worthy. Classic methods (question lists) do less well in this respect than more innovative methods. For example, the Conversation Company uses its communities as its most important research tool. The insights from a community can inspire managers and help to change staff behaviour.

Advantages and disadvantages of Facebook versus own community

We have been asked this question many times in recent years: what would be best for our brand – creating a Facebook community or building up our own community? As you might expect, both options have their advantages and disadvantages.

Advantages of a Facebook community

- The consumer is already on Facebook. Your company can therefore go directly to the market; you don't need to attract the market to you (which is much more difficult).
- The costs are more limited than the costs of an own community.
- Collaboration can immediately be transformed into activation, since everyone can 'watch in'.

Advantages of an own community

- You can consult with your consumers behind virtual 'closed doors'.
- You are the owner of all the data. You – and you alone – decide what happens. There are instances of Facebook groups suddenly disappearing because Facebook saw something it believed was against its rules. In your own community, you are the boss.
- There is more scope for in-depth conversations.

There is no doubt that a Facebook page is useful and relevant for every company. However, as a co-creation platform your own community is safer and more flexible than the Facebook environment. In reality, the two options complement each other. If you can afford it, go for both.

Organize for structural collaboration

To prepare your company properly for structural collaboration with fans, you need to do the following:

- Involve all your stakeholders in the collaboration. Your collaboration will have an impact on all the different networks within your organization. Involve the people who are most directly concerned with processing input from the market.

Let them follow the discussions with your community. The impact will be greater if they hear feedback and new ideas directly from consumers.

- Make sure that everyone is able to take part in the discussion: staff must be permitted to talk with fans. They must be able to ask questions of each other and both must be allowed to contribute to the final conclusions of any discussion. This creates positive motivation in both directions. Make sure that the company also gives enough feedback to fans. Let them feel that their input is valuable.

- Appoint a neutral moderator. The moderator (usually the community manager) plays an important role. Devote sufficient resources to make the community effective and manageable. Even if you delegate aspects of community management to an outside agency, you will still need someone inside the company who spends most of his or her time on these matters.

- Remember that transparent communication is essential. Be honest and unambiguous with the feedback you give to community members. These are the fans who are making great efforts free of charge on your company's behalf. The least that you can do in return is to communicate with them openly. As Professor Dr Rudy Moenaert puts it: 'Don't fake! Be!'

- Regard the community members as staff who are not on the payroll. The members of the community are almost like employees of your company. Their impact is as great as the impact of your own staff. The only difference is that you don't have to pay them. Be appreciative of this relationship and show your appreciation in a correct manner. If you offer a bonus to your staff following a successful campaign, don't forget to do something for the fans: their contribution will have been just as important.

Collaboration is the key to everything

In previous chapters, we have discussed the management of customer experience, conversations, content and collaboration. But it is this fourth C, collaboration, which is the key to the correct implementation of the first three. The communities of the Conversation Company provide input about every aspect of your activities. They help to give concrete shape and form to your content. They are crucial to your conversations and give feedback on your methods of working. They help you to map, evaluate and improve your touchpoints. And they do it all in close collaboration with your managers and your staff.

KEY CONVERSATION POINTS

Possible conversation starters

- One-off collaboration reflects an outdated checklist mentality.
- Structural collaboration means involving consumers in all types of decision making within your company.
- You need three types of community: staff, open and large, closed and small.
- With large, open communities, your primary task is to listen.
- Small, closed communities are the ideal platforms for collaborating closely with your customers.
- The customer can also become an (honorary) member of the board.
- Work with the right people: people with innovative ideas and social influencers.
- The people who help your company do so primarily from intrinsic motives. They do not need financial incentives.
- The company's role in its communities is to act as a moderator, but also to actively participate.
- Structural collaboration is central to the strategic and tactical thinking of the Conversation Company. Your content, conversation and customer experience planning should all be made in consultation with your customers.

Questions you must ask yourself

- Do you already have organic communities of fans within your company?
- In which elements (if any) of your decision-making processes are your consumers already involved?
- Does the voice of the consumer carry weight in your boardroom?
- What barriers exist within the company to structural collaboration with customers, and how can you remove these barriers?

Further information

A short video summary of Daniel Pink's book, *Drive* can be seen at: **www.youtube.com/watch?v=u6XAPnuFjJc.**

Part Four
How to become a Conversation Company in three easy steps

The fourth and last part of this book serves a different purpose to the first three parts. Until now, our objective has been to paint a picture of a modern, proactive company and how it should be run; a company that builds on its culture to generate conversations involving both its employees and its customers. In the next section, however, we will look at the concrete steps you need to take to transform your company into a Conversation Company. This involves a succession of internal change projects, which will help you to gradually move closer to the implementation of your vision. We will be offering plenty of practical and operational tips: regard these and the other information in this section as a step-by-step plan to be used by your conversation manager.

Chapter Twelve
Integrate customer-oriented thinking and social media in three steps

It begins today – and it never ends

A recent article in the *McKinsey Quarterly*[142] reports an interview with John Hayes, the CMO of American Express. Hayes hit the nail squarely on the head, when he said:

> If we bring a product to market, then the market will decide if that product has value. The market will conduct the conversation and will position the product accordingly. In other words, the market has control, not us. All we are finally responsible for is the financial results realised by the product... Marketing as such doesn't exist any more. Conversations relate to different departments: marketing, PR, service, product development, etc. The classic silo structure of a company no longer works. It has been replaced by networks and cross-functional teams in which customer-orientation stands central. I know of no single company that has adapted fully to this new way of working.

The message is clear: our traditional organizational structures and methods are no longer capable of responding to the needs of the modern market. In this part of the book we will discuss in concrete terms what change projects your company needs to undertake in order to face up to these new challenges.

In the following three chapters we will propose 10 strategic internal projects. All these projects are evolutionary in nature. For this reason, most of the projects will never actually be completed. Your mission as a Conversation Company starts today, but it will never end. The market is moving forward at a tremendous pace. Developing the ability to work flexibly and adapt quickly is the last important step in your metamorphosis into a Conversation Company. Reacting purposefully and with speed to new trends is the only way to be successful.

The three steps to integration

As part of the preparations for this book, we interviewed 25 senior managers.[143] Our purpose was to discuss their views about change projects. We talked to people in organizations that are already well on their way to becoming a true Conversation Company, as well as to people in organizations that had hardly started. In addition, we asked another 400 managers to complete a quantitative questionnaire about the integration of the conversation philosophy into their company.[144] The results of these studies prove that every company goes through similar processes in its attempt to build greater customer-orientation and conversational thinking into its operations.

The trajectory consists of three separate steps:

1 **The build-up of knowledge.** During this first step, the internal knowledge and conviction necessary to apply conversation management are built up in a structural manner. You follow a conscious training trajectory, making sure that you involve your legal and HR teams, as well as any other important internal partners. This creates the necessary internal consensus of support. Finally, you need to introduce the necessary hardware and software. These are the bases for a successful evolution.

2 **Pilot projects.** Implementing pilot projects offers important opportunities to learn, but these projects are also a way to demonstrate the added value that can be created by the new methods. This means that as well as accelerating your learning curve, they must also have a positive effect on your marketing and financial results. At the beginning of this phase, it is important to appoint a central person (the conversation manager) who is responsible for developing conversational thinking in your organization. This is also the phase in which you must start actively listening to conversations.

FIGURE 12.1

1.	**2.**	**3.**
THE BUILD-UP OF KNOWLEDGE	PILOT PROJECTS	INTEGRATION AND THE LEVER EFFECT

3　Integration and the lever effect. In this final phase your organization must embrace the concept of the Conversation Company fully by searching continuously for integration and the lever effect. The 4 Cs must be applied consistently and the gap between your company and the market must be closed. When this happens, a lever effect will be created. Everything you do will be magnified in a positive manner and your unused conversation potential will disappear.

Most companies have hardly started

Our research has revealed that the largest proportion (38 per cent) of companies in Europe and the United States are still in the first phase or have not yet started with their change process.[145] Another 14 per cent of companies claim to have already implemented the philosophy in full. The four sectors in which this is most likely to be the case are telecom, media, travel and foodstuffs. The financial market and the health industry are currently at the bottom of the class. As a general rule, service industries are also further along the change pathway than production industries. Similarly, the largest global companies have made less progress than regional companies with fewer than 500 employees.

The shining examples of conversation management include Google, Zappos, Cisco, Dell, Kodak, Intel, Starbucks and Best Buy. Yet notwithstanding the great advances they have already made, all these companies admit that there is still work to be done – or rather, that the work is never finished. The non-stop evolution of the market requires them to keep their eye continually on the ball. But if the journey to becoming a Conversation Company is a long one, it at least holds the fascination of being a true journey of discovery. There are no certainties: you are never quite sure what is going to happen and you never know in advance whether your plans will work. Everyone is exploring together and learning together. Surely this is something that you also want to be a part of?

CASE STUDY How Intel experienced the three steps

(Based on an interview in 2011 with Ekaterina Walter, Social Media Strategist at Intel.)

1. Extensive training for every employee

To begin with, Intel launched the Digital IQ Programme. This was an internal training programme designed to enhance the knowledge of every Intel employee with regard to the use of new media. It was an impressive programme, which can serve as a model for other companies to follow. It consists of no fewer than 100 separate modules and is based entirely on self-training. Each module has a short video, supplementary texts and a test. Once you have successfully completed the test, you can move on to the next module. Each module takes about 30 minutes to complete.

When the programme was first introduced in 2008, there was a degree of scepticism within the company. Within 10 months it was already clear that this scepticism was unfounded. By this time, Intel staff had already completed 18,000 modules and 16,000 hours of training and 68 per cent of the trainees found the content immediately useful in their daily work.[146] The key target groups were the sales and marketing people within the company. For these groups the training was compulsory. However, it was also opened to others in the company who might be interested (the only training for which this option was available). Within the key groups there were three different training levels. The highest and most specialized level was reserved for the digital marketing teams. The next level was focused on bloggers and communication managers. The lowest level was for sales and account managers, so that they could use online tools to contact their customers. This gradated method of working ensured maximum relevancy.

The training was later extended with a new module: Intel Digital IQ500. If staff managed to pass this test with success, they were authorized to talk in the name of Intel online. Intel was keen (and still is) for more and more of its employees to become spokespersons for the company. Ekaterina Walter, Social Media

Strategist at Intel, adds an important nuance to this decision: 'Your brand is only as strong as the culture that supports that brand. Because our company culture is clear and robust, it is relatively easy to let our staff talk about Intel online. But this will not be the case in every company. Training alone is not enough; the underlying culture has to be rock-solid.'

2. Blogs and wikis as pilot projects

As a next step, Intel founded its social media centre of excellence in 2009. This seven-strong team of social media experts was charged with integrating the conversation philosophy into all levels of the company. The members of the team were also responsible for carrying out a number of specific conversation-related tasks. For example, it was their job (initially, at least) to observe and, where necessary, participate in social media. In addition, they helped individual departments to plan their conversation strategies, in keeping with the overall general principles of the Conversation Company. In other words, the centre of excellence was intended to be more than just a help desk. It formulated proactive suggestions and recommendations for these other departments. The intention is that these departments, depending on the topics, will gradually take over the task of online participation. Intel has more than 1 million online mentions every month, so it is simply not possible for a small, dedicated team to answer every question. The facilitating work of the centre of excellence allows the departments to take on this role.

One of the first pilot projects at Intel was the development of a blog. Intel already had a number of employees with a private blog. This made it easier to create a basis of support for this new method of communication. This first blog was targeted at an IT public. It was later supplemented by a technology blog and a research blog. The CEO was also quick off the mark (he has had a blog since 2004). Within 24 hours he had received no fewer than 350 reactions. Since then, he blogs every month. Within no time at all, Intel soon had 60 employees blogging on behalf of the company. Today, that number has risen to over 2,000. The greatest return from the blog project was the contribution it made to the public perception of the company. Intel was keen to be known as a progressive organization. The use of blogs and their content strengthened this perception every day – and still does.

In addition to its blogs, Intel also developed an internal wiki: Intelpedia.[147] One of the Intel staff, Josh Bancroft, started this internal platform as long ago as 2005. Employees use Intelpedia to exchange knowledge with each other. By 2008, 8,700 people had already added content to the platform, which had registered more than 100 million page views. Roughly 500 pieces of new content are added to the site every day.

3. Integration, the lever and the challenge

In this phase the company wants to bring the conversations between its staff and the outside world to a higher level. The idea is to evolve from blogs to communities and structural collaboration with customers. With this aim in mind, the company launched the open port community, again aimed initially at an IT public. This community currently contains 40,000 members, who regularly consult the content or even make contributions of their own. In fact, just three months after the launch the majority of the content was already being provided by external visitors. In this way, the market is gradually becoming involved in Intel's decision-making processes.

At the same time, a lever effect is being created by the use of the company's social media accounts in support of marketing actions. Intel's reach is growing day by day. Staff contribute actively to this growth and many have become true Intel ambassadors.

The ultimate aim of Intel is to become more dynamic and more efficient. For a company with 80,000 employees, it is by no means evident to react quickly and flexibly to market change. Intel is a super-tanker, not a speed boat. Even so, the company is very clear about its objective: to make its processes shorter and more responsive. Ekaterina Walter sees a number of quick wins that can help Intel to move in the right direction.

> Trusting your staff and allowing them to make decisions is a first important step. The greatest delay in most companies is caused by endless meetings to discuss who is responsible for what. If staff are free to decide for themselves, everything moves much quicker. A second step is to limit the money spent on new tools and consultants. If you have good staff, there are an awful lot of things you can do for yourself. The third step is to invest in talented people. If you have the right men and women on board, it is easy to give them trust. Finally, don't always try and think of everything. You don't need to reinvent the wheel. Look at the market. Study the best examples. Use the knowledge created by your own projects.

Everyone is a marketeer

Nowadays, everyone is a marketeer. Everyone must have engagement. This means that every department in your organization must be involved in the change process. Like it or not, they are all 'interested parties'! Everyone can and must help in a direct or indirect manner to optimize your company's conversation potential.

All the commercial departments play a prominent role. Marketing, sales and customer service are directly responsible for providing your customers with a positive experience. These three departments must be closely involved with and collaborate together on the necessary change processes within your company.

It is also recommended that someone from senior management should play an active role in this process. In fact, bearing in mind the three levels of change discussed earlier (personal, structural and cultural), it is absolutely essential. The HR department also needs to be on board: the organization of training, the adjustment of evaluation procedures and the drawing up of new recruitment criteria are all key aspects in their domain. As far as R&D staff are concerned, they must be assisted to find ways of getting closer to the customer. In particular, their active and constructive participation is essential while you are setting up the necessary structural collaboration with your customers; after all, in future they will be working closely together. Other departments may be less fundamentally involved but can also lend their support. IT has a role to play in purchasing the required hardware and software. The legal department should be consulted to eliminate any possible risks your changes may imply. Finally, the social partners must be consulted. It is only when all the 'interested parties' are pulling in the same direction that it will be possible to create the lever effect that will launch your company to a future of growth and success.

The role of the CEO

If everyone has to be an 'interested party', this means that the CEO must also play a role. Many CEOs ask themselves what exactly they are supposed to do within the Conversation Company philosophy. Some of them are extrovert and enjoy taking part in conversations, which sends a powerful signal. But you need to be careful not to go to the other extreme: a Conversation Company in which the CEO seems not to understand the value of conversations can give entirely the wrong impression.

Conversations are about communication, and the CEO has important tasks to fulfil both in terms of internal and external communication. People are always interested to follow the opinions of leaders: just look at the average number of followers on the Twitter accounts of senior figures in the business world. They all score highly. People look up to leaders and like to follow them – and not only on Twitter.

A clear voice from the CEO on social media can offer several advantages. To begin with, the employees know that the top managers are also concerned with what they do. This will lead to a fall in the number of negative conversations and, more importantly, an increase in the number of positive ones generated by staff. In other words, in this instance the culture of the company is being made more tangible through the actions of its leader. The outside world will also follow what is happening and will conclude that the senior management in this company is 'approachable'.

Many CEOs are worried at the prospect of receiving 'personal' questions as soon as they have their own Twitter account. Others want to maintain their privacy and so regularly refuse to become friends on Facebook – which is their right, but which again is not always well received by customers. This is a real problem many companies are faced with. Of course, it can never be the intention that the CEO becomes a kind of personal help desk for consumers. So if you want to make your CEO a conversation-worthy touchpoint (and he or she certainly has that potential), you need to think carefully in advance how you are going to go about it. Provide facilitators to help the CEO with conversations.

It must certainly be the intention of any serious Conversation Company that the members of the senior management team take part in conversations. If not, your change process is likely to lose significant credibility. It is perhaps surprising, then, that at the time of writing just 65 per cent of senior managers in UK and US companies are active in social media.[148] This must change. There were moments in the past when everybody needed to learn to drive, or learn to work with a computer, or learn to use a mobile phone. Now, we all need to learn how to use social media – senior managers included! If you are an exponent of a philosophy in which everyone is a potential spokesperson, the company's top brass also need to take this responsibility seriously.

Can it be the same for every company?

Are we not missing something with our three-step plan? Is there not a risk that in future every company will be more or less the same? How will companies be able to differentiate themselves if everyone follows the same path?

Have you already asked yourself these questions while reading this book so far? It is, perhaps, an understandable reaction. It is indeed difficult to imagine that every company will seek to implement the same strategy. Even so, the research carried out by InSites Consulting showed clearly that the companies who most closely reflect the Conversation Company philosophy have all taken a remarkably similar route.

Does this mean that there are no longer any differences between companies? Of course not!

Even if companies follow identical trajectories, there will always be differences between them. Why? First and foremost because the three steps to change are carried out within the framework of the company culture – and every company culture is different. To give a simple example, this means that every company will draw up its own training programme specific to its own needs. What suits Intel might not suit Unilever -- and vice versa. Second, the pilot projects are also very different. Once again, these pilot projects are chosen on the basis of their relevance to specific company needs. For Intel this meant the development of a blog strategy, for ING (as we shall read shortly) it meant the creation of a webcare plan. Dependent upon these two variables – company culture and existing strategy – the final outcome will continue to vary from company to company.

Does this then mean that there will be no similarities? On the contrary, there will be plenty of similarities!

Just as every company is organized in accordance with the silo model at present, in the future companies will be organized along conversational lines. Just as every company at present arranges market research to learn more about its customers, in the future this will be done through direct customer communication. A number of elements of the new philosophy offer advantages to every company, so it is reasonable to expect that these will be adopted by every company. But the content and the implementation will continue to be different in almost every case.

The next three chapters will describe in detail the 10 projects every company needs to undertake in order to complete its transformation into a Conversation Company. Completing such a process usually takes between 24 and 48 months. The exact speed (like so many other things) is largely dependent upon the culture of your company (see the comments made at the end of Chapter 4). One of the most crucial steps is the selection of the right pilot projects. These projects must have sufficient impact to create both support and movement within the company with minimum delay. No company can afford to wait 48 months for impact! Both in the short term and the medium term, it is important that the change process develops momentum – and then keeps it. Be aware of the fact that this type of process will always create tension and frustrations between the leaders and the followers in your company. For some, things will be much too slow; for others, much too fast. You can help to reduce these tensions and frustrations to a minimum by working through the process in a step-by-step manner. Your leaders will be mentally in stage 3 while your followers are still in stage 1. Draw up a clear plan in advance and make sure that everyone keeps to it. In this way, everyone will have the same expectations.

So let's go to work – step by step

In the following three chapters we will be looking at each of the change phases in detail. Each phase will be linked to a number of internal strategic change projects. By following these guidelines, your organization will move closer, step by step, towards its ultimate goal: becoming a true Conversation Company. Good luck!

KEY CONVERSATION POINTS

Possible conversation starters

- Every company follows a similar trajectory on its journey to become a Conversation Company.
- Every department in your company must be involved in the change process.
- The change process consists of three phases: building up knowledge, implementing pilot projects, searching consciously for the lever effect.

Questions you must ask yourself

- Which phase is your company in at present?
- In which phase are your most important competitors?
- In which phase are your customers?
- Which people can you rely on in your company to play a pioneering role in the change process? Are you currently involving these people enough?
- Who are the pioneers among your top managers?
- Who will lead the change trajectory?

Further information

All the steps in the change process are shown in detail in the following research paper: **www.slideshare.net/stevenvanbelleghem/ the-social-dynamics-model-how-to-integrate-social-media-in-your-company**

Chapter Thirteen
Step 1: Building up knowledge and the necessary framework

Before we begin – time for a conversation audit

Before you start your process of structural change, we would recommend that you first take the time to conduct a thorough conversation audit of your company. By looking at yourself and your environment in a critical manner, you will gain clear insights into the current status of your company and your market. This information is crucial if you are to make the right decisions during the change process. It is difficult to plan out your route if you don't know where you are starting from.

The following analyses will help you to gain an accurate picture.

An external conversation scan

A first analysis will detail the current level of conversations relating to your brand and competing brands. What are people talking about? What are the basic sentiments expressed in these conversations?

Second, it is also important to establish a clear digital profile for the people in your target group. Who are your fans? How do they obtain their information?

Third, you need to establish exactly where your fans congregate. On which sites do most of their conversations take place? Is it Twitter or Facebook? Are there specialized forums for your sector? Do people converse online or offline?

Fourth, you need to look at the social media presence, behaviour and reach of all the key players in your market. Taken together, these elements will give you a clear impression of the conversations relevant to your company.

An internal conversation scan

This scan examines three specific aspects of your company. First, it draws up a conversation profile for your own employees. How knowledgeable are they about social media? Do you have any digital superstars on your payroll? Which members of staff talk spontaneously about your company? Who are your internal ambassadors? These insights will help you to draw up a relevant training plan. It will also help you to identify the employees who will be most willing to help you implement the conversation philosophy.

Second, it is useful to compile an inventory of the conversations already taking place inside your company. In most companies there will already be a number of loose, uncoordinated conversation activities. This can result in a mish-mash of overlapping websites and Facebook pages. Do you already have conversation guidelines and existing social media accounts? List these matters in detail, so that you know exactly what conversation potential is already being exploited.

Third, analyse the existing level of commitment to your brand. If your brand says something, how does the outside world react – and to what extent? Does the number of conversations increase if you launch a new product? If you organize a competition, how many people take part? Are your newsletters read or deleted?

All these matters will give you a good idea of the level of interaction that your company might initially expect when its starts its structural approach towards conversations.

A strengths and weaknesses analysis for customer-orientation

By combining the results of your internal and external audits, you will be able to draw up a strengths and weaknesses analysis for your conversation potential and the related levels of customer-orientation. This analysis will show in which conversation quadrant (see Chapter 5) your company is currently situated. Are you a boring, proud or worshipped company? Or are you perhaps already a Conversation Company?

In view of the fact that most conversations arise spontaneously as a result of your customers' experience of your products or your services, it is also advisable to take a close look at the current state of your customer-orientation. Are you customer-friendly? Where can you improve? Are there any 'irritations' inherent in your processes? For example, do customers have to pay an extra administrative charge if they want to change their subscription with your company? Is your 'money-back' guarantee genuine, or are there get-outs in the small print? This is by no means an easy exercise to conduct. You must re-examine matters that until now have always seemed straightforward and self-evident. You no doubt had good reasons for introducing these measures, but what do your customers think about them? Make a list of anything that might be a negative conversation starter. Evaluate these potential customer irritants one by one. Do you really need them? Can they be replaced with something more acceptable? Get rid of what you can and soften the impact of the things that you need to retain. Be strict in your assessment!

Drawing up a first conversation dashboard

Lastly, it is useful to draw up a dashboard at the very start of your change process. This dashboard will be used to measure a limited number of parameters relating to conversations. This makes it easier to follow and evaluate your progress. After all, you need to know whether your chosen trajectory is having the desired effect. To begin with, keep it simple and measure the three most important criteria: the number of conversations, the sentiments in the conversations and the impact of the conversations. Do this for your own company and for your most important competitors. At a later stage, add the reach of your social media accounts and those of your rivals.

Three strategic projects of this phase

Armed with the details from your audits, you are now ready to begin your process of structural change. During this first phase you need to construct a solid foundation on which the further development of your conversation strategy can be built. To do this, you should make use of these three strategic projects:

- **Project 1: Build up the required levels of knowledge.**
  Most companies possess relatively little in-house knowledge
  relating to social media and conversation management.
  This will slow down the evolution and growth of your
  company. The provision of relevant and far-reaching training
  for all your staff is therefore an essential step if you wish to
  be successful.

- **Project 2: Don't postpone the difficult conversations.** Some
  departments will be more willing to join in the conversation
  game than others. Our surveys have shown that people in the
  legal department, IT managers and corporate communications
  staff are generally more reluctant (although there are always
  exceptions). For this reason, it is important to involve the 'foot
  draggers' in your plans at an early stage. Make allies of these
  people. Encourage them to be part of the change consensus.
  The HR department is another key partner whose commitment
  you need to secure. Many HR procedures will undergo
  structural change, so you need to have your HR managers
  on board from the outset.

- **Project 3: Provide the right infrastructure.** In order to
  implement the philosophy of the Conversation Company fully,
  your staff will need the right software and hardware. In addition,
  a clear online presence is required. Choose the right channels
  and manage them continuously.

FIGURE 13.1

Project 1: Build up the required levels of knowledge

CASE STUDY AB-inBev

(Based on an interview in 2011 with Jef Vandecruys, Global Project Leader digital connections, AB-inBev.)

The brewing giant AB-inBev believes firmly in training its staff to meet the challenges of social media and the digital world. So much is evident from its decision to set up 'The Global Digital University' in Palo Alto, where top trainers such as Eric Schmidt (CEO Google) and Mark Zuckerberg (CEO Facebook) give lessons to senior managers.

The 'university' is a 10-day programme that is organized each year. So far, more than 250 AB-inBev managers have had the opportunity to take part. The first training was for the entire board of directors. The most important objective is: creating awareness of evolutions in the field of social media and their impact on consumer marketing. After the first inspirational sessions, the participants learn about more practical matters via an internal digital platform which summarizes the best practices of different well-known brands.

Almost every company organizes training of one kind or another, but very few as yet devote adequate attention to conversation training. At present, only 30 per cent of companies in the UK and the United States offer training of this kind to their personnel.[149] This 30 per cent is already further along the pathway that leads towards true conversation management. Their courses vary widely in terms of depth and content, but underline the crucial point that proper conversation training is a basic requirement for building the strong foundations necessary for change.

Our numerous interviews revealed that the companies that have made most progress to date in this field opt for a combined programme of the AB-inBev kind. This often begins with an inspirational workshop, which stimulates the desire of the participants to work at the conversation potential of their company. This workshop does not concentrate on the technological aspects, but rather on the impact of conversations on brands. These evolutions are discussed at a strategic level and are communicated with a positive and enthusiastic message. In ideal circumstances, every employee should have the chance to follow such a workshop, but this will be indispensable for senior and middle managers.

The workshops are allied to a separate programme of self-study, geared to the more specific requirements of particular functions and/ or levels of experience. On the one hand, there is a need to answer a wide variety of basic tactical questions. For example, many people have trouble getting to grips with Twitter. Others may have difficulty with the setting of Google alerts. At the same time, more advanced social media users want answers to more complex questions. For this reason, it is strongly recommended to organize your training to reflect different levels of basic knowledge. In the previous chapter, we described how Intel drew up different profiles for its training programme. Cisco adopts a very similar approach. Both companies make some elements of the programme compulsory and other elements optional. Everything is geared to the operational responsibilities of the member of staff concerned. At the end of each module there is a test. This is necessary to allow managers to see who has learnt his or her lessons well and is consequently ready to play an effective role in conversations. A self-study programme of this kind is efficient and remains confined to the digital environment. This is useful for companies who find it difficult to give their personnel 'live' access to social media. The employees will only be allowed to use social media once they have shown that they have acquired the minimum basic skills in the 'practice arena' provided by the self-study training modules. This approach is becoming more and more popular, particularly with larger companies.

An internal online platform where employees can share experiences is also a useful tool. Companies such as AB-inBev and Cisco build in-house knowledge platforms with the specific objective of inspiring their staff to embrace conversation management. These internal sites give details of cases and examples drawn from the company's own projects. Lessons to be learnt are discussed and exchanged. In this way, the theoretical training is supplemented with first-hand, practical information.

A third and final option is the setting up of an internal team of experts who can advise their colleagues about the implementation of their conversation projects. Training is essential but is not a guarantee of success. In the harsh world of daily practice people are regularly confronted with problems that the training programmes simply do not cover. At such moments, it is useful to have someone that you can turn to for guidance. The quicker you can appoint a person (or team) as the pioneer(s) of your change project, the quicker you will achieve impact. Pioneers are the facilitators of change. Through their advisory role, they help to enhance the level of practical knowledge in your company.

Reverse mentorship

Reverse mentorship is a new training concept that is rapidly growing in popularity. It involves the digital illiterates in your company being tutored by your most skilled digital experts. In other words, the training is not organized 'top–down', but is based on individual knowledge and experience. The idea is to bring your digital 'natives' (your most media-aware staff, often in lower grades) into contact with your digital 'dummies' (often staff in senior management positions). This has a double advantage. It allows your senior managers to learn about the digital world in depth, while at the same time giving the 'natives' an insight into the processes of wider company management. By combining these two different worlds, it is often possible to create magic. The learning curve of young and old alike accelerates dramatically and there is a general increase in the company's overall digital awareness.

CASE STUDY
Edelman bases its training on the principles of combat sports

Edelman is a worldwide player in the PR sector, with more than 3,600 employees in over 50 countries. One of its most recent challenges was to transform itself from an 'ordinary' PR company to a PR company in the digital era. In an interview in 2011 Phil Gomes, Senior Vice President of Edelman, described how he approached the responsibility of making Edelman's global operations more digitally aware. One of the first steps was to rewrite the job profiles of all staff to reflect the requirements of digital communication. Tasks such as 'observing conversations' and 'managing a consumer community' were something totally new in the PR industry. Once the new profiles had been written, it was clear that most staff needed to learn new competencies in order to carry out their new responsibilities effectively.

Initially, the company began a programme where the trainees came together in the same location to receive their training. This was not only very expensive, but took little account of people's deadlines and agendas. In short, it was not cost-effective. The idea gradually grew that self-training might be a better way forward. The structure of this training is based on the hierarchy used in combat sports such as judo. Employees are awarded digital 'belts' in different colours: white, yellow, orange, green, blue, brown or black. Every time they completed a module and its related test with success, they were awarded a new belt. Each module consists of 8–12 short exercises. Each exercise is based on a five-minute film. The employees are free to set their own training tempo. If someone 'wins' a new belt, his or her profile on the internal communication platform is immediately updated. Cheating is avoided by providing a sufficiently wide range of questions for each level. This means that each test contains a different selection of questions, so that answers cannot easily be passed on from one employee to another. Moreover, the training is regularly updated to reflect market evolutions. If newer trainings need to be created, the black belt employees are automatically reduced to a lower level. Once they have completed the new training successfully, they get their black belt back again. More recently, more specialized levels of training have been added to the programme. Completion of these additions does not earn the trainee a new belt, but rather a digital badge which is added to his or her internal profile – for example a badge that shows that you are an expert in managing PR crises. Many people like this competitive element, and it is also useful when putting together teams for external projects.

In just a few years' time, Edelman has managed to train over 1,000 black belts. This means that one third of its workforce now has an in-depth knowledge of the latest digital evolutions – which not only represents a huge added value for the company, but also for its customers.

Project 2: Don't postpone the difficult conversations

Your change project will not be easy. For this reason, it is necessary to secure the agreement of all relevant parties before you start to apply the conversation philosophy in practice. This can cost considerable time and effort, particularly in large companies. In small companies, it is sometimes enough just to get the necessary agreement from one or two top people. Departments which are regarded as 'difficult to convince' in this respect include legal, corporate communication and IT. In large companies it is also necessary to obtain the tacit consent of the social partners, so that everyone is on the same wavelength. Without wishing to generalize, this is often easier said than done. Change brings uncertainty, and uncertainty is something that employees (and their representatives) do not like. The best way to avoid problems is to involve all these 'reluctant' partners in your plans at the earliest possible stage. Do not attempt to camouflage the problems and potential pitfalls. Explain your objectives clearly and tell everyone that you need their help to create a workable framework which will allow you to realize these objectives to the benefit of all concerned. Show them that the opportunities are greater than the risks. Your intuition may sometimes tell you to do some things behind the backs of your stakeholders. This is a serious mistake. Attempting to discuss these matters at a later stage will be much more difficult, with powerful negative emotions on both sides.

In this initial phase, the HR department is another key partner. Your company culture and your staff are the basic building blocks of the Conversation Company. This obviously has important HR implications. First and foremost, your company values need to be defined and managed. There can be no culture without values, and it is the job of the HR department to formulate these values. This is a fundamental task. Moreover, it is a task which needs to be tackled before the change process can begin. Are your current values in keeping with the conversation philosophy? Are they compatible with what you are trying to achieve? Do they need to be reworded in light of your new objectives? Once your values have been set, their daily management is another crucial element in the efficient running of the Conversation Company. The HR team must draw up an operational plan which will allow the core values to infuse all levels of the organization.

In addition, there will also be a need for revised recruitment criteria. When appointing new staff, you will first need to look for a good fit with the new company values. From now on, this will be more important than good qualifications and/or technical skills. For example, retailer Decathlon only employs active sportsmen and women. Whoever serves in one of their specialized sport departments must actually be a practitioner of that same sport. Recruiting the wrong people – however talented – can only lead to disappointment on both sides. In particular, new staff must be aware and accept that the company wants to focus on the customer. This kind of customer-mindedness is difficult to learn; you either have it or you don't. Take on people who are generally helpful by nature; they are more likely to understand and be willing to respond to customer needs.

In some cases, new function profiles may also need to be drawn up. The job content of various functions will inevitably change.

For example, staff involved in customer service will certainly be required to converse with consumers online, which may not have been the case until now. In addition, a number of new functions will be created (such as community manager). Once again, it will be the responsibility of the HR department to rewrite (or write) these job descriptions. Staff evaluation procedures will also need to be amended to reflect the new competencies. By and large, employees behave in accordance with the expectations set down in their personal perform-ance plans, which in turn are based on their evaluation parameters. This means that if you want to change their behaviour, you first need to change the evaluation parameters. By communicating your revised expectations clearly to your people, you will make the new approach more tangible. Your staff have the ability to make or break your con-versation project. Invest the necessary time to explain your objectives carefully and convince them of their importance.

Most companies will also need a conversation guide, usually referred to as a social media policy. This policy specifies what your employees are allowed and not allowed to say online. Once again, the drawing up of this policy is self-evidently an HR task. A good conversation guide is written in a positive and enthusiastic style, with more dos than don'ts.

Finally, the HR department is responsible for appointing a conver-sation manager. They must ensure the recruitment of someone with the right profile; someone who can play a pioneering role in the change process that lies ahead; someone who can act as a facilitator for the different departments as he or she seeks to cope with the difficulties inherent in the transformation to a true Conversation Company.

CASE STUDY
UCB involved everyone and concluded an innovation partnership

PatientsLikeMe is the largest community of patients in the world (see wikipedia.org). When the brother of James Heywood was diagnosed with a rare disease, his family found no one who was able to talk to him about his condition. There were just too few people with the same problem. It was like looking for a needle in a haystack. This was when James decided to set up PatientsLikeMe. He searched for people with the exact same illness. However small the group was, they would be able to find each other via this online platform. And it worked.

His brother found fellow sufferers with whom he could converse. But the site continued to grow and soon became a major success story. Sadly, Heywood's brother died of his condition, but the initiative lives on because it meets a universal need we all have: being in touch with people who are in the same position as ourselves.

In 2009 the pharmaceutical company UCB entered into an innovative partnership with PatientsLikeMe. The two companies agreed to collaborate on an open community for epileptics. People from all over the world can exchange their thoughts and experiences of the disease. The purpose is to improve the personal environment of patients. They help each other and UCB to look for elements that can make their lives better. In this way, UCB is seeking to position itself as an expert in the market. At the same time, it is effectively fulfilling its company mission: to be closer to the patients.

Why have we cited the UCB case study? It seems to be just a simple partnership. But it isn't. UCB is the first pharmaceutical company that has ever succeeded in setting up a patient community of this kind. The legal departments in the health sector are the most difficult of all to convince of the merits of the conversation philosophy. René Hansen, Global Director of marketing innovation and health technology at UCB, was the main architect of the agreement. He realizes that it was only possible because of the creation of an internal consensus within the company.

> UCB already started in 2008 with inspiration workshops to convince our staff about the needs of the modern-day patient. These workshops were attended by colleagues from marketing and sales, but our colleagues from the legal and medical departments also sat in on the sessions. It didn't always run smoothly, but after a time people began to understand that this is the only way forward. By involving everyone in the project from the start, we managed to get everyone on board.

Remember: the sooner you deal with the difficult conversations inside your own company, the sooner your structural change process can begin.

Project 3: Provide the right infrastructure

This project lays the foundations for your social media approach. The purpose of social media (see Chapter 6) is to build up reach and make possible effective structural collaboration with your customers. The following project will help you to achieve the first of these objectives.

For this project you will need to:

- Clear up your social media battlefield. Many companies already have several different Facebook accounts. Others have a Facebook page with one fan and no content. Some have even had their Twitter accounts hijacked by enthusiastic customers. These are all examples of social media dramas. The challenge is to build up a consistent and transparent image of your company through your presence on social media. To do this, it is useful to have your most important social media tools in your own hands. In the United States and the UK 68 per cent of companies have their own Facebook page and 56 per cent have a Twitter account. More than half have a LinkedIn page and 42 per cent are on YouTube. The smaller social network sites have been less adopted: 11 per cent for Flickr, 5 per cent for Slideshare and 8 per cent for Foursquare.[150] Build up the social media structure you need. Remove overlapping and old accounts that no longer serve their purpose. Give proper shape and form to your social media battlefield, so that you can present a clear and consistent image of your company and its culture.

- Turn your staff into fans. Your first followers must be your own staff. But the Conversation Company wants more fans than employees, and this balance must be right from the start. Once your social media accounts are in place, encourage your own people to follow the company online. Make sure that the pages look attractive and immediately contain relevant and interesting content. This will motivate your staff to share these pages with others in their circle of family and friends. And this is how you get the social media ball rolling...

- Publicize your touchpoints. This sounds obvious but is often overlooked. Add Facebook and Twitter buttons to your website, in your e-mail signatures, in your out of-office replies, etc. Remind members of your target group as often as you can that you are now an online participator in conversations. Don't assume that they will come looking for you; you need to go looking for them – and let them know where you are! Facilitation is the key.

- Provide the necessary hardware and software. If you expect your staff to be active in social media, it would be pretty short-sighted not to give them the right tools to do the job. Make sure that they have good-quality computers and the correct software support. If, for example, Twitter is important for your company, make sure you install Tweetdeck. If you expect your people to check on Twitter during the weekend, provide them with smart phones and tablets. It will motivate them and make your customers happy.

The role of the social media policy

'If a company needs a policy to tell its staff what they can and cannot do online, then the HR policy of that company has failed,' says Professor Dr Rudy Moenaert. Hard words, perhaps, but nonetheless true. Too many companies have recruited too many employees who do not fit in with their culture. Or even worse: there is no clear culture. In these situations you will need a social media policy, because your HR policy has indeed failed. Having said this, most large companies see a need for a policy of some kind to give themselves, their managers and their staff a more comfortable feeling of security. We prefer to call this kind of policy a 'conversation guide'. This summarizes in a short, simple and positive manner what employees can do during online conversations.

The most important success indicator is the build up of knowledge within your company

How do you know when you have been successful in this phase? You have been successful when the average level of knowledge in your company with regard to conversations, social media and customer-orientation has clearly increased. Most companies communicate their successful online campaigns to underline the new direction that the company is taking. But it is only when they begin to publicize how many of their employees have followed conversation training that you know that they are starting to work structurally. In January 2011 Dell announced that 5,000 members of staff had already been trained. By mid-March this figure had risen to 8,000.[151] These figures confirm the company's successful structural approach.

KEY CONVERSATION POINTS

Possible conversation starters

- Before you begin, conduct an internal and external conversation audit. It is impossible to follow the right route if you don't know where you are starting from.

- A training trajectory is a fundamental requirement for success. Combine inspirational workshops with an extensive self-training programme. Create an internal knowledge platform and set up a panel of experts who can give more specific advice.

- Right from the very beginning, make alliances with people in the legal, IT and corporate communication departments. Agree a framework in which everyone feels comfortable.

- Lay the foundations for your successful presence on social media. Clear up your social media battlefield by terminating unnecessary online accounts. Encourage your own staff to be your first followers and fans. Provide your employees with the right hardware and software, so that they can participate in conversations actively and effectively.

- Your most important success indicator is the average level of your staff's knowledge in relation to conversations and customer-oriented thinking.

Questions you must ask yourself

- What training has your company given about conversations?
- What training trajectory is suitable for your company?
- Which departments should you invite to participate in the preparations for your change project?
- Which aspects of your HR policy are good and which need to be changed urgently?
- On which social media do you need to focus?

Further information

Take a look at: **www.patientslikeme.com**.

Chapter Fourteen
Step 2: Choosing and implementing your pilot projects

Three strategic projects of this phase

In this phase, you start with real conversation projects. The proof of the conversation philosophy is to be found in its practical implementation. This is the focus for this phase and we will concentrate on the following three projects:

- **Project 4: Appoint a conversation manager.** Somebody needs to take charge of your change process. This leadership role is the task of the conversation manager. Depending on the size of your company, this person may need to surround himself or herself with a conversation team. In this case, we usually speak of a centre of excellence. This team acts as a facilitator for other staff in the organization. Its members are in the picture with regard to all your pilot projects, share experiences and take the lead in all the most important matters. They serve as a guide, an internal consultant and a helping hand.

- **Project 5: Define pilot projects on the basis of impact and feasibility.** During your change process, the pilot projects are the single most important weapon to create a basis of support within the company for the conversation philosophy. These projects must show that the new philosophy has impact. It is therefore vital to choose projects that can deliver tangible results. At the same time, the projects will also accelerate the learning curve of the company as a whole.

- **Project 6: Create a listening culture.** To close the gap between your company and the market, it is essential to listen to conversations between consumers. A listening culture goes

FIGURE 14.1

much further than just passive listening. Active listening and the rapid implementation of what you learn are the essential elements of this new culture.

Project 4: Appoint a conversation manager

(For full details of the role of conversation manager, see Van Belleghem[152] and **www.theconversationmanager.com.**)

There is occasionally discussion about the content of the conversation manager's job. Some people see the role as an operational function, with the most important task being the direct handling of conversations with online consumers on behalf of the brand. To some extent this is true, but as a definition it is too narrow and too operational. The conversation manager helps the company to think in function of the conversation philosophy. He or she is the central project manager with the responsibility of turning the company into a Conversation Company.

In large companies, this job is too extensive to be tackled by a single person. For this reason the tasks are shared with a centre of excellence in a team led by the conversation manager. The core tasks of this team are: determining strategy, and planning; developing processes; and managing resources and knowledge.

Strategy and planning involves:

- writing the overall strategy vision relating to conversations;
- guiding the implementation of the pilot projects;
- assuming direct responsibility for flagship projects;

- actively managing and enhancing the internal consensus of support in favour of change.

Developing processes involves:

- compiling and updating the conversation guide;
- acting as a facilitator for the rewritten HR processes;
- drawing up the procedures for active listening (see later);
- drawing up the procedures for structural collaboration with the market (see later).

Managing resources and knowledge involves:

- assuming responsibility for the setting up of a training and knowledge programme in collaboration with HR;
- sharing lessons learnt internally with relevant teams;
- acting as an internal consultant for all relevant teams;
- assessing the means required in terms of time and money.

The goal of this central team is to increase efficiency and accelerate the learning curve within the company. This will lead to the more rapid standardization of processes. In addition, it will create clarity within your organization. If there is no central team, sooner or later discussions will arise about who is ultimately responsible for the change process. Similarly, in the beginning there is a chance that no one will be prepared to assume responsibility. Once the first good results have been achieved and the level of risk diminishes, suddenly everyone will want to play. These discussions about who are the true pioneers (and who are not) can cost your company a small fortune in both time and money. Avoid this problem by allocating the responsibility to a single team from the outset. Putting together this team is your single biggest investment in your transformation to a Conversation Company. To give you some idea: a recent study has shown that on average international companies invest USD 270,000 per year in their centres of excellence.[153] Having said this, our own studies have revealed that just 56 per cent of companies have appointed a single responsible person or team for their change project.[154] Clearly, there is still a lot of work to be done.

Some people think that the terms 'conversation manager' and 'community manager' are confusing. Yet the distinction is clear: the conversation manager assumes the strategic role outlined above; the community manager is responsible for the running of the different collaboration platforms with the market. Both are important, but their responsibilities are very different.

CASE STUDY Even eBay has a centre of excellence

Every company needs a facilitator for its internal process of change. Even eBay, one of the most successful social network sites in the world, has its own centre of excellence.[155] The members of the team are responsible for helping different departments, including HR, strategy and corporate communication, to reduce their unused conversation potential. They are also responsible for conversation strategy, for the integration of this strategy into all marketing planning and for actively listening to consumer conversations. They are not occupied full time with matters relating to the change process. They are drawn from other teams within the company and therefore have other responsibilities as well. The only full-time responsible officer is the conversation manager. The team comes together once a month to monitor and follow up its plans. Ali Croft and Jill Hunley, two members of the team, recommend that companies create such a team without delay, even if it is only small to begin with.[156]

You also need to accept that there is no such thing as a perfect solution. Once you start listening to conversations, the software, no matter how good, will never do exactly what you want. So start small, choose conversation parameters that are workable, and build up from there. Once things are up and running, you can optimize and expand.

Project 5: Define pilot projects on the basis of impact and feasibility

Laying good foundations is important, but the real proof of change rests in the implementation of your projects. In this phase you need to choose a number of projects to begin with. When considering your choice, it is advisable to pick more than one project. To create a consensus of support within the company, it is useful to have a number of strings to your bow. This allows people to discover the benefits of the new philosophy in different areas of your operations. A good project has a single person responsible for its implementation. This must be clear right from the start. If it is an important project, the conversation manager should assume this role. However, by involving as many other people as possible at an early stage, you can build up a groundswell of support for change. You don't want your team of experts or centre of excellence to find themselves isolated on an island within your company. An uninhabited island can be appealing – but not for long! For this reason it is advisable to involve different departments in your change projects. In the Conversation Company everyone must be made aware that they are jointly responsible for the optimization of conversation potential. So make sure that it is not just the staff in the commercial departments who are involved in your opening projects. HR and R&D are also interesting departments to engage in your pilot phase.

To make your final choice, use a feasibility/return matrix. This matrix is based (as the name implies) on two axes.

Feasibility is estimated on the basis of the likely degree of difficulty of the project (eg whether internal processes need to be amended before its implementation) and the known availability of resources (time and money).

Return needs careful consideration. Pilot projects must have an immediate impact. Determine clearly beforehand what your objectives and your expectations are. These might involve an increase in the number of conversations, the creation of sales leads or a direct increase in sales.

In the analysis of pilot projects, it is important to regard both dimensions as being equally valid. Research has shown that managers are inclined to attach more weight to feasibility. This focus is too narrow and can lead to a fall in productivity and impact. The strategic opportunity (return) is just as important as practical realization.[157]

By combining these two dimensions, you can create four quadrants:

- **Disappointment.** This quadrant is a trap you must avoid. A project may require little effort to implement with success (and has been chosen for that reason) but will yield next to nothing in terms of positive return. This results in disappointment at the conclusion of the project and hinders your further evolution as a Conversation Company.

FIGURE 14.2

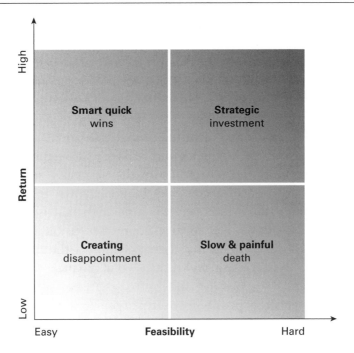

- **Slow and painful death.** This is another quadrant you should avoid like the plague! Some projects cost plenty of time, energy and money but produce zero return. This type of project can bring your change process to a grinding halt.

- **Smart quick wins.** Choose two or three projects to place in this quadrant. They cost little effort, but provide immediate and visible return. This will increase the support for change, and can even help to accelerate the pace of that change considerably.

- **Strategic investments.** Chose one or two projects that will fit this quadrant. They require greater initial investment and effort, but produce concrete added value in the long run. These projects will teach your team that conversation management requires a structural approach. You cannot change everything overnight with easy quick fixes. When the results of these projects become clear in due course, they will strengthen the resolve of your organization to become a true Conversation Company.

Companies that are fairly advanced in terms of conversation thinking recommend starting a fan community as one of the projects in this phase.[158] This external project has the advantage of helping to combine a number of your other internal change projects. Via a fan community you can listen to an important part of your target group. In addition, you are developing a first form of structural collaboration with your customers, while simultaneously enhancing your flexibility and speed of response. Your fans will be ready to help and feedback will be quick and plentiful: of that you can be sure.

A second project recommendation relates to investment in your own media. In addition to setting up the necessary social media accounts, the creation of a company blog can often result in considerable added value. Moreover, it is a medium that is fully under your control. It allows you to give your own vision with regard to anything and everything that is happening in the market. And if your blog is a success, it will reduce your reliance on expensive classic media.

A third interesting possibility is to organize a product launch focused primarily on the conversation philosophy. Choose a product with clear conversation potential, plan on that basis and exploit the opportunities that are created.

All three of these suggestions would, if successfully implemented, score high on the return dimension. All three would have an immediate impact on your company. All three have longer-term strategic implications. The efforts required will be considerable, but so will be the gains. 'He who dares, wins.'

CASE STUDY Yelo product launch

In December 2010 Telenet, a major player in the Belgian telecom sector, launched a new service: Yelo. Yelo makes it possible to watch television on your iPhone or iPad, wherever there is a Telenet internet connection in the vicinity. You simply log in via your customer details and can then follow the entire programme schedule, just as if you were sitting at home in your armchair. In view of the innovative nature of this new service, Telenet was keen to be the first to launch it. However, at the beginning of December the project was not 100 per cent ready.

In an interview in 2011, the Telenet CEO, Duco Sickinghe, said that he believes strongly in the conversation philosophy. He wants to transform his organization into a true Conversation Company. In this respect he saw the launching of Yelo as an opportunity – and as a test case. And so he took a brave decision: to launch an unfinished product onto the market. He reasoned that the basic functionality of the product was good, so that the customer could use it as intended.

During the launch period every effort was made to utilize every ounce of conversation potential. The press conference was broadcast live on the net. Interested customers – including Vincent Van Quickenborne, the Minister for ITC and the Economy – could pose questions direct to Duco online via Twitter. Since Van Quickenborne has 20,000 followers, this immediately gave a huge boost to the visibility of Yelo. Telenet also invited influential bloggers in the sector to be the first to try out the new product. In addition, Telenet customers had a similar opportunity to use the new service on a free trial basis and were asked to provide feedback about the new service. Their comments were used to further refine the product during its finishing phase.

Alongside this public communication, Telenet also set up a research community.[159] In this community, 100 enthusiastic fans worked structurally at the further refinement of Yelo. Together they provided between 35 and 40 suggestions for the possible improvement of the product, 50 per cent of which were adopted during the first update.

By using this major pilot project as an example, Telenet immediately underlined the value of several important aspects of the Conversation Company: structural collaboration, building a listening culture and improving online reach.

CASE STUDY ING launches webcare

(Based on an interview in 2011 with Erik Van Roekel, Senior Social Media Manager at ING, and Harold Reusken, Senior Press Officer at ING.)

The first important conversation project undertaken by ING in the Netherlands was the development of a webcare strategy. Via webcare customers can be helped in real time through social media. In particular, customers with complaints or problems can be assisted with a minimum of delay. This quickly changed many negative conversations about ING into positive ones. In other words, there was a clear short-term return for the company.

Members of the management team were convinced to undertake this project by Erik Van Roekel, the Senior Social Media Manager, and Harold Reusken, the Senior Press Officer, who had already conducted an 'unofficial' experiment to help a complaining blogger. The first reactions were positive and so helped to lower the threshold for the senior management team. Moreover, in the aftermath of the 2008 financial crisis ING had reformulated its mission statement – 'the customer is central' – in much stronger terms. The webcare project was a perfect way to put this wish into everyday practice. It was also a very concrete project with which to start the change process – which is never a bad thing. This meant that everyone understood the objectives and was aware of the expectations. The relevance for ING was obvious. The return was assessed on the basis of the evolution of the net promoter score, an indicator that is used throughout the company.

Once the webcare scheme was up and running, the positive reactions quickly began to follow. Even if it was not always possible to solve all the problems, the customers were pleased that they had been given a chance to be heard. The blogging social media experts also responded favourably to the initiative. About 100 problem cases were solved each month and 43 per cent of the conversations took place on Twitter. The project was positively evaluated by the ING board and is now a permanent element within the wider ING service strategy. Just as importantly, it helped to change the thinking of many ING employees in favour of further organizational change in the direction of conversation management, which is now scheduled for the period 2011–12.

Project 6: Create a listening culture

Right from the very first days of social media, there has been much hype about 'listening to the customer'. Thanks to social media, conversations between customers are now transparent and traceable. Companies have rediscovered the existence of mouth-to-mouth advertising. In recent years, 70 per cent of companies in the UK and the United States have started to monitor conversations.[160] However, only half of these companies listen in a structural manner; mostly their efforts are ad hoc. In 80 per cent of listening companies, the listening is confined to just a part of the organization.[161]

A listening culture means that on the one hand the company listens to the market and on the other hand adjusts its decision-making processes to reflect what it hears. It is a combination of observation and action. If your company has a listening culture you monitor consumer conversations. This gives you answers to questions you never even knew you had. You systematically learn more about the consumer. You begin to sense what is being said about your company and your brand in the market place. These insights become increasingly more relevant. You use them to improve the quality of your products and services. You listen to the customers and thank them for their input. You take action based on what they have said and let them know what you have done.

The following elements are used to give shape and form to a listening culture:

- **Listening software.** The Conversation Company possesses the right software which will allow it to listen to customer feedback in real time. This software is capable of analysing the conversations on specialized forums, Facebook, Twitter and other social media sites.

- **Call-to-action reports.** The listening team must pass on insights gleaned from conversations on a regular basis to the rest of the company. These reports give details of the conversation status and a list of concrete points for action. A person responsible for implementation is allocated to each action point. Our interviews taught us that passive reports with lists of figures have insufficient impact. If each department can be told to perform specific tasks which will result in specific benefits, the relevance levels increase significantly.

- **Your own listening community.** This is where the first moves towards structural collaboration take place. In addition to listening to market conversations, the Conversation Company builds up its own research community from among its own fans and followers. These communities are a continuous digital version of the traditional focus group. The communities usually consist of between 50 and 150 fans who are committed to helping your brand. You should discuss all your ideas with these people. The future of your company will not be created, but co-created. This community will provide you with inspirational ideas about the daily lives and behaviour of the members of your target group.

- **Setting and implementing objectives.** You only become a truly active listener when you start setting your own objectives. How many consumer ideas do you want to explore further? What time frame will you allow before taking action? How will you link this action back to the market? For what type of decisions will you give weight to the observations gathered during your listening?

CASE STUDY Cisco builds its listening culture step by step

(Based on an interview in 2011 with Lasandra Brill of Cisco.)

The listening culture of Cisco has evolved strongly in recent years. Lasandra Brill concludes that the company has gone through various phases to reach this position. During the first phase conversations were listened to only sporadically. If there was a specific reason, Cisco would decide to start conversations with a limited number of individuals. The second phase was more experimental. Use was made of various free applications to gain insights into conversations. The third phase saw the first efforts to create a broad basis of support for a conversation-based philosophy. People became more aware of the conversations taking place about the brand, and their importance. The data became richer and more relevant. This naturally led to the question: 'what are we going to do with all this information?' In the fourth phase the listening finally began to have an impact. More departments started listening to conversations in real time. Customers' problems were tackled and solved. The company's processes in R&D and commercial departments were attuned to market input. In 2011, Cisco now finds itself in the fifth phase, the most aspirational phase, the phase in which decisions, budgets and investments all reflect feedback from outside the company.[162]

The most important success indicator is the impact of the pilot projects

In this phase, the most important parameter for measuring success is the feedback that you receive about your pilot projects. What is the perception of the market about your first steps in conversation? The reactions of your customers are extremely important. Perhaps your activities have been noticed by bloggers and journalists. If so, this is a positive signal. Moreover, you have been provided with plenty of free information which can be of great value in your further development towards a Conversation Company. Remember, however, that internal perception is just as crucial as external perception. The reactions of your colleagues and management will determine the speed at which the following phases of change will be implemented. In addition to this qualitative feedback, the objective facts are also essential if you want to evaluate your efforts meaningfully. Compare the actual results with the objectives you set beforehand. This will show you exactly where you stand. After five or so pilot projects, you will have acquired a mass of additional knowledge and experience. You will begin to get a feeling for what works and what doesn't. Once you have gained sufficient confidence, based on the good results of these pilot schemes, the next step is to integrate your conversation strategy into every aspect of your company (step 3).

Once the first two phases have been completed, your company has already undergone a significant evolution. Your company culture is more sharply focused. Your plans to live out your company values in your daily operations are complete. Your HR procedures have been refined to motivate and facilitate your staff. Your social media are both present and professional. You have appointed a conversation manager. You have processes in place to listen actively to consumers. And you have initiated and successfully completed a number of pilot projects which have had an immediate impact on your organization. You have achieved much and can be rightly proud of what you have done. But don't kid yourself: the hardest part is still to come!

KEY CONVERSATION POINTS

Possible conversation starters

- Appoint a conversation manager at an early stage in your change process. He or she will facilitate your transformation into a Conversation Company.

- The tasks of a conversation manager are to determine strategy and planning, to develop processes and to manage resources (time and money).

- Choose a limited number of pilot projects. Make sure that these are all projects which will have an immediate impact on your organization. A combination of quick wins and strategic long-term gains is ideal. Make well-considered decisions, based on the feasibility/return matrix.

- A listening culture goes much further than mere listening. Every member of staff must gain insights into the conclusions of the conversations with the market. Listening must become active listening. Implement any relevant findings as quickly as possible.

- Your most important parameter for success is the feedback you receive about your pilot projects. How did the market react? What do your staff think? What were the objective results?

Questions you must ask yourself

- Would one of your present employees make a good conversation manager?
- Do you need a conversation team or can a single person manage the task? Who will take part in your centre of excellence?
- What quick wins can you implement tomorrow?
- Does your organization listen? If so, is your listening active or passive? How can the processing and communication of conversation insights be improved?

Further information

Use these links for interesting information on:

- the eBay centre of excellence: **www.slideshare.net/ influencepeople/ali-croft-monitoring-social-media-ebay**
- the listening culture at Cisco: **http://blogs.cisco.com/socialmedia/ social-media-listening-and-engagement-journey/#more-21405**.

Chapter Fifteen
Step 3: The way to full integration and the lever effect

Four strategic projects of this phase

This is the phase in which major structural change takes place. It is also the phase in which the conversation lever will begin to take effect. All your efforts and investments will ensure a greater impact on all your activities. To integrate the conversation philosophy fully into the workings of your organization, you will first need to complete four challenging projects:

- **Project 7: Make the four Cs fully operational.** The four Cs must be used structurally in the management of your company. As a result of the steps you have already taken, customer experience and conversations will already have been mobilized. In this phase you will work further at content management and will build up the necessary communities to activate structural collaboration with the market.

- **Project 8: Search consciously for the lever effect.** You have invested heavily in your culture, in your people and in many organizational changes. You must search consciously for a lever effect, so that all remaining unused conversation potential in your company will be effectively exploited.

- **Project 9: Implement agile management.** If you involve consumers in your activities, they expect to see quick results. In this phase you will need to shorten the implementation time of all your processes. This includes the flexibility to identify and respond to new trends with a minimum of delay. Developing this speed and flexibility will be the last and

FIGURE 15.1

1. THE BUILD-UP OF KNOWLEDGE

2. PILOT PROJECTS

3. INTEGRATION AND THE LEVER EFFECT

possibly greatest challenge on your way to becoming a Conversation Company.

- **Project 10: Work with new success indicators.** To change the behaviour of your company, it is necessary to change its objectives. The personal objectives of staff have already been adjusted (see Chapter 13). To integrate the conversation philosophy completely into your daily activities at every level of your organization, you will need to work with new success indicators, both for individual departments and for the company as a whole.

Project 7: Make the four Cs fully operational

In the second part of the book we discussed the four Cs in some detail. In this phase you must make them fully operational throughout the company.

Your investments in your culture and the changes made to your HR policy will already have provided an improved customer experience policy. Customer experience is now more central to the manner in which you recruit staff and organize their training. The stronger culture provides a more consistent level of customer experience. This latter step is one of your most important measures to better exploit unused conversation potential.

By now, you also manage your conversations both proactively and reactively. Your central listening team and the listening culture you have built up ensure that your company now observes, facilitates and participates in conversations online. In addition to the reactive management of these conversations, your content strategy stimulates positive conversation starters. Your company provides daily content updates and communicates non-stop, 24/7.

In this final phase you must now create an atmosphere of collaboration. In theory, decisions will no longer be taken without the prior consultation of your staff (internal decisions) and the market (external decisions). You must also use this phase to build up the necessary internal and external communities that will allow you to forge true structural collaboration (assuming that this has not already been done during your pilot projects). Work with a combination of large-open and small-closed communities.

The knowledge you have acquired in the first two phases will now stand you in good stead. For example, your internal audits may have helped you to find digital superstars and brand ambassadors. These people will be vital in helping you to spread your content and establish a far-reaching structural partnership with the market.

Project 8: Search consciously for the lever effect

As a result of your previously implemented internal change projects, you will already have achieved much. Your staff have been properly trained. Your social media reach has been expanded. You have developed communities of loyal fans with whom you work closely. These are all examples of conversation assets for your company. The conversation lever will now allow you to use these assets to the full.

Your conversation manager has the task of facilitating the use of this lever for every member of staff. You will need a conversation plan for every commercial activity. Teach your employees how to use this lever when they are launching a new product, or when you change your company logo, or break bad news, or conclude a take-over, or recruit new staff, or introduce a new CEO... You must make it second nature to manage your conversations as well as possible in every situation.

The conversation lever is applied by the consistent practical implementation of the four Cs in every action undertaken by your company. In the Introduction we described how these four pillars often result in unused conversation potential in many companies. Now you are going to use those same four pillars to create a conversation lever, so that in your company, at least, unused conversation potential will be a thing of the past.

Customer experience: how can we optimize the experience of our actions?

- Foresee online channels to extend the scope and impact of offline events.
- Foresee offline conversation starters.
- Involve the right touchpoints and make them all conversation-worthy.
- Train relevant staff to provide only top experiences.

Conversation: what conversations do we need to conduct to create even more conversations?

- Be ready to observe the reactions to particular actions and campaigns.
- Follow relevant conversations in advance, to see if you may need to intervene.
- Prepare thorough answers for questions you are expecting.

Content: what additional content can we create to optimize conversations?

- Foresee formal content that others can share.
- Train people in the making of informal content.
- Foresee a content plan for the entire duration of any activity.
- Foresee a content 'exclusive' for loyal customers.

Collaboration: which people are good conversation sources and are willing to help?

- Test your ideas beforehand with your community.
- Look for customers who can help you.
- Look for staff who can help you.
- Look for other opinion makers who can help you.
- Determine the role of the CEO.
- Appoint someone who is responsible for listening to feedback and develop procedures to implement the lessons of this first feedback immediately.
- Keep all internal networks fully informed of your plans.

CASE STUDY
Cisco uses the conversation lever for a product launch

(Based on an interview in 2011 with Lasandra Brill of Cisco.)

Cisco possesses some very important conversation assets: millions of fans on Twitter, hundreds of blogging employees, a conversation-minded management, a centre of excellence and various customer communities.

Since 2008 the company has been using these assets to support its product launches. For example, each product launch is broadcast live on the web, which produces a reach for these events which is 90 times greater than would otherwise be the case. In addition, the company invests in relevant content, writing for a number of trendsetting and informative blogs. For its launches, this information is shared by more than 1,000 other blogs. Cisco also makes attractive and amusing films for YouTube, which regularly pass the 1 million viewers mark. Impressive? It becomes even more impressive when you consider the cost of achieving this reach, which is just one sixth of what it used to be with traditional marketing methods (thanks largely to lower travel costs and a lower media budget, both the result of direct online transmission).

Achieving greater impact with less expense is the ultimate purpose of the conversation lever. To achieve this, Cisco uses the four Cs to maximum effect:

- **Customer service.** The product presentation is broadcast live and thereby becomes a conversation-worthy touchpoint.
- **Conversation.** During the launch, feedback is monitored and replies given, if necessary. Cisco participates actively in online conversations about the launch.
- **Content.** Cisco's new products are attractively presented in full detail. Interesting articles and quality video images are prepared and released.
- **Collaboration.** The product team and the conversation manager facilitate and manage everything.

  Colleagues and managers tweet, blog and send Facebook messages about the launch to everyone in their social media networks. Customers are involved with the launch, so that engagement is enhanced. This results in numerous additional conversations. Opinion makers find the content interesting and share it with others.

CASE STUDY 'Star-player' at Heineken

(Based on a presentation by Heineken at the IAB Europe Conference, 2011.)

For many years Heineken has been one of the main sponsors of the Champions League. As you might expect, this is not cheap. In view of the high level of investment, Heineken decided to try and create an additional and highly conversation-worthy touchpoint. This was the Heineken Star-player. Star-player is a mobile application that offers football fans a number of extra interactive possibilities during the Champions League matches. For example, the users can try and guess when the first goal will be scored or can choose the 'man of the match'. The application works in real time and is linked to each game. In just a few months Star-player has attracted thousands of users. This means that while they are watching the game on television, the fans are also linked for a full 90 minutes to the Heineken brand.

Project 9: Implement agile management

The term 'agile management' describes the ability of a company to adjust quickly to changing circumstances. In the UK and the United States, 71 per cent of managers see this as a priority for their organization.[163] Agile management is often confused with speed. Responding quickly to blog posts and tweets is not enough to be considered as an agile company. Of course, that is part of the matter, but it is the easy part. The difficult part is making your company sufficiently flexible so that it can react quickly in the right manner to the right trends. This also means that it is necessary to shorten the length of your production processes. A customer who sends you what he or she regards as valuable information wants more than just 'thank you for your feedback tweet, we'll see what we can do'. This customer wants to see your product amended – and wants to see it amended in six weeks, not six months. No matter how large your organization is, you need to try and develop the mentality of a small company. Ekaterina Walter, Social Media Strategist at Intel, sees this as the biggest challenge facing the company. 'Intel made major efforts to integrate conversational thinking into its activities. The hardest aspect was to make the company fast and flexible. Intel is a super-tanker, but in future we will need to manoeuvre like a speedboat. Our marketing processes need to halve their implementation time if we want to follow the pace set by the market.'

An agile company makes a quarterly, monthly, weekly or even a daily planning. The first step to becoming agile is to move away from traditional year planning. If you only do a planning and budgetary exercise once each year, you have little option but to stick to it, come what may. But the future is now changing so rapidly that yearly planning makes your company sluggish. Real-time feedback requires real-time action – and for this you need plenty of flexibility. By planning your budget and your operations on a quarterly basis, you automatically become more flexible.

In particular, an agile company needs to have a marketing budget that is 100 per cent flexible. In my book *The Conversation Manager*[164] I recommended that 20 per cent of the marketing budget should be kept flexible. I now realize that this is nowhere near enough. Besides, this buffer was often the first thing to be scrapped when it became necessary to make savings. As a result, the desired objective – flexibility – was never achieved. Hence my more radical suggestion in this present book: make your marketing budget completely flexible! As a company, you have a mission and a vision, linked to specific plans. You need to make budgetary estimates to realize these plans. But you can leave the concrete filling in of these estimates until the moment is ripe.

By investing in micro-trends, you can ensure that you never react too late to a new trend. The Conversation Company is constantly prepared to try out new things: new media, new technology, new websites... Even if a new trend does not immediately seem to be a good match for your culture, there is still no harm in finding out how it works. By keeping your eye on the ball and taking the latest micro-trends seriously, you can be sure that you do not miss out on any important evolutions. Your centre of excellence is the ideal place to test these trends. This does not mean, of course, that you need to adjust your processes every time a bright new idea comes along. The most important thing is to learn, experiment and see which way the wind is blowing.

Similarly, agile does not imply that you need to decide everything on gut-feeling. On the contrary, an agile company is highly analytical. During its testing of new trends, the Conversation Company will measure as many relevant parameters as possible in great detail.

Moreover, this will immediately be linked to an assessment of the likely impact of the trend, product, medium, etc. Over a longer period, this will allow you to a make a valid and well-founded comparison of all these innovations, to see which of them (if any) may really be of use to your organization.

Finally, an agile company has no problems with 'bad meeting' mentality. In the United States, there is something like 11 million meetings per day. That is equivalent to 3 billion each year![165] Very many of these meetings are inefficient and ineffective. We have all sat through seemingly pointless meetings, asking ourselves 'what on earth am I doing here?' – meetings with no agenda, no decisions and no follow-up. And if you do actually decide something, a new meeting is necessary before you can decide something else. Everyone 'important' needs to be consulted. If you add to this holidays, sickness and the intervention of other 'priorities', important decisions can sometimes be delayed for weeks, if not months. In the intervening period, your company may be missing dozens of new opportunities. Thanks to its network structure and its access to its own communities of customers, the Conversation Company can leave this meeting mentality far behind.

CASE STUDY
Google: best example of an agile company

Google sees becoming more agile as it biggest challenge.[166] According to CEO Larry Page, Google's chief rivals – Facebook and Groupon – are much more adaptive and flexible. Even so, notwithstanding its giant size Google still manages to retain a high degree of flexibility. This is supported by the willingness of its culture to accept failure (see earlier). Agile marketing can only succeed if 'open' is one of your core cultural values. Google is continuously working in a 'beta' environment. This means that staff are encouraged to spend 20 per cent of their time thinking up innovative new ideas. When they are nearly ready, these ideas are launched onto the market. Some succeed (like Google Earth); others fail (like Google Wave). But this risk of being first is always worth taking. By structurally investing part of its time in micro-trends, the company is always ready to jump on the next big trend when it arrives.

CASE STUDY

Atlassian increases its efficiency via agile management

(See also Pink, 2009, 2010.)[167]

Atlassian is an Australian company that employs about 200 staff. Some time ago, members of the management team concluded that they were not progressing quickly enough in terms of innovation and internal IT projects. To turn things around, they decided to conduct a radical experiment. Every quarter, they gave their IT team a free day. During this day, the team members were asked to work at a solution for a concrete problem. They were free to choose the problem themselves. The only condition was that within 24 hours they must be ready to present their proposals to the rest of the company. The results were amazing. The amount of work produced in a single day was phenomenal and each time yielded a crop of innovative new ideas which helped to remove several long-standing problems faced by the company.

Project 10: Work with new success indicators

Objectives determine people's behaviour. In the period leading up to an Olympic Games, athletes have just one objective: to achieve the Olympic minimum. Give people an objective, and they will work systematically towards it. To succeed in the challenge of becoming a Conversation Company, a company needs its employees to change their behaviour. This means that your organization will need a new set of success indicators. These indicators go further than measuring social media reach or the number of new leads, which are two of the most frequently-used criteria.[168] But these are no longer sufficient to give a total view of the impact created by your change process.

The Conversation Company makes use of the following indicators at company level:

- **Financial returns.** The evolution in turnover and profit is the most important parameter. By following this evolution during and after the change it will become clear what financial effects have resulted from your more efficient exploitation of your conversation potential.

- **Savings.** When the number of conversations increases, it becomes less necessary to pay for expensive advertising. This will allow you to slash your budget for traditional marketing. Your communities will also help you to conduct market research in a cheaper and more efficient manner. Farming out a number of your management tasks to your customers will also make you more cost-effective as a company.

- **New customers.** Conversations will lead to an increase in the number of new customers. You should measure the evolutions in this total as the number of conversations gradually swells.

- **The number of extremely satisfied customers.** Do not check your customer-friendliness surveys to see what your average score is; check to see how often you score 10 out of 10. Extremely satisfied customers are a conversation goldmine. By only looking at the maximum scores, you force your company to adopt an extreme approach towards its conversational thinking.

- **The number of extremely satisfied employees.** The same principle outlined in the last point applies for your staff. Your most satisfied members of staff are your most valuable ambassadors. Here, too, you must focus on extremes to secure the right behaviour.

- **Conversations.** The Conversation Company wants to eliminate unused conversation potential. To follow this evolution, you must measure the number of conversations, the sentiments contained in those conversations, the impact of those conversations and the extent of your reach on social media.

- **Knowledge and integration of conversation thinking.** Keep count of the number of employees you have trained in the new way of thinking. Monitor the percentage of business plans where the conversation philosophy is respected and integrated.

Financial success indicators are self evident. The real flywheel effect is created by the positive spiral that develops between super-satisfied customers and super-satisfied staff. If the staff are happy, the customers sense this – and happiness is infectious. This positive experience will lead to new positive conversations, in which more staff and customers will be involved. Activating the flywheel effect costs time and effort – but it is worth both. The change trajectories in your transformation process can lend a helping hand in this respect. Once the flywheel is turning, it requires little further exertion to keep it going. And this is when you will really start to see the influence on your financial parameters.

Your change process never comes to an end

Once you have progressed through the three steps of change – building up knowledge; implementing pilot projects; and achieving full integration and leverage – your company will possess the right assets and the right mentality to behave as a fully fledged Conversation Company.

As a reminder, these are the 10 projects that your company must implement to achieve this transformation:

- Project 1: Build up the required levels of knowledge
- Project 2: Don't postpone the difficult conversations
- Project 3: Provide the right infrastructure
- Project 4: Appoint a conversation manager
- Project 5: Define pilot projects on the basis of impact and feasibility
- Project 6: Create a listening culture
- Project 7: Make the four Cs fully operational
- Project 8: Search consciously for the lever effect
- Project 9: Implement agile management
- Project 10: Work with new success indicators.

The change projects and the management of the four Cs are part of a never-ending process. These are all matters at which you will need to work ceaselessly, day after day, month after month, year after year. The Conversation Company is never finished. The world continues to change – and you must change with it.

This is it...

You've made it! You have finally arrived at the end of this book. Congratulations!

Now the real work can begin: the building of your own Conversation Company. I wish you every success! The purpose of this book is to offer you a new business philosophy and to suggest the tools that will be necessary to implement that philosophy. I hope that I have succeeded in that task and I look forward to seeing the first results of your efforts.

I adore feedback and conversations. Please feel free to let me know what you think of the book and where you do not agree with it. I would also love to hear about your practical experiences. On Twitter you can find me at **@Steven_InSites**. Or you can e-mail **Steven@InSites.eu**. If you would like to keep in touch with new examples and ideas, you can surf to my blog: **www.theconversationmanager.com**.

PS – You have 48 hours

I hope that this book will have changed your thinking, but what I really want is to change your behaviour. People who know me will tell you that I always end a story by setting a task and a deadline. If you have been inspired and gained insights while reading this book, I have an important mission for you: do something with your plans within the next 48 hours. If you don't – and I speak from experience – there is a good chance that you will do nothing at all. If you have good intentions (and I am sure that you do), link them immediately to positive action. People who announce their '48-hour to dos' on Twitter (#conversationcompany) will get a special mention in our blog. And if what you propose is really exceptional... well, you'll see.

Just 47 hours and 59 minutes to go: you'd better get started! #goodluck.

KEY CONVERSATION POINTS

Possible conversation starters

- To make the four Cs fully operational, during this final phase you must develop structural collaboration and a content strategy.

- You must actively manage the conversation lever. You have built up numerous conversation assets and you must now apply these to every activity in your company. This will allow you to extract greater added value from everything you do.

- The conversations must make use of the four Cs.

- The conversation manager facilitates the use of the conversation lever throughout the company.

- The Conversation Company has the ability to adjust quickly to the market. The development of flexibility and adaptability is the last step in your change transformation.

- Use new success indicators that will allow you to monitor the evolution of the Conversation Company.

The change process never ends. You must continuously manage the Conversation Company on the basis of the four key pillars: customer experience, content, collaboration and conversations.

Questions you must ask yourself

- Does your company already have a community? Can you define a project to create a new community?

- What content is your company sharing today? How frequently do you share new content? What topics do you focus on? Which people can help you to prepare content?

- Does your company work with an annual plan? How rigid is your planning in general?

- Do you invest in micro-trends?

- Do you have a meeting culture?

- What percentage of your decisions are taken in collaboration with your staff and your customers?

- Does every department believe in the conversation philosophy? Are you already in a position to integrate this philosophy fully throughout the company?

- Which conversation success indicators are you already using? Which indicators can you introduce immediately? What is the current state of your conversation assets? Which assets are well developed and which ones are lagging behind?

- How and when are you going to start your change process?

Further information

Use these links for further interesting information on:

- Cisco using the conversation lever for a product launch: **www.socialmediaexaminer.com/cisco-social-media-product-launch**;

- the Heineken Star-player: **http://youtube.com/watch?v=XP5yySEZub8.**

Epilogue

Children show the way

Congratulations! You made it to the end of this book. I hope it has given you some inspiration. Perhaps you are already dreaming of a fascinating change process in your own company? Or perhaps you are a little uncertain, worried even, at the prospect of this long and uncertain journey? To remove these uncertainties, I have a last important tip for you: learn from children!

As I write these words, my son Siebe is just two years old. It is a fantastic age. He is starting to talk, starting to move around all by himself, scuttling here, there and everywhere.

There is nothing I like more than to simply sit and watch him at play, trying out something new or just messing about with his toy cars.

As I sit and observe him, I am struck by how much we adults could learn from the attitude and behaviour of this tiny young man, and so many others like him. There are four things in particular that make me really jealous. Four things that can also help you to realize your transformation into a Conversation Company.

First, children of this age always tell the truth, the whole truth and nothing but the truth. At congresses and seminars we all talk about the importance of openness and transparency, but – if we are really honest – we have to admit that we still have a long way to go before this becomes a reality. Many companies find it hard to let go of the need to control. Do you remember the example of Softcat, where the staff decide the level of the boss's wages? I can't see that happening everywhere – not yet, at least.

Something else that children are good at – much better than we grown-ups – is living in the present. If something goes wrong, they feel bad at the time; but five minutes later they have forgotten all about it! The smallest possible positive distraction immediately restores their positive feeling. Adults have lost that ability. In some companies, people carry a whole rucksack of bad experiences around with them, with corresponding cynicism and sarcasm as a result. And the longer you carry the rucksack, the heavier it becomes.

The third aspect is the desire to try out something new every day. As I have written elsewhere, I am a big fan of the saying: 'Your mind is like a parachute: to make it work properly, you have to open it first.' Children have no problem with this open-minded approach; many managers do. Stepping out of your comfort zone, taking a risk with something new: this is not something that many people will undertake lightly! You can see this easily enough: just compare your marketing plan for 2011 with your plan for 2010. In most cases, 90 per cent of the content will be exactly the same. 'We did it last year, so why shouldn't we do it this year?' Routine is the enemy of change. And change requires a lot more energy than routine.

The fourth thing I so admire about my two-year-old son is his determination. If he tries something new and it doesn't work, there will be an initial moment or two of frustration, but this is immediately followed by a second attempt – and, if necessary, a third, fourth and fifth attempt. In short, he keeps on trying until he succeeds. The best example of this is the transition from crawling to walking. It cost him weeks of effort (as it does every child), but he got there in the end. The pride in his eyes (true, mixed with a little fear) spoke volumes. This is something else we grown-ups have lost: the ability to carry on when it costs us an extra effort. If we try something new and it fails, we stop after the first attempt (or the second attempt at most). We 'delegate' it, or outplace it, or say that it is not suitable for our company.

In the rapidly changing times in which we live, it would be useful for all of us if we occasionally reasoned more like a child. The ability to adjust and to persevere are two of the most important qualities of the successful entrepreneur and manager of the future. And you will find it easier to adapt to constantly changing circumstances if you have the courage to take a leaf out of a child's book. So why not give it a try?

Steven Van Belleghem

Notes

1   InSites Consulting (2010) 'Stop the paradox' study [Online: accessed 8 December 2011] **www.slideshare.net/stevenvanbelleghem/presentations**

2   Society of Digital Agencies (2010) '2010 Digital Marketing Outlook' [Online: accessed 8 December 2011] **http://societyofdigitalagencies.org/2011/02/2011-digital-marketing-outlook-released/**

3   InSites Consulting (2011) 'Social media integration' study [Online: accessed 8 December 2011] **www.slideshare.net/stevenvanbelleghem/stop-the-paradox**

4   InSites Consulting (2010) 'Stop the paradox' study [Online: accessed 8 December 2011] **www.slideshare.net/stevenvanbelleghem/presentations**

5   Keller, E (2007) Opening speech, Womma Summit

6   InSites Consulting (2011) 'Social media around the world' study [Online: accessed 8 December 2011] **www.slideshare.net/InSitesConsulting/social-media-around-the-world-2011-9537752**

7   InSites Consulting (2009) 'ConAir' study

8   Keller Fay Group and Google (2011) 'Word of mouth and search' study [Online: accessed 12 December 2011] **www.kellerfay.com/news-events/googlekeller-fay-research-word-of-mouth-and-the-internet/**

9   Verhaeghe, A and Schillewaert, N (2007) 'A new way of measuring buzz', Esomar W3 Conference, InSites Consulting

10 Richins, M (1983) 'Negative word-of-mouth by dissatisfied consumers: a pilot study', *Journal of Marketing*, **47** (1), pp 68–78.
    Mahajan, V, Muller, E and Kerin, R (1984) 'Introduction strategy for new products with positive and negative word-of-mouth', *Management Science*, **30** (12), pp 1389–404
    Herr, P, Kardes, F and Kim, J (1991) 'Effects of word-of-mouth and product-attribute information on persuasion: an accessibility-diagnosticity perspective', *Journal of Consumer Research*, **17** (4), pp 454–62

11 InSites Consulting (2010) 'Stop the paradox' study [Online: accessed 8 December 2011] **www.slideshare.net/stevenvanbelleghem/presentations**

12 *Contagious Magazine* (2010) 'A marathon of personal addresses from Isaiah makes the web smell a little spicier' [Online: accessed 9 December 2011] **www.contagiousmagazine.com/2010/07/old_spice_1.php**

13 Symphony IRA data (2010) **www.symphonyIRI.co.uk**

14 *Advertising Age* (2010) 'Old Spice fades into history' [Online: accessed 9 December 2011] **http://adage.com/article/viral-video-charts/digital-megan-fox-boots-isaiah-mustafa-viral-chart/146030/**

15 Hendricks, S (2011) 'Het enorme succes van #TVoh op twitter', ('The enormous success of #tvoh on Twitter'), *Marketing Facts* [Online: accessed 9 December 2011] **www.marketingfacts.nl/ berichten/20110122_het_enorme_succes_van_tvoh_op_twitter/**

16 Drell, L (2011) 'The Voice: how a TV show became a 24/7 social media conversation', *Mashable* [Online: accessed 8 December 2011] **http://mashable.com/2011/06/15/the-voice-social-media-nbc/**

17 InSites Consulting (2011) 'What people share' study

18 InSites Consulting (2011) 'Social media around the world' study [Online: accessed 8 December 2011] **www.slideshare.net/InSitesConsulting/ social-media-around-the-world-2011-9537752**

19 IAB Conference Europe (2011) 'How Diageo's digital strategy started' [Online: accessed 8 December 2011] **www.slideshare.net/ stevenvanbelleghem/how-diageos-digital-strategy-started**

20 InSites Consulting (2011) 'Social media around the world' study [Online: accessed 8 December 2011] **www.slideshare.net/ InSitesConsulting/social-media-around-the-world-2011-9537752**

21 InSites Consulting (2011) 'Social media around the world' study [Online: accessed 8 December 2011] **www.slideshare.net/ InSitesConsulting/social-media-around-the-world-2011-9537752**

22 *Customer Think* (2008), 'HP demo days turn employees into ambassadors' [Online: accessed 8 December 2011] **www.customerthink.com/article/ hp_demo_days_employees_brand_ambassadors**

23 Glanz, B (2009) 'The story of Johnnie the Bagger' [Online: accessed 8 December 2011] **www.barbaraglanz.com/action/johnny-story-vimeo.html**

24 InSites Consulting (2010) 'Stop the paradox' study [Online: accessed 8 December 2011] **www.slideshare.net/stevenvanbelleghem/presentations**

25 InSites Consulting (2011) 'What people share' study

26 InSites Consulting (2011) 'What people share' study

27 InSites Consulting (2011) 'Social media integration' study [Online: accessed 8 December 2011] **www.slideshare.net/ stevenvanbelleghem/stop-the-paradox**

28 InSites Consulting (2011) 'What people share' study

29 InSites Consulting (2010) 'Stop the paradox' study [Online: accessed 8 December 2011] **www.slideshare.net/stevenvanbelleghem/ presentations**

30 Ariely, D (2008) *Predictably Irrational: The hidden forces that shape our decisions*, New York, HarperCollins

31 McCracken, G (2009) *Chief Culture Officer: How to create a living, breathing corporation*, New York, Basic Books

32 Jenkins, H (2006) *Fans, Bloggers and Gamers: Media consumers in a digital age*, New York University Press

33 Hinssen, P (2011) *Digitaal is het nieuwe normaal* (*The New Normal*), Brussels, Lannoo Campus

34 InSites Consulting (2010) 'Stop the paradox' study [Online: accessed 8 December 2011] **www.slideshare.net/stevenvanbelleghem/presentations**

35 InSites Consulting (2010) 'Stop the paradox' study [Online: accessed 8 December 2011] **www.slideshare.net/stevenvanbelleghem/presentations**

36 McNeil, G (2010) 'The Nordstrom way to customer service excellence' [Online: accessed 11 December 2011] Slideshare: **www.slideshare.net/ parature/the-nordstrom-way-to-customer-service-excellence**

37 McKinsey (2009) Telco study

38 Spector, R and McCarthy, P (2005) *The Nordstrom Way to Customer Service Excellence*, New Jersey, John Wiley & Sons

39 Michils, M (2011) *Open Boek* (Open Book), Brussels, Lannoo Campus

40 Hsieh, T (2010) *Delivering Happiness*, New York, Hachette

41 Desphandé and Webster (1989) 'Organizational culture and marketing: defining the research agenda', *Journal of Marketing*, (1) pp 3–15

42 Yip, G (1995) *Total Global Strategy: Managing for worldwide competitive advantage*, New York, Prentice Hall

43 Schneider, B and Rentsch, J (1988) 'Managing climate and cultures: a future perspective', in J. Hage (ed), *The future of organization*, pp 181–200), Lexington MA, Lexington Books
Ojo, O (2009) 'Impact assessment of corporate culture on employee job performance', *Business Intelligence Journal*, 2 (2) pp 388–97

44 Hofstede, G and Hofstede, G J (2005) *Cultures and Organizations: Software of the mind*, New York, McGraw-Hill

45 Nayar, V (2010) *Employees First, Customers Second: Turning conventional management upside down*, Boston, Harvard Business Publishing

46 *Frankwatching* (2011) 'Één minuut op het wereldwijde web' (One minute on the worldwide web) [Online: accessed 12 December 2011] **www.frankwatching.com/archive/2011/07/01/infographic-day-1-minuut-op-het-wereldwijde-web/**

47 Grossman, L (2010) 'Twitter can predict the stock market' *Wired* [Online: accessed 12 December 2011] **www.wired.com/ wiredscience/2010/10/twitter-crystal-ball/**

48 Foremski, T (2010) 'HP study shows Twitter predicts success of movies', *Silicone Valley Watcher* [Online: accessed 12 December 2011] **www.siliconvalleywatcher.com/mt/archives/2010/04/hp_study_shows.php**

49 Bernoff, J and Shadler, T (2010) *Empowered: Unleash your employees, energize your customers, transform your business*, Boston, Harvard Business Publishing

50 Wauters, R (2009) 'Best Buy goes all Twitter crazy with @Twelpforce', *Techcrunch* [Online: accessed 12 December 2011] **http://techcrunch.com/ 2009/07/21/best-buy-goes-all-twitter-crazy-with-twelpforce/**

51 Treacy, M and Wiersema, F (2000) 'Three paths to leadership', *Harvard Business Review* [Online: accessed 12 December 2011] **www.profitmatters.ca/Articles/customer_intimacy.htm**

52 Moenaert, R, Robben, H and Gouw, P (2008) *Visionary Marketing: Building sustainable business*, Brussels, Lannoo Campus

53 Sidhu, J (2003) 'Mission statements: Is it time to shelve them?' *European Management Journal*, 4, August, pp 439–46

54 Lencioni, P (2002) 'Make your values mean something', *Harvard Business Review*, 1 July 2002 [Online: accessed 12 December 2011] **http://hbr.org/product/make-your-values-mean-something/an/R0207J-PDF-ENG**

55 Ransdell, E (2007) 'The Nike story? Just tell it!', *Fastcompany.com* [Online: accessed 12 December 2011] **www.fastcompany.com/magazine/31/nike.html**

56 Hsieh, T (2010) *Delivering Happiness*, New York, Hachette

57 Collins, J and Porras, J (1994) *Built to Last: Successful habits of visionary companies*, New York, HarperCollins

58 InSites Consulting (2011) 'Social media integration' study [Online: accessed 8 December 2011] **www.slideshare.net/stevenvanbelleghem/stop-the-paradox**

59 InSites Consulting (2011) 'Social media integration' study [Online: accessed 8 December 2011] **www.slideshare.net/stevenvanbelleghem/stop-the-paradox**

60 InSites Consulting (2009) Brand identification research

61 InSites Consulting (2009) Brand identification research

62 InSites Consulting (2011) 'Social media integration' study [Online: accessed 8 December 2011] **www.slideshare.net/stevenvanbelleghem/stop-the-paradox**

63 InSites Consulting (2011) 'Social media integration' study [Online: accessed 8 December 2011] **www.slideshare.net/stevenvanbelleghem/stop-the-paradox**

64 Van den Bergh, J and Behrer, M (2011) *How Cool Brands Stay Hot: Branding to generation Y*, London, Kogan Page

65 Oosterveer, D (2011) 'Authenticiteit verslaat sociale media als marketing topic' ('Authenticity beasts social media as a marketing topic') *Marketing Facts* [Online: accessed 12 December 2011] **www.marketingfacts.nl/berichten/20110705_authenticiteit_verslaat_social_media_als_marketingtopic/**

66 InSites Consulting (2010) Brand leverage research

67 Li, C (2010) *Open Leadership: How social technology can transform the way you lead*, San Francisco, Jossey-Bass

68 Lashinsky, A (2006) 'Chaos by design', *Fortune Magazine*, **154** (7)

69 O'Dell, J (2011) 'How Egyptians used Twitter during the January crisis', *Mashable* [Online: accessed 12 December 2011] **http://mashable.com/2011/02/01/egypt-twitter-infographic/**

70 Halliday, H (2010) 'Gap scraps logo redesign after protests on Facebook and Twitter', *Guardian*, 12 October

71 *Contagious Magazine* (2011) 'Nokia plan B, C... X' [Online: accessed 12 December 2011] **www.contagiousmagazine.com/2011/02/nokia_16.php** *Wall Street Journal* (2011) 'Nokia "plan B" a hoax?' [Online: accessed 12 December 2011] **http://online.wsj.com/article/SB10001424052748704657704576150021377871258.html**

72 Geller, J (2011) 'Open letter to BlackBerry bosses: senior RIM exec tells all as company crumbles around him' [Online: accessed 12 December 2011] **www.bgr.com/2011/06/30/open-letter-to-blackberry-bosses-senior-rim-exec-tells-all-as-company-crumbles-around-him/**

73 Verelst, J (2011) 'G1000 moet democratie redden' ('G1000 to save democracy'), *De Morgen* [Online: accessed 12 December 2011] **www.demorgen.be/dm/nl/3625/De-Formatie/article/detail/1277411/2011/06/11/G1000-moet-democratie-redden.dhtml**

74 Nicolas, S (2011) 'The way we do things around here', *Director Magazine* [Online: accessed 12 December 2011] **www.director.co.uk/MAGAZINE/2011/3_march/culture_64_07.html**

75 Van Belleghem, S (2009) *The Conversation Manager*, Brussels, Lannoo Campus

76 Parr, B (2011) 'Google search becomes more social: integrates Flickr, Twitter & Quora', *Mashable* [Online: accessed 12 December 2011] **http://mashable.com/2011/02/17/google-social-search-2/**

77 Keller Fay Group and Google (2011) 'Word of mouth and search' study [Online: accessed 12 December 2011] **www.kellerfay.com/news-events/googlekeller-fay-research-word-of-mouth-and-the-internet/**

78 *McKinsey Quarterly* (2008) 'Building the Web 2.0 enterprise: McKinsey global search results' [Online: accessed 12 December 2011] **www.mckinseyquarterly.com/Building_the_Web_20_Enterprise_McKinsey_Global_Survey_2174**

79 Maslow (1943); for details see **http://en.wikipedia.org/wiki/Maslow's_hierarchy_of_needs**

80 Adams, S (2011) 'Personal blogging at work' increases productivity, *Forbes Magazine* [Online: accessed 12 December 2011] **www.forbes.com/sites/susanadams/2011/03/01/personal-blogging-at-work-increases-productivity/**

81 Solis, B (2011) *Engage: The complete guide for brands and businesses to build, cultivate, and measure success in the new web*, New Jersey, John Wiley & Sons

82 Verdonck, L (2011) 'Porsche: zo bedank je 1 miljoen fans' ('Porsche: so thank you one million Facebook fans'), *Marketing Facts*

[Online: accessed 13 December 2011] **www.marketingfacts.nl/ berichten/20110221_porsche_1_000_000_facebook_fans_bedankt/**

83 InSites Consulting (2011) 'Social media around the world' study [Online: accessed 8 December 2011] **www.slideshare.net/InSitesConsulting/ social-media-around-the-world-2011-9537752**

84 InSites Consulting (2011) 'Global mobile adoption and usage' study

85 Hibbard, C (2010) 'How Twitter helped Discovery Channel during a hostage crisis', *Social Media Examiner* [Online: accessed 13 December 2011] **www.socialmediaexaminer.com/discovery-channel-case-study/**

86 Elliott, A (2011) 'Power to the people: 3 tasty crowdsourcing case studies', *Mashable* [Online: accessed 13 December 2011] **http://mashable.com/ 2011/02/20/crowdsourcing-case-studies/**

87 Oosterveer, D (2011) 'KLM 24 uur per dag te bereiken via sociale media' ('KLM 24 hours a day via social media'), *Marketing Facts* [Online: accessed 12 December 2011] **www.marketingfacts.nl/berichten/20110722_klm_24_ uur_per_dag_te_bereiken_via_sociale_media/**

88 Van Keulen (2011) 'Tjalling Smit (Director E-Acquisition) over online bij KLM, metasearch, display testing en Twitter' ('Tjalling Smit (Director E-Acquisition) over onlineat KLM, metasearch, display testing and Twitter' *Marketing Facts* [Online: accessed 13 December 2011] **www.marketingfacts.nl/berichten/20110224_tjalling_smit_e_acquisition _klm_metasearch_display_testing_twitter/**

89 *Marketing Tribune* (2011) 'KLM opnieuw social met Delfts blauwe tegel-campagne' ('KLM delft Blue tile again with social campaign') [Online: accessed 13 December 2011] **www.marketingtribune.nl/nieuws/ klm-opnieuw-social-met-delfts-blauwe-tegel-campagne/**

90 Van Roekel (2010) 'Briljante guerilla-marketingcampagne van Heineken' ('Brilliant guerilla marketing campaign from Heineken'), *Marketing Facts* [Online: accessed 12 December 2011] **www.marketingfacts.nl/ berichten/20100316_briljante_guerilla-marketingcampagne_van_ heineken/**

91 *Online University Data* (2010) '50 online university professors on Twitter worth following' [Online: accessed 13 December 2011] **http:// onlineuniversitydata.com/2010/50-online-university-professors-on-twitter-worth-following/**

92 Deighton, J and Kornfield, L (2010) 'Harvard business school executive education: balancing online and offline marketing', *Harvard Business Review* [Online: accessed 13 December 2011] **http://hbr.org/product/harvard-business-school-executive-education-balanc/an/510091-PDF-ENG**

93 InSites Consulting (2010) 'Stop the paradox' study [Online: accessed 8 December 2011] **www.slideshare.net/stevenvanbelleghem/presentations**

94 Van Belleghem, S (2009) *The Conversation Manager*, Brussels, Lannoo Campus

95 *Contagious Magazine Special Report* (2011) 'Real-time marketing' [Online: summary accessed 12 December 2011] **www.contagiousmagazine.com/2011/05/real-time_marketing.php**

96 Jaffe, J (2010) *Flip the Funnel: How to use existing customers to gain new ones*, New Jersey, John Wiley & Sons

97 Hsieh, T (2010) *Delivering Happiness*, New York, Hachette

98 Solis, B (2011) *Engage: The complete guide for brands and businesses to build, cultivate, and measure success in the new web*, New Jersey, John Wiley & Sons

99 Mainwaring, S (2011) *We First: How brands and consumers use social media to build a better world*, New York, Palgrave Macmillan

100 Bernoff, J and Shadler, T (2010) *Empowered: Unleash your employees, energize your customers, transform your business*, Boston, Harvard Business Publishing

101 InSites Consulting (2010) 'Stop the paradox' study [Online: accessed 8 December 2011] **www.slideshare.net/stevenvanbelleghem/presentations**

102 McCarthy, P (2011) 'Case study: Ben & Jerry fair tweets', Womma [Online: accessed 13 December 2011] **http://womma.org/word/2011/08/10/case-study-ben-jerry%E2%80%99s-fair-tweets/**

103 De Ruyck, T *et al* (2010) 'How fans became future shapers of an ice-cream brand', Research paper for Esomar Qualitative 2010, InSites Consulting & Unilever

104 *Bevnet Magazine* (2009) 'Stopping soda's slide' [Online: accessed 13 December 2011] **www.bevnet.com/magazine/feature/2009/stopping_sodas_slide/**

105 Kumar, J, Petersen, J and Leone, P (2007) 'How valuable is word of mouth?', *Harvard Business Review* [Online: accessed 13 December 2011] **http://hbr.org/2007/10/how-valuable-is-word-of-mouth/ar/1**

106 Court, D *et al* (2009) 'The consumer decision journey', *McKinsey Quarterly* [Online: accessed 13 December 2011] **www.mckinseyquarterly.com/The_consumer_decision_journey_2373**

107 Richardson, A (2010) 'Touchpoints bring the customer experience to life', *Harvard Business Review* blog [Online: accessed 13 December 2011] **http://blogs.hbr.org/cs/2010/12/touchpoints_bring_the_customer.html**

108 InSites Consulting (2011) 'Social media around the world' study [Online: accessed 8 December 2011] **www.slideshare.net/InSitesConsulting/social-media-around-the-world-2011-9537752**

109 Van der Stighelen, G (2010) 'Think before you promise' blog post [Online: accessed 13 December 2011] **http://guillaumevds.posterous.com/think-before-you-promise**

110 Reichheld, F (2006) *The Ultimate Question: Driving good profits and true profits*, Boston, Harvard Business Publishing

111 Fortune, S (2011) 'Cadillac taps Ritz-Carlton to transform their customer service experience', *psfk* [Online: accessed 13 December 2011] **www.psfk.com/2011/03/cadillac-taps-ritz-carlton-service-consultants-to-elevate-the-customer-service-experience.html**

112 Van Belleghem, S (2009) *The Conversation Manager*, Brussels, Lannoo Campus

113 InSites Consulting (2008) 'Future talking' study

114 Willaerts, C (2011) *The Conversity Model: Making money with social media*, Brussels, Lannoo Campus

115 Friedman, B (2011) 'Whole foods subtle social media marketing plan', *Social Media Today* [Online: accessed 13 December 2011] **http://friedmansocialmedia.com/blog/2011/07/27/whole-foods-markets-subtle-social-media-marketing-plan/**

116 De Maagt, P (2011) 'Four dimensions of social sales', *www.polledemaagt.com* [Online: accessed 13 December 2011] **www.polledemaagt.com/blog/models-frameworks/four-dimensions-of-social-sales/**

117 Hall, E (2011) 'Heinz launches limited edition ketchup on Facebook in UK', *Advertising Age* [Online: accessed 13 December 2011] **http://adage.com/article/global-news/heinz-launches-limited-edition-ketchup-facebook-u-k/149316/**

118 InSites Consulting (2011) 'What people share' study

119 InSites Consulting, *Pub* and VmmTV (2010) 'Top spots' study

120 Van Belleghem, S (2009) *The Conversation Manager*, Brussels, Lannoo Campus

121 Lee, E (2011) 'Foursquare to users: nice check-in, now please write something', *Ad Age Digital* [Online: accessed 13 December 2011] **http://adage.com/article/digital/foursquare-users-nice-check-write/229026/**

122 Scott, D (2011) *Real-time marketing and PR: How to instantly engage your market connect with customers, and create products that grow your business now*, New Jersey, John Wiley & Sons

123 Slideshare (2009) 'Content marketing case study' [Online: accessed 14 December 2011] **www.slideshare.net/HubSpot/content-marketing-case-study**

124 De Clerck, J-P (2011) 'Hoe Hubspot succesvol werd' ('How successful was Hubspot: Mike Volpe lessons') [Online: accessed 14 December 2011] **www.marketingfacts.nl/berichten/20110315_mike_volpe_hoe_hubspot_succesvol_werd/**

125 InSites Consulting (2011) 'Social media integration' study [Online: accessed 8 December 2011] **www.slideshare.net/stevenvanbelleghem/stop-the-paradox**

126 *Contagious Magazine Special Report* (2010) 'Brand communities'
[Online: summary accessed 14 December 2011]
www.contagiousmagazine.com/2010/06/contagious_2.php

127 De Ruyck, T *et al* (2011) 'Engage, inspire, act: how Unilever changed the
hearts, minds and actions of their R&D employees in 6 weeks' time',
Amsterdam, InSites Consulting & Unilever; Esomar Publications

128 *Frost & Sullivan* (2011) 'R&D/Innovation and product development
priorities' survey results [Online: accessed 14 December 2011]
www.frost.com/prod/servlet/cio/246147934

129 Cook, S (2008) 'The contribution revolution', *Harvard Business Review*
[Online: accessed 14 December 2011] **http://hbr.org/search/
Scott%252520Cook%2525202008/**

130 Verhaeghe, A *et al* (2011) 'Crowd interpretation', Amsterdam, Illustre &
Cleas; Esomar Publications

131 Van Dijk (2011) 'The effects of co-creation on brand and product
perceptions', Wageningen NL, Faculty of Social Sciences, Wageningen
University; see more information at: **Joycediscovers.wordpress.com**

132 McCracken, G (2009) *Chief Culture Officer: How to create a living,
breathing corporation*, New York, Basic Books

133 *Contagious Magazine Special Report* (2011b) 'C-commerce'

134 De Ruyck, T *et al* (2010) 'How fans became future shapers of an ice-cream
brand', Research paper for Esomar Qualitative 2010, InSites Consulting &
Unilever

135 Cook, S (2008) 'The contribution revolution', *Harvard Business Review*
[Online: accessed 14 December 2011] **http://hbr.org/search/
Scott%252520Cook%2525202008/**

136 Pink, D (2009) *Drive: The surprising truth about what motivates us*,
New York, Penguin Group USA

137 InSites Consulting (2011) 'Social media around the world' study
[Online: accessed 8 December 2011] **www.slideshare.net/
InSitesConsulting/social-media-around-the-world-2011-9537752**

138 Boudreau, K and Lakhani, K (2009) 'How to manage outside innovation',
MIT Sloan Management Review [Online: accessed 14 December 2011]
**http://sloanreview.mit.edu/the-magazine/2009-summer/50413/
how-to-manage-outside-innovation/**

139 Schillewaert, N (2011) 'Online research: now & next, 2011', conference
notes, *International Journal of Market Research*, 53 (4)

140 Sawhney, M, Verona, G and Prandelli, E (2005) 'Collaborating to create:
the internet as a platform for customer engagement in product information',
Journal of Interactive Marketing, 19 (4), pp 4–17

141 De Ruyck, T *et al* (2011) 'Engage, inspire, act: how Unilever changed the
hearts, minds and actions of their R&D employees in 6 weeks' time',
Amsterdam, InSites Consulting & Unilever; Esomar Publications

142 *McKinsey Quarterly* (2011) 'How we see it: three senior executives on the future of marketing [Online: summary accessed 14 December 2011] **www.mckinseyquarterly.com/How_we_see_it_Three_senior_ executives_on_the_future_of_marketing_2835**

143 InSites Consulting (2011) 'Social dynamics' model [Online: accessed 14 December 2011] **www.slideshare.net/stevenvanbelleghem**

144 InSites Consulting (2011) 'Social media integration' study [Online: accessed 8 December 2011] **www.slideshare.net/stevenvanbelleghem/stop-the-paradox**

145 InSites Consulting (2011) 'Social media integration' study [Online: accessed 8 December 2011] **www.slideshare.net/stevenvanbelleghem/stop-the-paradox**

146 Solis, B (2011) *Engage: The complete guide for brands and businesses to build, cultivate, and measure success in the new web*, New Jersey, John Wiley & Sons

147 Lasica, J (2010) 'The story of Intelpedia: a model corporate wiki', *www.socialmediabiz* [Online: accessed 14 December 2011] **www.socialmedia.biz/2010/07/08/the-story-of-intelpedia-a-model-corporate-wiki/**

148 InSites Consulting (2011) 'Social media integration' study [Online: accessed 8 December 2011] **www.slideshare.net/stevenvanbelleghem/stop-the-paradox**

149 InSites Consulting (2011) 'Social media integration' study [Online: accessed 8 December 2011] **www.slideshare.net/stevenvanbelleghem/stop-the-paradox**

150 InSites Consulting (2011) 'Social media integration' study [Online: accessed 8 December 2011] **www.slideshare.net/stevenvanbelleghem/stop-the-paradox**

151 Swallow, E (2011) 'How to: build a social media education program for your company', *Mashable* [Online: accessed 14 December 2011] **http://mashable.com/2011/01/18/social-media-training/**

152 Van Belleghem, S (2009) *The Conversation Manager*, Brussels, Lannoo Campus

153 Owyang, J (2011) 'Program plan: the social media center of excellence', Web Strategy [Online: accessed 15 December 2011] **www.web-strategist.com/ blog/2011/04/04/program-plan-the-social-media-center-of-excellence/**

154 InSites Consulting (2011) 'Social media integration' study [Online: accessed 8 December 2011] **www.slideshare.net/stevenvanbelleghem/stop-the-paradox**

155 Owyang, J (2011) 'Program plan: the social media center of excellence', Web Strategy [Online: accessed 15 December 2011] **www.web-strategist.com/ blog/2011/04/04/program-plan-the-social-media-center-of-excellence/**

156 Croft, A and Hunley, J (2010) 'eBay social media case study', *Slideshare* [Online: accessed 15 December 2011] **www.slideshare.net/ influencepeoples/ali-croft-monitoring-social-media-ebay**

157 Moenaert, R *et al* (2010) 'Strategic innovation decisions: what you foresee is not what you get', *Journal of Innovation Management*, 27 (6), pp 840–55 [Online: accessed 15 December 2011] **http://onlinelibrary.wiley.com/ doi/10.1111/j.1540-5885.2010.00755.x/abstract**

158 InSites Consulting (2011) 'Social media integration' study [Online: accessed 8 December 2011] **www.slideshare.net/stevenvanbelleghem/stop-the-paradox**

159 InSites Consulting (2011) 'The launch of Telenet Yelo', Amsterdam, Esomar Publications

160 InSites Consulting (2011) 'Social media integration' study [Online: accessed 8 December 2011] **www.slideshare.net/stevenvanbelleghem/stop-the-paradox**

161 InSites Consulting (2010) 'Stop the paradox' study [Online: accessed 8 December 2011] **www.slideshare.net/stevenvanbelleghem/ presentations**

162 Marx, S (2011) Cisco blog: 'Social media listening and engagement journey' [Online: accessed 15 December 2011] **http://blogs.cisco.com/ socialmedia/social-media-listening-and-engagement-journey/#more-21405**

163 InSites Consulting (2011) 'Social media integration' study [Online: accessed 8 December 2011] **www.slideshare.net/stevenvanbelleghem/stop-the-paradox**

164 Van Belleghem, S (2009) *The Conversation Manager*, Brussels, Lannoo Campus

165 Horton, M (2010) 'How 3 billion meetings per year cost time, money and productivity in the enterprise' Social Cast blog [Online: accessed 15 December 2011] **http://blog.socialcast.com/how-3-billion-meetings-per-year-waste-time-money-and-productivity-in-the-enterprise/**

166 Efrati, A and Morrison, S (2011) 'Chief seeks more agile Google', *Wall Street Journal* [Online: accessed 15 December 2011] **http://online.wsj.com/ article/SB10001424052748704115404576096332781525252.html**

167 Pink, D (2009) *Drive: The surprising truth about what motivates us*, New York, Penguin Group USA
Pink, D (2010) 'Work smarter: Atlassian', *Wired Magazine* [Online: accessed 15 December 2011] **www.wired.co.uk/magazine/archive/2010/04/ features/work-smarter-atlassian**

168 InSites Consulting (2011) 'Social media integration' study [Online: accessed 8 December 2011] **www.slideshare.net/stevenvanbelleghem/stop-the-paradox**

About the author

Steven Van Belleghem is also the author of best-selling book *The Conversation Manager*. He is one of the Managing Partners at InSites Consulting and a part-time Marketing Professor at the Vlerick Business School. His passion is for helping clients with strategic and tactical issues around conversations, word-of-mouth and social media.

Together with the team at InSites Consulting, he helps companies to get a grip on current consumers through branding, advertising and integrating conversations in their entire company strategy. As an author and Marketing Professor, he also lectures and teaches throughout the world on conversations and social media.

About InSites Consulting

InSites Consulting was established in 1997, and although a marketing research company, the founders never really wanted to be market researchers. InSites Consulting really is a crazy blend of academic visionaries, passionate marketers and research innovators that are determined to challenge the status quo of marketing research.

Over the last 10 years the company has grown at an amazing rate of 35 per cent per year. Today there's more than 130 employees working in five offices (BE, NL, UK, RO, US) getting their energy from helping world-leading brands to improve their marketing efforts and to develop deeper connections with consumers on a global scale. InSites Consulting has been rewarded with no less than 15 international awards.

The recipe for success: a never-ceasing enthusiasm, a lot of hard work, a culture of sharing, and permanent innovation in research methods and marketing thought leadership. And last but not least: positively surprising clients every day.

More information on **www.insites-consulting.com.**

Index

NB: page numbers in *italic* indicate figures or tables